Food Systems Resilience

Edited by Ana I. Ribeiro-Barros,
Daniel S. Tevera, Luís F. Goulao
and Lucas D. Tivana

Published in London, United Kingdom

Food Systems Resilience
http://dx.doi.org/10.5772/intechopen.95206
Edited by Ana I. Ribeiro-Barros, Daniel S. Tevera, Luís F. Goulao and Lucas D. Tivana

Contributors
Dorcas Stella Shumba, Shivani Sood, Harjeet Singh, Suruchi Jindal, Adane Atara Debessa, Degefa Tolossa, Berhanu Denu, Bart de Steenhuijsen Piters, Emma Termeer, Deborah Bakker, Hubert Fonteijn, Herman Brouwer, Elke Stedefeldt, Rayane Stephanie Gomes De Freitas, Tanya Zerbian, Mags Adams, Neil Wilson, Jasper Okoro Godwin Elechi, Ikechukwu U. Nwiyi, Cornelius Smah Adamu, Dikabo Mogopodi, Samuel Raditloko, Inonge Chibua, Mesha Mbisana, Banyaladzi Paphane, Kriengsak Chareonwongsak, Fernando Teixeira

First published in London, United Kingdom, 2022 by IntechOpen
IntechOpen is the global imprint of INTECHOPEN LIMITED, registered in England and Wales, registration number: 11086078, 5 Princes Gate Court, London, SW7 2QJ, United Kingdom
Printed in Croatia

British Library Cataloguing-in-Publication Data
A catalogue record for this book is available from the British Library

Additional hard and PDF copies can be obtained from orders@intechopen.com

Food Systems Resilience
Edited by Ana I. Ribeiro-Barros, Daniel S. Tevera, Luís F. Goulao and Lucas D. Tivana
p. cm.

This title is part of the Sustainable Development Book Series, Volume 1
Topic: Sustainable Economy and Fair Society
Series Editor: Usha Iyer-Raniga
Topic Editor: Antonella Petrillo

Print ISBN 978-1-80355-003-9
Online ISBN 978-1-80355-004-6
eBook (PDF) ISBN 978-1-80355-005-3
ISSN 2753-6580

For EU product safety concerns:
IN TECH d.o.o., Prolaz Marije Krucifikse Kozulić 3, 51000 Rijeka, Croatia,
info@intechopen.com or visit our website at intechopen.com.

IntechOpen Book Series

Sustainable Development

Volume 1

Aims and Scope of the Series

Transforming our World: the 2030 Agenda for Sustainable Development endorsed by United Nations and 193 Member States, came into effect on Jan 1, 2016, to guide decision making and actions to the year 2030 and beyond. Central to this Agenda are 17 Goals, 169 associated targets and over 230 indicators that are reviewed annually. The vision envisaged in the implementation of the SDGs is centered on the five Ps: People, Planet, Prosperity, Peace and Partnership. This call for renewed focused efforts ensure we have a safe and healthy planet for current and future generations.

This Series focuses on covering research and applied research involving the five Ps through the following topics:

1. Sustainable Economy and Fair Society that rclates to SDG 1 on No Poverty, SDG 2 on Zero Hunger, SDG 8 on Decent Work and Economic Growth, SDG 10 on Reduced Inequalities, SDG 12 on Responsible Consumption and Production, and SDG 17 Partnership for the Goals

2. Health and Wellbeing focusing on SDG 3 on Good Health and Wellbeing and SDG 6 on Clean Water and Sanitation

3. Inclusivity and Social Equality involving SDG 4 on Quality Education, SDG 5 on Gender Equality, and SDG 16 on Peace, Justice and Strong Institutions

4. Climate Change and Environmental Sustainability comprising SDG 13 on Climate Action, SDG 14 on Life Below Water, and SDG 15 on Life on Land

5. Urban Planning and Environmental Management embracing SDG 7 on Affordable Clean Energy, SDG 9 on Industry, Innovation and Infrastructure, and SDG 11 on Sustainable Cities and Communities.

The series also seeks to support the use of cross cutting SDGs, as many of the goals listed above, targets and indicators are all interconnected to impact our lives and the decisions we make on a daily basis, making them impossible to tie to a single topic.

Meet the Series Editor

Usha Iyer-Raniga is a professor in the School of Property and Construction Management at RMIT University. Usha co-leads the One Planet Network's Sustainable Buildings and Construction Programme (SBC), a United Nations 10 Year Framework of Programmes on Sustainable Consumption and Production (UN 10FYP SCP) aligned with Sustainable Development Goal 12. The work also directly impacts SDG 11 on Sustainable Cities and Communities. She completed her undergraduate degree as an architect before obtaining her Masters degree from Canada and her Doctorate in Australia. Usha has been a keynote speaker as well as an invited speaker at national and international conferences, seminars and workshops. Her teaching experience includes teaching in Asian countries. She has advised Austrade, APEC, national, state and local governments. She serves as a reviewer and a member of the scientific committee for national and international refereed journals and refereed conferences. She is on the editorial board for refereed journals and has worked on Special Issues. Usha has served and continues to serve on the Boards of several not-for-profit organisations and she has also served as panel judge for a number of awards including the Premiers Sustainability Award in Victoria and the International Green Gown Awards. Usha has published over 100 publications, including research and consulting reports. Her publications cover a wide range of scientific and technical research publications that include edited books, book chapters, refereed journals, refereed conference papers and reports for local, state and federal government clients. She has also produced podcasts for various organisations and participated in media interviews. She has received state, national and international funding worth over USD $25 million. Usha has been awarded the Quarterly Franklin Membership by London Journals Press (UK). Her biography has been included in the Marquis Who's Who in the World® 2018, 2016 (33rd Edition), along with approximately 55,000 of the most accomplished men and women from around the world, including luminaries as U.N. Secretary-General Ban Ki-moon. In 2017, Usha was awarded the Marquis Who's Who Lifetime Achiever Award.

Meet the Volume Editors

Ana I. Ribeiro-Barros, Ph.D., is the director of the Tropical College, University of Lisbon (ULisboa). She obtained a Ph.D. in Plant Molecular Biology from Wageningen University, the Netherlands. She is also a senior researcher, head of the lab, and professor at the School of Agriculture, ULisboa, and an invited professor at Nova University Lisbon (NOVA), Eduardo Mondlane University (UEM), and Gorongosa National Park (GNP). She is a member of the Coordination and Scientific Committees of the doctoral program "Tropical Knowledge and Management" (NOVA), Master in Biotechnology (UEM), and Master in Conservation Biology (GNP); and a national expert for Food and Nutrition Security and Sustainable Agriculture - High-Level Policy Dialogue EU-Africa. Her research expertise and interests are centered on biodiversity, environmental sustainability, agro-ecological approaches, and food and nutritional security.

Daniel S. Tevera is an Extraordinary Professor in the Department of Geography, Environmental Studies, and Tourism, University of the Western Cape, South Africa. He has received widespread recognition for his research on urban food systems, African migration, urban informality, and environmental security. He has extensive research experience in southern Africa. He has participated in the African Food Security Urban Network, as a national team leader. He has been a visiting scholar at Oxford University, UK, Gothenburg University, Sweden, Dartmouth College, USA, and Friedrich-Schiller University, Germany. He is the inaugural Programme Director of the Leadership for Environment and Development in Southern Africa (LEAD-SA).

Lucas Daniel Tivana has a Ph.D. in Food Engineering and has been a senior lecturer at Eduardo Mondlane University, Mozambique, since 1998. His research and teaching activities cover several areas such as food handling, storage and processing, food microbiology, food chemistry, and food analysis, and include advising national and international Ph.D. and master's students. His research is focused on developing post-harvest technologies suitable for smallholder farmers in Sub-Saharan Africa. He has served as PI in a Regional Project under the Agricultural Productivity Programme for Southern Africa (APPSA). He also served as a consultant to national institutions such as the Ministry of Agriculture and international organizations such as the Food, Agriculture, and Natural Resources Policy Analysis Network (FANRPAN).

Luís F. Goulao has a Ph.D. in Agronomic Engineering and is a professor at the University of Lisbon's School of Agriculture (ISA) focusing his research to link agriculture and food and nutritional security with development outcomes, with an emphasis on tropical regions' contexts and global impact. He is a member of the coordination board of the Linking Landscape, Environment, Agriculture and Food (LEAF) research unit, heading the "Plant Science & Crop Production" research group. He is also a member of the Coordination and Scientific Committees of Doctoral Programmes "Sustainability Science," "Development Studies," and "Agricultural Innovation in Tropical Food Chains." Dr. Goulao is co-chair of the Thematic Interdisciplinary Network "Rede AGRO" and a member of the coordination committee of the Interdisciplinary "College Food, Farming and Forestry (F3)" at the University of Lisbon.

Contents

Preface

Food and nutrition security are prerequisites to achieving the United Nations Sustainable Development Goals (SDGs) of poverty eradication (SDG 1), hunger eradication (SDG 2), good health and wellbeing (SDG 3), reduced inequalities (SDG 10), sustainable cities and communities (SDG 11), and responsible consumption and production (SDG 12). However, meeting these ambitious goals within the next 10 years, given the current global scenario, will be challenging. On one hand, the exponential growth of the world's population, which is anticipated to reach about 10 billion in 2050, mainly living in cities and under diet transition, will necessarily result in a significant increase in food demand. On the other hand, climate change projections such as an increase in temperature and greenhouse gases, erratic rainfall patterns, and increased frequency of extreme weather events, accompanied by the reduction of arable land by as much as 50% in 2050, impose major food production challenges. In addition, the world is also facing unprecedented health, social, political, and economic impacts. The COVID-19 pandemic has exacerbated the vulnerability of local food systems, especially in the global South through food supply disruption and contraction. Additionally, the armed conflict in Ukraine and the economic sanctions on Russia will likely change the arrangements of global trade of major staple agricultural commodities and the energy markets, directly or indirectly impacting food availability, food supply, and food prices and therefore challenging food security in the most vulnerable settings. Thus, accelerating the development and implementation of a nutrition-sensitive agricultural research and development agenda is now more relevant than ever to transform current food systems to ensure healthy and inclusive diets that are environmentally sustainable and affordable on the global scale. This book presents a set of chapters that discuss some of the major challenges and achievements for food systems resilience. It is divided into two sections, the first of which is devoted to key issues of global interest (Chapters 1–4) and the second of which includes case studies (Chapters 5–10).

Section Overview

Section 1 focuses on the transformation of food systems towards resilience. The first two chapters employ a global context approach to address the key factors undermining food systems' resilience and sustainability. Chapter 1 (by B. de Steenhuijsen Piters et al.) unpacks the intertwined connections between food system resilience, food policies, and global food markets. The authors argue that because of shocks (e.g., COVID-19) and crises in global food systems (e.g., the global food price crisis of 2008) it has become difficult to achieve food and nutrition security for all. The chapter concludes that to achieve national food systems goals, policymakers and key stakeholders must have a common understanding of what food system resilience entails, to allow transformation actions that anticipate, prevent, absorb, and adapt to the impacts of shocks and stressors.

Chapter 2 (by J. O. Godwin Elechi) focuses on global food system transformation for resilience. The author argues that the current global food systems are unsustainable because, on one hand, more than 800 million people globally are chronically undernourished, while on the other hand, food systems are releasing a third of all greenhouse gases and are responsible for 80% of biodiversity loss. Therefore, scaling up existing food systems cannot be the way forward in order to achieve SDG 2 on ending hunger by the year 2030. The chapter also highlights that the challenge is to renovate, to find sustainable ways of producing more local food, especially in Sub-Saharan Africa (SSA) where many countries rely on food items sourced from distant producers. Therefore, the transformation of global food systems, including the entire operational environment (cropping, harvesting, post-harvesting, and distribution) and consumption, is essential to make the entire system more efficient and more environmentally friendly. For that, government policy intervention along with the behavioral change from producers, consumers, and food distributors will be required.

Chapter 3 (by D. S. Shumba) addresses the importance of Weather Index Insurance (WII) to manage food production uncertainties, using the dataset of pilot projects that have been launched across SSA since the early 2000s. This chapter explores the gap between the assertion that WII is a promising risk transfer mechanism for smallholder farmers in SSA and the realization that, even where microfinance is made available, subscription rates among smallholder farmers rarely rise.

Chapter 4 (by D. Mogopodi et al.) discusses a global food safety concern that is related to the presence of mycotoxin contaminants in everyday food, recognizing that mycotoxins pose a threat to human health and food security, which is frequently neglected in SSA food systems. The authors discuss mycotoxin's impact on food availability and public health and provide analytical and preventive strategies that aim to increase the quality of products while avoiding food wastage.

Section 2 presents six case studies that address different topics and geographies in Africa, Asia, Latin America, and Europe. Chapters 5 (by T. Zerbian et al.) and 6 (by K. Chareonwongsak) discuss the food insecurity shocks and stressors imposed by the COVID-19 pandemic at a community level (Preston community, NW England, UK) and at a country level (Thailand), highlighting the importance of self-sustained communities to mitigate food insecurity crises in both settings. Chapter 5 builds on the new challenges for food production, distribution, and consumption posed by the COVID-19 pandemic and the exacerbating effects on the existing socioeconomic inequalities that hinder access to food. The chapter focuses on the dynamic interactions of local food initiatives and derives its findings from a social network analysis (SNA) conducted during the summer of 2020. The authors pinpoint that pre-existing social conditions, such as a previously organized local food network in partnership with local authorities, have enabled some communities to self-organize and respond favorably to the COVID-19 crisis and discuss the role of current models of emergency food provisioning, advocating stronger collaborative bonds within already organized networks. Chapter 6 provides an analysis of the status of food insecurity and food system resilience during the COVID-19 crisis in Thailand. It proposes the adoption of a "Food Self-Sustained Community" (FSSC) model that addresses food security at the community level. It also shows how, through pre-emptive planning, a community can switch local food production seamlessly to a self-sufficient and resilient model that prepares it for future crises, so that the community can produce enough food for all members without relying on outside sources.

Chapter 7 (by A. A. Debessa et al.) discusses the nexus between coping strategies and resilience to recurrent food insecurity shocks in the community of Boricha,

Sidana National Regional State, Ethiopia. The authors address the coping strategies employed by households when exposed to food insecurity shocks and highlights that households use various consumption-based coping strategies that range from compromising the quality of food to food rationing. Repeatedly occurring food shortage has also forced some households to employ resilience erosive coping mechanisms such as selling reproductive assets. Such coping strategies limit the capacity of households to cope with future food insecurity-related shocks. Coordinating crisis management based on humanitarian intervention with households' livelihood assets protection and resilience strengthening is the major policy objective of this study.

Chapter 8 (by R. S. Gomes and E. Stedefeldt) focuses on food safety as an intrinsic component of food security and a shaper of food systems. It discusses the "commercial restaurant" system and the "kitchen worker" subsystem from the perspective of building resilience in food safety. It discusses that relationship maps built for the system and subsystem guide the presentation and discussion of structural, organizational, social, and symbolic aspects and elements. Examples include risk perception of foodborne diseases, cognitive illusions, sociological aspects, the social dimension of taste, humanization, and working conditions and precariousness of work in kitchens. The chapter concludes by providing some recommendations for promoting food safety resilience in commercial restaurants.

Chapter 9 (by F. Teixeira) discusses the environmental pressures that the Montado/Dehesa systems are experiencing, leading to an impoverishment of the floristic composition of the understorey. The chapter examines the potential for using legume–rhizobia symbiosis to increase biological nitrogen fixation (BNF) and avenues for research. It also discusses the co-colonization of the roots of legumes with arbuscular mycorrhizal (AM) fungi and the effects on P and Mn uptake. The chapter highlights a better understanding of the relationships between soil pH, organic matter content (SOM), microbial community, soil P content, and the plant strategies to mobilize it, as well as plant effects on the soil solution concentrations of Mn, as important for the management of these systems. The increase of BNF in these systems, through the breeding of tolerant cultivars to acidic soils and a stepwise legumes enrichment, alongside soil fertility management, may contribute to increasing biomass production and SOM content.

The final chapter (by S. Sood et al.) addresses the importance of effective and efficient systems for the early diagnosis of biotic stress in crops through deep learning models, using wheat-rust pathogenic interaction as a model. Rusts are plant diseases caused by obligate fungi parasites. They are usually host-specific and cause greater losses of yields in crops, trees, and ornamental plants. Wheat is a staple food crop bearing losses specifically due to three species of rust fungi namely leaf rust (Puccinia triticina), stem rust (Puccinia graminis), and yellow rust (Puccinia striiformis). About 100% yield loss has been reported by the stem and yellow rust, while a 50% yield loss has been reported by leaf rust. Under this scenario, the need for an effective and efficient system that allows the identification and classification of these diseases at early stages was recognized. The chapter reports the results from the use of a deep learning-based convolutional neural network (i.e., VGG16) transfer learning model for wheat disease classification on the CGIAR image dataset. The deep learning models produced the best results by tuning the various hyper-parameters such as batch size, number of epochs, and learning rate.

Collectively, the book addresses some major challenges of food systems associated with a diversity of agricultural contexts and priorities, disclosing distinct but complementary entry points to advance resilience. Within this context, the transformation of the current food systems towards sustainability and resilience should include smart and innovative approaches across all components of the food system – from supply chains to consumer behavior and diets – that ensure both the production of nutritious foods at affordable costs and the reduction of food wastage and the valorization of sub-products. Understanding the complexity of food systems and shaping actions and policies to their different categories that range from "rural and traditional" to "industrialized and consolidated" is mandatory to identify priority areas of intervention. Only with resilient and sustainable food systems, contextualized according to geographic and socioeconomic realities, and adjusted to 21st-century societal expectations, the world would be able to meet the SDG targets. Actions targeting different drivers that govern food systems are mandatory to this endeavor. And time is of the essence.

The editorial team acknowledges all chapter contributors. Acknowledgments are also due to the School of Agriculture, University of Lisbon – Forest Research Center (UIDB/00239/2020) and Linking Landscape, Environment, Agriculture and Food Research Centre (UIDB/04129/2020), Department of Geography, Environmental Studies and Tourism, University of the Western Cape, and Faculty of Agronomy and Forest Engineering, Eduardo Mondlane University.

Ana I. Ribeiro-Barros
Forest Research Center,
School of Agriculture,
University of Lisbon,
Lisbon, Portugal

Daniel S. Tevera
Department of Geography, Environmental Studies and Tourism,
University of the Western Cape,
Western Cape, South Africa

Lucas D. Tivana
Faculty of Agronomy and Forest Engineering,
Eduardo Mondlane University,
Maputo, Mozambique

Luís F. Goulao
Linking Landscape, Environment, Agriculture,
School of Agriculture,
University of Lisbon,
Lisbon, Portugal

Section 1

Food Systems Transformation towards Resilience

Chapter 1

Perspective Chapter: Food System Resilience – Towards a Joint Understanding and Implications for Policy

Bart de Steenhuijsen Piters, Emma Termeer, Deborah Bakker, Hubert Fonteijn and Herman Brouwer

Abstract

The COVID-19 crisis is just one in a series of shocks and stressors that exemplify the importance of building resilient food systems. To ensure that desired food system outcomes are less fluctuating, policy makers and other important stakeholders need a common narrative on food system resilience. The purpose of this paper is to work towards a joint understanding of food system resilience and its implications for policy making. The delivery of desired outcomes depends on the ability of food systems to *anticipate*, *prevent*, *absorb*, and *adapt to* the impacts of shocks and stressors. Based on our literature review we found four properties of food systems that enhance their resilience. We refer to these as the **A B C D** of resilience building: Agency, Buffering, Connectivity and Diversity. Over time, many food systems have lost levels of agency, buffering capacity, connectivity or diversity. One of the principal causes of this is attributed to the governance of food systems. Governance is inherently political: as a result of conflicting interests and power imbalances, food systems fail to deliver equitable and just access to food. Moreover, the impacts of shocks and stressors are not evenly distributed across actors in the food system. This paper has highlighted the importance of more inclusive governance to direct food system transformation towards such higher levels of resilience. We conclude that we cannot leave this to the market, but that democratic and before all independent, credible institutions are needed to create the necessary transparency between actors as to their interests, power and influence.

Keywords: food system, resilience, COVID-19, agency, governance

1. Introduction

Food system resilience presents a paradox: even when global food markets prove to be quite resilient in the face of different shocks and crises, desired outcomes such as food and nutrition security are not ensured *for al and all timesl*. To ensure that desired food system outcomes are less fluctuating, policy makers and other important stakeholders need a common narrative on food system resilience. The purpose of this paper is to work towards a joint understanding of food system resilience and its implications for policy making.

The impacts of the global COVID-19 pandemic remind us of the importance of food systems that can withstand and recover from shocks. The COVID-19 crisis has impacted everyone's life in some way. However, some people live in more vulnerable contexts than others and have different levels of response capacity, hence they experience more profound impacts. The world's poorest people already dealt with unstable livelihoods and chronic food insecurity before the pandemic. This means low- and middle-income countries (LMIC) have a less advantaged starting point in the face of shocks and crises.

The COVID-19 crisis is just one in a series of shocks and stressors that exemplify the importance of building resilient food systems. The global food crisis of 2008 revealed how a convergence of different market shocks and disruptions in food production can cause dramatic increases in global food prices and food shortages [1]. The 2008 food price crisis has, in many cases, compounded the impacts of existing shocks and crises, such as droughts, floods, conflict and insecurity. Despite its apparent resilience under the pressure of the COVID-19 pandemic so far, the global food system remains vulnerable. The blockage of the Suez Canal in 2021 shows how a small technical or human failure can bring global transport to a sudden standstill [2]. COVID-19 related measures, such as restrictions in movement of goods and people, have had direct implications for people's livelihoods, food affordability and food access [3].

The delivery of desired outcomes depends on the ability of food systems to *anticipate*, *prevent*, *absorb*, and *adapt to* the impacts of shocks and stressors. Food system resilience issues are far from simple to solve. The complex interdependencies within our food systems involve all aspects of life: natural, political, economic, social and cultural. It is therefore key to start from a common understanding between all stakeholders of what food system resilience entails. From there, we can identify the steps that are needed to reform the governance of food systems to obtain and secure the outcomes that we need as a society. This is also the challenge for the United Nations Food Systems Summit, due late 2021, which will create the momentum to acknowledge where we are in building more resilient food systems, and where we want to go.

Key messages

Building food system resilience is necessary to withstand shocks and stressors and maintain progress towards desired outcomes: food and nutrition security and equitable livelihoods for all in a healthy ecosystem.

We identify four key properties of building resilient food systems: ensuring **A**gency, creating **B**uffers, stimulating **C**onnectivity, and enhancing **D**iversity throughout the system.

Implementing these properties will enhance the capacity of food systems to anticipate, prevent, absorb, and adapt to the impacts of shocks and stressors.

Building resilience through these key properties requires transformation of the entire system and this raises questions about the politics and governance of markets and broader food systems.

2. Towards a joint understanding: What is food system resilience?

A **food system** includes all processes, actors and activities associated with food production and food utilisation, from growing and harvesting to transporting and consuming [4]. A food system also encompasses the wider **food environment**, from markets and trade to policies and innovation. The main challenge for food systems globally is to increase the supply of safe and healthy food in an inclusive and sustainable way. This is reflected in the desired **outcomes** of a well-functioning food system, which include (**Figure 1**):

Shocks and stressors.

The ability of our food system to deliver desired outcomes directly depends on its capacity to deal with natural and man-made disturbances: shocks and stressors. *Shocks* refer to a sudden event that impacts on the functions of a system and its components, as seen for example with COVID-19 and locust plagues. A *stressor* can be defined as a long-term trend that undermines the functioning and increases the vulnerability of a system. The most acute stressor threatening the current global food system is climate change, which in turn leads to a variety of shocks, such as extreme weather events or crop diseases.

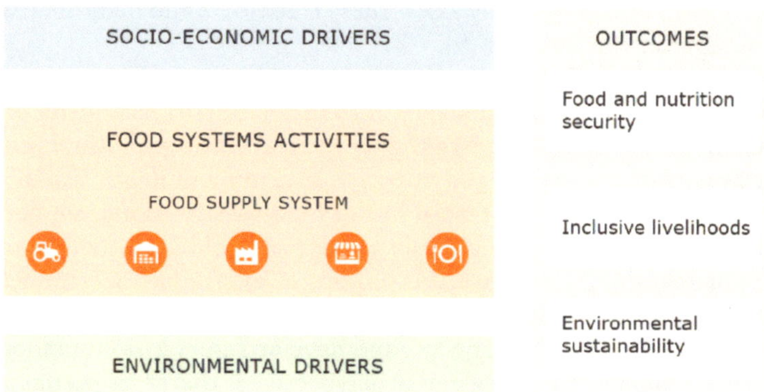

Figure 1.
Simplified visualisation of a food system. Source: adapted from Van Berkum, Dengerink and Ruben [4].

- the production of sufficient, safe and healthy food for our growing world population
- the equitable distribution of costs and profits
- being adaptable to climate change and using land and natural resources sustainably

In this paper we refer to **food system resilience** as the capacity of food systems to deliver desired outcomes in the face of shocks and stressors. The concept of resilience has its origins in ecological stability theory, explaining the capacity of ecosystems to return to their original state after a disturbance [5]. In the past decades, resilience thinking has been applied in various disciplines (such as ecology, economics and risk management) and different definitions of the concept exist according to the discipline for which they have been developed [6]. In relation to food systems, resilience thinking has been applied to address the complex interactions between nature and society with a focus on maintaining human well-being within planetary boundaries [7]. However, there is confusion and contestation about what the concept means and how it can be measured. This is especially true for the resilience of food systems, where multiple types of resilience interact (such as agricultural, economic, political and social resilience), raising the question of whether a unified conceptualisation of food system resilience is possible. In this context, one suggestion could be to identify context-specific challenges and policy implications using a 'resilience lens', and translating resilience to contextual, measurable indicators [8]. This paper is an effort to identify starting points to apply such a resilience lens in policy environments.

Considering increasing concerns about undesired outcomes, as well as the rate and scale of global challenges such as climate change, population growth and loss of biodiversity, there is increasing reference to the need for profound, systemic changes in our food systems. Such changes are also referred to as food system **transformation**, raising questions on how these are identified, prioritised and promoted through public policy instruments, private sector responses or civil society agency. The sum of these can be referred to as food system **governance**. Effective governance of food systems needs to take into account that resilience is not a unified, absolute measure, as interventions that make food systems more *robust* to shocks and stressors may also lead to associated vulnerabilities. The key is to continually assess these **trade-offs** and determine whether they are an acceptable consequence [9].

In other words, enhancing food system resilience involves a more complex task than just ensuring the stable delivery of food and nutrition security or other desired outcomes. For example, expanding or intensifying agricultural production may positively contribute to food and nutrition security, but it will also increase the likelihood of pollution and potential loss of biodiversity. Moreover, benefits and losses are often not distributed evenly across stakeholders in food systems. As resilience is not an absolute measure, it is important to take into account who has the power to define it [10]. The awareness of such interactions and trade-offs is at the core of approaches to describe, diagnose, and develop interventions in food systems. Thinking about resilience from a systemic perspective is therefore particularly useful for policymakers who formulate strategies for food system interventions. Building on a common conceptual understanding of resilience in food systems is necessary to avoid that the concept causes confusion and miscommunication between different stakeholders.

Following the concepts used by the Organisation for Economic Co-operation and Development (OECD), the Food and Agriculture Organisation (FAO), and the Scientific Group of the UN Food Systems Summit, we distinguish five key capacities that together determine the ability of food systems to handle shocks and stressors: anticipation, prevention, absorption, adaptation and transformation:[11–13].

The projected rise in food and nutrition insecurity on a global scale is driven by different **shocks and stressors** that often overlap or interact. We can categorise them in the following four clusters [14, 15] with some illustrative examples:

- climate change, variability and extremes *(e.g., erratic rainfall, droughts)*
- conflict and insecurity *(e.g., displacement, civil unrest, terrorism)*
- economic downturns and market disruptions *(e.g., food price spikes of 2008)*
- other unexpected shocks *(e.g., the sudden outbreak of desert locusts, a pandemic)*

In summary: conceptual clarity and purpose of building food system resilience are needed for effective communication between stakeholders who define together the governance of food systems. Five capacities of food system to respond to shocks and stressors emerge from recent literature, as well as four distinct clusters of shocks and stressors. In the next sections we explore reasons why food systems are not resilient,

Anticipation	Capacity to manage risks and plan strategies to deal with shocks when they occur.
Prevention	Preventive actions to mitigate the effects of expected shocks or stressors.
Absorption	The ability to cope immediately with the effects of shocks and stressors.
Adaptation	The capacity to adapt strategies and actions while maintaining stable functioning of the system.
Transformation	The capacity to transform the entire system.

how food systems evolve after shocks and stresses, and what emerges from literature as key properties of resilient food systems.

3. Why are food systems not resilient and what are the consequences?

Shocks and stressors rarely happen in isolation and always impact on the wider food system, creating potential trade-offs between different outcomes, such as food and nutrition security, environmental sustainability and secured livelihoods for all. Climate change and global warming increase the incidence of extreme weather conditions and impact the entire ecosystem. Increasingly unpredictable weather and extreme weather incidents mean that farmers are regularly faced with high yield losses. Furthermore, agriculture itself is caught in a double bind: the sector as a whole contributes over 10 per cent to global greenhouse gas emissions, yet it needs to produce sufficient food to feed the growing world population. Public health shocks, such as COVID-19, may compound with economic shocks, which will in turn negatively impact on food and nutrition security. Cases of protracted crises, where conflict, coupled with weather or health shocks, cause severe food insecurity, exemplify the complex interactions between shocks, stressors and the food system.

Even before COVID-19, from 2005 to 2016, developing countries were experiencing an average of 260 natural disasters a year, killing 54,000, affecting 97 million and costing USD 27 billion annually [16]. FAO estimates that 23 per cent of the economic loss and damage due to natural disasters is related to the agricultural sector – which significantly impacts on the ability of disaster victims to rebuild and recover.

Stagnating outcome 1: **Food and nutrition security** (SDG 2, 3, 6) Despite the global commitment to end hunger by 2030 (SDG 2) and decades of decline in world hunger, the most recent estimates show that if recent rates of increase persist, the global number of undernourished people in 2030 would exceed 850 million [18].	Stagnating outcome 2: **Equitable livelihoods** (SDG 1, 5, 8, 10, 11) Action Track 4 of the Food System Summit emphasises how inequality and power imbalances constrain the ability of food systems to deliver poverty reduction and equitable livelihoods. For the first time in over 20 years, global extreme poverty levels rose in 2020 as COVID-19 compounded the impacts of conflict and climate change [19].	Stagnating outcome 3: **Sustainability** (SDG 6, 13, 15) Climate change is threatening all aspects of the food system. Although global ambitions to tackle climate change were set in the Paris Agreement, the global community is a long way off track meeting either the 1.5 or 2 degrees targets. As a result of this, the frequency and severity of natural disasters is expected to increase, exacerbating food insecurity and poverty [20].

Table 1.
Three areas where SDG progress is stagnating.

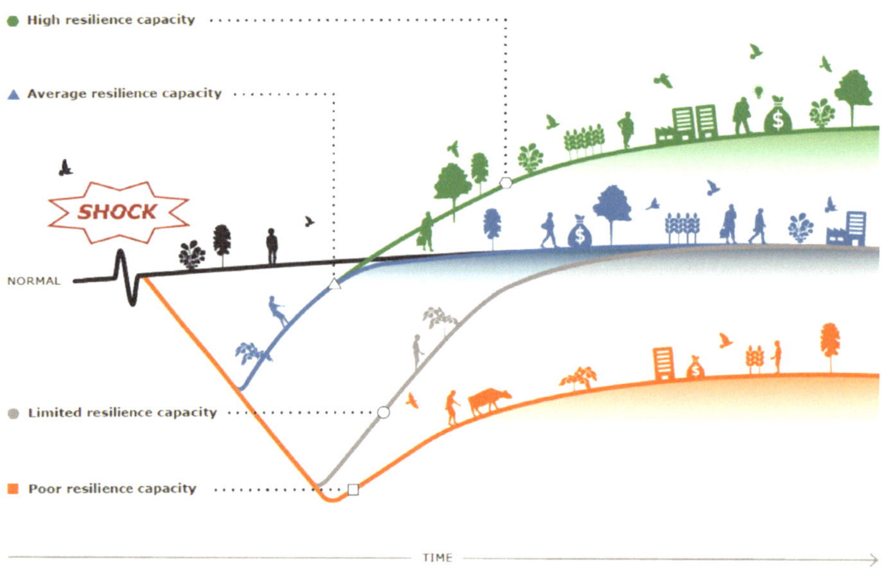

Figure 2.
The capacity of a food system to respond to shocks and stressors. Source: This paper.

Repeatedly, we see shocks trigger systemic crises that disrupt the entire food system, including social services, the economy, and the environment.

The capacity to manage risks and to adapt to changes is unevenly distributed across nations, regions, communities, and households. The poor are especially vulnerable and liable to become trapped in vicious cycles of decline due to shocks and stressors. This poverty and vulnerability trap means that recovery to pre-disaster levels of well-being becomes increasingly difficult [17].

To ensure that food systems can deliver desired outcomes for future generations, resilience building should go hand in hand with sustainable development. After all, a resilient system is a system that can be sustained in the long term. In 2015, the international community agreed on 17 Sustainable Development Goals (SDGs) to be met by 2030, in an effort to build a more sustainable world. Even though progress has been made towards this end, progress on many of the goals is either stagnating or lost, partly due to the recent COVID-19 crisis (see **Table 1**). This stagnation demonstrates the urgency in designing our food system from a resilience perspective. If it were designed as such, our food systems could have average to even high resilience capacities, rewarding us with the stable or enhanced delivery of the desired outcomes (as stated in the SDGs) despite the occurrence of shocks and stressors (see **Figure 2**).

An example of a food system with a high resilience capacity is found in Ireland, where the shock of the 2008 economic crisis was absorbed by making investments in the dairy sector. This sector became a driver of growth for the whole Irish economy in the following decade, [21] and the shock eventually became the trigger for a new pathway of opportunities. Unfortunately there are many more examples of food systems where the opposite happens: shocks and stressors expose underlying weakness in resilience capacity.[1] This can result in deterioration of desired food system outcomes such as food and nutrition security, living income, or protection of natural resources.

[1] See, for early evidence of impact of Covid-19 on agriculture, e.g. [22]. Also: [23].

4. What can be done to make food systems more resilient?

To understand how food systems can be more resilient we need to explore the role that resilience capacities play in relation to shocks and stressors. We propose to subdivide these capacities according to three phases of a shock/stressor scenario: the first two capacities (*anticipation* and *prevention*) relate to the phase prior to the occurrence of any shocks. The third capacity (*absorption*) plays the largest role during the occurrence of a shock, while the last two capacities (*adaptation* and *transformation*) are most relevant in the aftermath of the shock and influence the recovery towards post-shock food and nutrition security (the upward trajectory in **Figure 2**). This subdivision is more subtle when examining stresses, since these play out over longer time spans. In this context, it is an interesting question whether the effect of COVID-19 on the food system qualifies as a shock or a stressor.

The first two resilience capacities (*anticipation* and *prevention*) are the closest linked to the shock type or stress itself. For instance, the anticipation of extreme weather events is greatly aided by the distribution of accurate and up-to-date satellite data amongst all stakeholders, allowing preventive action against floods to strengthen local water defences.

To prepare for our future challenges, we need to transform food systems towards food and nutrition security for all in such a way that the economic, social, cultural and environmental bases to generate food security and nutrition are safeguarded for future generations [24]. This is a complex task that requires strong collaboration across disciplines and national borders. First, the need and urgency of this task should be acknowledged. Then, efforts can be made to direct policy objectives towards making food systems more resilient. Regarding these policy objectives, literature on resilient food systems identifies various important measures to consider, ranging from regional and local production and distribution, diversification of production, environment and responses, improved rural infrastructure, accessibility and local self-organisation.[2] From these, we derive four summarising aspects that define the response capacity of food systems. These four properties are not exhaustive, but they are always recognisable in systems that are resilient. We suggest that policy makers and other stakeholders recognise what we present as the **A B C D** of resilience building (**Figure 3**):

1. **A**gency: the means and capacities of people to mitigate risks and to respond to shocks.

2. **B**uffering: resources to fall back on in the face of shocks and stressors.

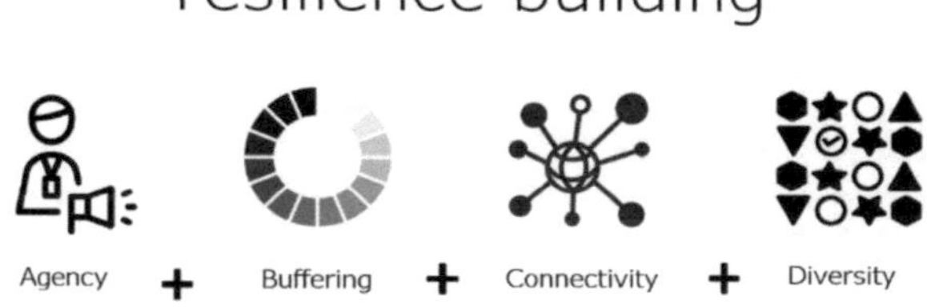

Figure 3.
The ABCD of food system resilience building. Source: This paper.

[2] See, for example: [25–30].

3. **C**onnectivity: the interconnection of and communication between actors and market segments.

4. **D**iversity: diversity at different scales and in different places, from production to consumption and from farm level to regional diversity.

4.1 Agency

Human agency is a key factor in determining how individuals and society respond to change, disruptions and crises. Agency can be understood as the ability of people to choose their actions and execute them as they see fit. By emphasising agency, we go beyond the view of vulnerable people as passive victims in the face of external threats or crises. Agency is strongly related to adaptive capacity: the necessary resources for people and systems to adapt and learn, but agency also allows for anticipation and prevention. So far, discussions on food system resilience have focused in large part on resilience at system-level, for example maintaining stable trade relationships. This aggregated view has resulted in much less attention to understanding the role of human agency in the adaptation at the heart of resilient food systems [31]. For example, in situations of protracted crises, people have developed coping strategies, ranging from informal early warning systems to community seed systems, that contribute to the resilience of their livelihoods [32].

- *Understanding individual behaviour, as well as community responses, is essential to strengthening the resilience of a system as a whole.*

4.2 Buffering

Buffering in food systems can be understood in a broad sense: from buffering strategies by subsistence farmers to the creation and maintenance of national food stocks. Buffering may result in higher costs and lower long-term profit but increase the overall resilience of a system. For example, small- and medium-sized enterprises may choose to increase their savings accounts instead of investing all profits in the growth of their business, in preparation for shortfalls in sales. Buffering strategies are essential for enhancing the absorption capacities in a system. Creating buffers can be seen as an action in anticipation of a shock or stressor. In the financial world, buffering strategies in the form of maintaining adequate capital levels are a crucial part of the risk management toolkit:[33] financial buffers ensure business continuity in the face of low-frequency high-impact events by absorbing the resulting losses and maintaining solvability [34]. Policies may also impact on the buffering capacity of a food system, such as the creation of national food stocks or by providing direct financial support to people and businesses that struggle during a shock.

- *Buffering in food systems should be acknowledged as an economic asset and be preserved or strengthened at the level that is most appropriate (individual, firm, region), even if it may lead to lower economic returns.*

4.3 Connectivity

In every system, connectivity refers to the nature and strength of the interactions between the various components. Maintaining and building connectivity at the community, company, and country level helps to build resilience and guard against negative outcomes [35]. Improved connectivity in agricultural value chains improves a food system's capacity to respond to shocks and stressors and is an essential contributor to adaptation and transformation capacities. Connectivity can manifest both in terms of physical infrastructure (roads, ports, airports) and communication infrastructure (internet access), as well as in terms of the existence of economic, political and social relationships between actors and nations. For instance, when a dominant trade partner experiences reduced supplies (e.g., due to local droughts), one has to switch to other suppliers to secure access to food. In this sense, connectivity offers an important protection against local and distant shocks, but it also exposes an actor to unforeseen price fluctuations imposed by alternative supply networks. At the community level, strong infrastructure can ensure mobilisation of support in times of need. At the business level, companies with access to multiple markets can more easily switch between commodities or divert products globally, thereby continuing their business operations [35].

- *Strengthening connectivity at different levels (community, private sector, country) with different means (infrastructure, communication networks, relationships) is a crucial component of a resilient food system.*

4.4 Diversity

Resilient systems are diverse systems. Diversity means that a loss of one resource may be compensated by another. A shortage can be mitigated by a surplus elsewhere.[3] Evidence from studies on the resilience of ecosystems indicates that biodiversity is an important contributor to system stability and continuity [41]. More diverse farming systems have greater capacity to absorb the effects of shocks and stressors, and this capacity stabilises food supplies through value chains to consumer markets [42]. According to a large and growing body of research, a diverse farm system – household plots, mixed multi-crop farms, variety in farm type and size – does indeed enhance the availability and consumption of diverse foods needed for a healthy diet [43]. What is required is a fundamentally different model of agriculture based on diversifying farms and farming landscapes, optimising biodiversity and stimulating interactions between different species, as part of holistic strategies to build long-term resilience, healthy agro-ecosystems and secure livelihoods. Together, a varied and balanced diet, a wide range of crops and foodstuffs, and a diverse system of production and distribution, make a more resilient, stable and healthier food system. ([44], p. 73)

- *It is key to recognise the importance of diversity – not just in nature, but also in the entire food system, including production, consumption, economy, governance and society.*

5. Governance for food system resilience

Most food systems across the globe do not deliver all the outcomes that society expects. Over time, many food systems have lost levels of agency, buffering capacity,

[3] See, for example: [36–40].

connectivity or diversity. One of the principal causes of a food system's failure to evolve in desired directions is its governance.

Governance encompasses the rules, authorities and institutions that coordinate, manage and steer food systems: not just government, but also markets, cultural traditions and networks, and non-state actors such as businesses and civil society organisations [45, 46]. Governance is inherently political: as a result of conflicting interests and power imbalances, food systems fail to deliver equitable and just access to food. Moreover, the impacts of shocks and stressors are not evenly distributed across actors in the food system. There are significant differences in vulnerability and response capacities between different groups of people, sectors and regions. Socio-political differentiation and economic inequality are often overlooked in relation to food system resilience, but these factors need to be taken into account to effectively address unequal impacts and outcomes. For example, monopolies by big private sector players, at the expense of a multitude of smaller players, have a potentially negative impact on the overall resilience of food systems. Political economic analysis of the governance model will expose any imbalances in power and interests. Such imbalances are increasing worldwide in food systems where concentration of big corporations is observed. Concentrated firms can shape markets, shape technology and innovation agendas, and shape policy and governance frameworks [47].

Momentum, commitment and a large support base is needed for system transformation. Commitments to actions that are understood and underwritten by many stakeholders have a higher chance of being implemented than those agreed upon by few stakeholders. Multi-stakeholder approval also increases public support for such actions – which can be direly needed in challenging circumstances. Getting a large and diverse enough group of stakeholders on board also increases the "solution space": the pool of resources, creativity and agency needed to develop new innovations in food systems. However, the necessary diversity of actors and values will result in processes of negotiation and contestation. This requires careful and deliberate facilitation of multi-stakeholder processes to build trust and relationships, manage potential conflicts, and prevent elite capture [48]. In addition, multi-sectoral policies are needed to address trade-offs and interdependencies of food system actors and components. This requires boundary spanning capabilities [49] and policy integration in order to connect the different policy subsystems [50]. For example: integrated programmes, coordination schemes, participatory analysis, and multi-stakeholder platforms can help to connect different governance levels and sectors.

Lastly, the challenges of food system transformation call for experimentation, not only in technologies and instruments, but also in concrete governance processes. Various multi-stakeholder collaborations, appropriate to different levels and cultures of governance, need to be tried and tested. New kinds of formal and informal institutions, conflict resolution options that are mediated or legislated, and the generation and use of new kinds of data will be needed. Both bottom-up and top-down innovation will be required, aiming for a broad portfolio of innovation projects, where risks, failures and uncertainties are embraced [51]. Much innovation will happen spontaneously – but most will need financial, legal or policy support to break through and change current food system governance regimes. This support can be delivered at different levels: it can aim to shift structural system characteristics, which prevent innovation; it can be geared towards promoting smaller innovations that offer small wins; or finally, the support can be focused on enabling rapid processes for testing and adapting the innovation to the relevant context.

6. Conclusions and recommendations

Initially, the COVID-19 pandemic caused panic about the impacts on food supply at a global scale. Now that worries about basic food supply have mostly faded, attention has moved to broader concerns about the effects of different shocks and stressors on food and nutrition security, economic livelihoods, sustainability, biodiversity and healthy ecosystems. Partially overlapping components of food systems of growing, producing, distributing and consuming food have shown differentiation in terms of resilience. In fact, many food systems do not deliver outcomes such as healthy diets and environmental sustainability, and fail to positively contribute to the livelihoods of large numbers of producers and consumers alike. Over time, food systems have delivered more and new foods, as well as economic opportunities for many people – in part through investments in research and innovation. At the same time, food systems continue to contribute heavily to global warming, waste problems, pollution, obesity, chronic disease and social inequality. This is why we argue that building food system resilience is not only important to withstand and recover from shocks and stressors, but also to maintain progress towards desired outcomes, such as food and nutrition security and equitable livelihoods for all. Even if a system is resilient, specific groups in society may still be vulnerable. A resilient system should therefore also be fair, equitable and inclusive – which implies that building resilience is an inherently political process, aiming for a transformation of the entire food system.

In this paper, we have identified four key properties of building resilient food systems: ensuring agency, creating buffers, increasing connectivity, and enhancing diversity throughout the system. These are certainly not stand-alone or quick-fix solutions. An integrated and context-sensitive approach that focuses on strengthening these properties will certainly increase the capacity of food systems to anticipate, prevent, absorb, and adapt to the impacts of shocks and stressors. This requires tailor-made interventions with attention to potential trade-offs. For example, creating an enhanced balance between reliance on global food markets (import dependency) and domestic food production (self-sufficiency) requires investments in market and value chain development, including incentives for midstream value chain actors and campaigns ("nudging") that bring about changes in consumer behaviour to favour domestic produce. **Table 2** offers some more examples of observed challenges and policy entry points related to these four key properties.

AIn the first sections of this paper we highlighted that more shocks and stressors to food systems can be anticipated in the nearby future. These challenges seem to be unavoidable, but higher levels of resilience will make our food systems better prepared and capable of absorbing their effects without jeopardising essential contributions by food systems to our livelihoods. This paper has highlighted the importance of more inclusive governance to direct food system transformation towards such higher levels of resilience. We conclude that we cannot leave this to the market, but that democratic and before all independent, credible institutions are needed to create the necessary transparency between actors as to their interests, power and influence. Aligning these interests is never easy, and must be accompanied by collective negotiation and conflict management processes especially in cases where interests strongly diverge. Besides this, actors will need to be mobilised and incentivised to contribute their resources, innovation capacities and outreach to constituencies in society, ranging from consumers to producers and everybody in between. This requires working with everyone with a stake in food systems to try to look at things

	Observed challenges	Policy entry points
A	The COVID-19 crisis shows many food system actors lack financial, social or natural capital to act according to their priorities.	Food system policy should consider human behaviour as central: people are at the heart of food system dynamics. This can be achieved through more inclusive modes of food system governance.
B	In LMICs, buffers have disappeared due to budgetary reasons and government reforms. The great dependency on imports for many of these countries leads to increased vulnerability in the face of shocks.	Policies that serve as buffers (such as social protection programmes or financial support) are crucial to mitigate the impacts of shocks. Food system actors – from primary producers to consumers – should be supported to build buffers.
C	Reduced connectivity, for example, due to closed borders and restrictions of movement of people and goods, increases the chance of harmful impacts after shocks.	In the face of a global, national or local shock or stressors, connectivity should be considered as key to keeping up the flow of goods, people and services. This includes public communication and requires acknowledging that too much connectivity may have downsides, such as spreading a threat, such as bird flu.
D	Modernisation of farming systems focusing on the maximisation of yields has resulted in the progressive loss of biodiversity associated with monocropping and overspecialisation.	Policy should stimulate diversity – in policy measures and production – to limit vulnerability when a shock occurs. Traditional production systems practiced risk management through diversification before specialised production became the norm.

Table 2.
Summary of the ABCD of food system resilience building.

differently and collaborate [52]. This is key to create the conditions for transformation towards sustainable, inclusive and resilient food systems.

Acknowledgements

The authors would like to acknowledge funding from the Wageningen University & Research Programme on "Food Security and Valuing Water" that is supported by the Dutch Ministry of Agriculture, Nature and Food Quality.

Author details

Bart de Steenhuijsen Piters[1*], Emma Termeer[2], Deborah Bakker[2], Hubert Fonteijn[3] and Herman Brouwer[4]

1 Food Systems, Wageningen Economic Research, Netherlands

2 Wageningen Economic Research, Netherlands

3 Biometris, Wageningen Plant Research, Netherlands

4 Wageningen Centre for Development Innovation, Netherlands

*Address all correspondence to: bart.desteenhuijsenpiters@wur.nl

References

[1] Headey, D. (2011). Rethinking the global food crisis: The role of trade shocks. Food Policy, 36(2), 136-146; Headey, D., & Fan, S. (2010). *Reflections on the global food crisis: How did it happen? How has it hurt? And how can we prevent the next one?* (Vol. 165). IFPRI. Retrieved from: https://www.ifpri.org/publication/reflections-global-food-crisis

[2] The Guardian (2021). *At least 20 livestock ships caught in Suez canal logjam*. 26 March 2021. Retrieved from: https://www.theguardian.com/environment/2021/mar/26/at-least-20-livestock-ships-caught-in-suez-canal-logjam

[3] Béné C., Bakker D., Chavarro Rodriguez M., Even B., Melo J., and Sonneveld A. (2021). Impacts of COVID-19 on people's food security: foundations for a more resilient food system. Report prepared for the CGIAR COVID-19 Hub Working Group 4, CGIAR.

[4] Van Berkum, S., Dengerink, J. & Ruben, R. (2018). *The food systems approach: sustainable solutions for a sufficient supply of healthy food*. Wageningen Economic Research. The Hague.

[5] Holling, C.S. (1973). Resilience and stability of ecological systems. Annual Review of Ecology and Systematics, 4(1), 1-23.

[6] Tendall, D. M., Joerin, J., Kopainsky, B., Edwards, P., Shreck, A., Le, Q. B., ... & Six, J. (2015). Food system resilience: defining the concept. Global Food Security, 6, 17-23.

[7] Folke, C., Biggs, R., Norstrom, A.V., Reyers, B. & Rockstrom, J. (2016). Social-ecological resilience and biosphere-based sustainability science. Ecology and Society, 21(3), 41.

[8] Wassenaer, L. van, Oosterkamp, E., Van Asseldonk, M. & Ryan, M. (2021 in publication). Food system resilience: ontology development and impossible trinities. *Agriculture and Food Security.*

[9] Janssen, M.A. & Anderies, J.M. (2007). Robustness Trade-offs in Social-Ecological Systems. International Journal of the Commons, 1(1), 43-65.

[10] Dewulf, A., Karpouzoglou, T., Warner, J., Wesselink, A., Mao, F., Vos, J., Tamas, P., Groot, A., Heijmans, A., Ahmed, F., Hoang, L., Vij, S. & Buytaert, W. (2019). The power to define resilience in social–hydrological systems: Toward a power-sensitive resilience framework. Wiley Interdisciplinary Reviews: Water, 6(6), e1377.

[11] Hertel, T.W., Elouafi, I., Ewert, F. & Tanticharoen, M. (2021). Building Resilience to Vulnerabilities, Shocks and Stresses – Action Track 5. A paper from the Scientific Group of the UN Food Systems Summit. 8 March 2021. Retrieved from: https://www.un.org/sites/un2.un.org/files/5-action_track-5_scientific_group_draft_paper_8-3-2021.pdf

[12] OECD (2020). *Strengthening agricultural resilience in the face of multiple risks*. Paris. OECD Publishing. Retrieved from: https://doi.org/10.1787/2250453e-en

[13] UN FAO (2020). *Resilience: FAO in Emergencies*. Retrieved from: http://www.fao.org/emergencies/how-we-work/resilience/en/

[14] UN FAO (2018). *Conflicts and climatic shocks aggravate current food insecurity in many countries*. 20 September 2018. Rome. http://www.fao.org/news/story/en/item/1153461/icode/

[15] UN FAO Regional Office for Africa (2020). *Building Resilient Food and Agriculture Systems in the Context of Climate Change, Conflicts and Economic Downturns: Addressing the Humanitarian-Development-Peace Nexus in Africa*. 26 October 2020. Retrieved from: http://www.fao.org/3/nc665en/nc665en.pdf

[16] UN FAO (2017). *The impact of disasters and crises on agriculture and food security*. Rome. http://www.fao.org/3/I8656EN/i8656en.pdf

[17] Brown, K. & Westaway, E. (2011). Agency, Capacity, and Resilience to Environmental Change: Lessons from Human Development, Well-being, and Disasters. Annual Review of Environment and Resources, 36, 321-342.

[18] UN FAO, IFAD, UNICEF, WFP & WHO (2020). *The State of Food Security and Nutrition in the World 2020*. Rome, FAO. Retrieved from: http://www.fao.org/3/ca9692en/ca9692en.pdf

[19] World Bank (2020). *Updated estimates of the impact of COVID-19 on global poverty: the effect of new data*. Washington, World Bank. Retrieved from: https://blogs.worldbank.org/opendata/updated-estimates-impact-covid-19-global-poverty-effect-new-data

[20] United Nations (2020). *The Sustainable Development Goals Report 2020*. New York. Retrieved from: https://unstats.un.org/sdgs/report/2020/The-Sustainable-Development-Goals-Report-2020.pdf

[21] Brouwer, H., Guijt, J., Kelly, S. & Garcia-Campos, P. (2021). Ireland's journey towards sustainable food systems. The processes and practices that made a difference. Rome, FAO.

[22] FAO (2021) *Agricultural livelihoods and food security in the context of COVID-19: Results from household surveys in 11 countries with high pre-existing levels of food insecurity – Cross-country monitoring report, May 2021*. Rome. https://doi.org/10.4060/cb4747en

[23] Fan, S., Pandya-Lorch, R., Yosef, S. (eds) (2014) *Resilience for Food and Nutrition Security*. Washington DC: IFPRI. DOI: http://dx.doi.org/10.2499/9780896296787

[24] Scientific Group for the UN Food Systems Summit (2021). *Food Systems: Definition, Concept and Application for the UNFSS* (by Von Braun, Afsana, Fresco, Hassan, Torrero). Retrieved from https://sc-fss2021.org/wp-content/uploads/2021/04/Food_Systems_Definition.pdf.

[25] Béné, C. (2020). Resilience of local food systems and links to food security – a review of some important concepts in the context of COVID-19 and other shocks. Food security, 12, 805-822.

[26] Hodbod, J. & Eakin, H. (2015). Adapting a social-ecological resilience framework for food systems. Journal of Environmental Studies and Sciences, 5, 474-484.

[27] Schipanski, M.E., MacDonald, G.K., Rosenzweig, S., et al. (2016). Realizing Resilient Food Systems. BioScience, 66(7), 600 610.

[28] Seekell, D., Carr, J., Dell'Angelo, J. et al. (2017). Resilience in the global food system. Environ. Res. Lett, 12.

[29] Worstell, J. & Green, J. (2017). Eight qualities of resilient food systems: toward a sustainability/resilience index. Journal of Agriculture, Food Systems, and Community Development, 7(3), 23-41.

[30] Toth, A., Rendall, S. & Reitsma, F. (2016), Resilient food systems: a

qualitative tool for measuring food resilience. Urban Ecosyst, 19, 19-43.

[31] Bristow, G. & Healy, A. (2014). Regional Resilience: An Agency Perspective. Regional Studies, 48(5), 923-935.

[32] SNV & WUR (2021). *Covid-19 & Agriculture Review #3: Understanding vulnerabilities and resilience strategies in the context of COVID-19*. May 2021. Retrieved from: https://snv.org/cms/sites/default/files/explore/download/snv_wur_covid-19_agriculture_review_3_compressed.pdf

[33] Bui, C., Scheule, H., & Wu, E. (2017). The value of bank capital buffers in maintaining financial system resilience. Journal of Financial Stability, 33, 23-40.

[34] Bode, C., Wagner, S.M., Petersen, K.J. & Ellram, L.M. (2011). Understanding responses to supply chain disruptions: insights from information processing and resource dependence perspectives. The Academy of Management Journal, 54(4), 833-856.

[35] Love, D., Allison, E.H., Asche, F. et al. (2020). Emerging COVID-19 impacts, responses, and lessons for building resilience in the seafood system. Retrieved from: https://www.researchgate.net/publication/342504946_Emerging_COVID-19_impacts_ responses_ and_ lessons_for_building_resilience_in_the_seafood_system

[36] Benton, T.G., Bieg, C., Harwatt, H., Pudasaini, R. & Wellesley, L. (2021). *Food system impacts on biodiversity loss: three levers for food system transformation in support of nature*. Chatham House Research paper. London. https://www.chathamhouse.org/sites/default/files/2021-02/2021-02-03-food-system-biodiversity-loss-benton-et-al_0.pdf

[37] Leslie, P. & McCabe, J.T. (2013). Response diversity and resilience in social-ecological systems. Current Anthropology, 54(2), 114-143.

[38] Levia, D.F., Creed, I.F., Hannah, D.M., Nanko, K., Boyer, E.B. et al. (2020). Homogenization of the terrestrial water cycle. Nature geoscience, 13, 656-658.

[39] Wageningen University & Research (n.d.). *DiverIMPACTS – crop diversity as the foundation for sustainable European production chains*. Project page. https://www.wur.nl/en/project/DiverIMPACTS-crop-diversity-as-the-foundation-for-sustainable-European-production-chains-1.htm

[40] Wageningen University & Research (2016). *Plant diversity is a key factor to the resilience of Amazon forests.* News article. 9 September 2016. https://www.wur.nl/en/newsarticle/Plant-diversity-is-a-key-factor-to-the-resilience-of-Amazon-forests.htm

[41] Oliver, T.H. (2015). Biodiversity and resilience of ecosystem functions. Trends in Ecology & Evolution, 30, 673-684.

[42] Lee, J. van der, Kangogo, D., Özkan Gülzari, S., Dentoni, D., Oosting, S., Bijman, J., Klerkx, L. (2020 submitted). Resilience assessment in farming systems: a review.

[43] IPES-Food (2016). *From Uniformity to Diversity: a paradigm shift from industrial agriculture to diversified acroecological systems*. International Panel of Experts on Sustainable Food Systems. Retrieved from: http://www.ipes-food.org/_img/upload/files/UniformityToDiversity_FULL.pdf

[44] Report of the 5th SCAR Foresight Exercise Expert Group (2020*). Resilience and transformation. Luxembourg. Publications Office of the European Union.*

Retrieved from: https://scar-europe.org/images/FORESIGHT/FINAL-REPORT-5th-SCAR-Foresight-Exercise.pdf

[45] Hooghe, L., & Marks, G. (2003). Unraveling the Central State, but How? Types of Multi-level Governance. American Political Science Review, 97(2), 233-243.

[46] Stoker, G. (1998). Governance as theory: five propositions. International Social Science Journal, 50(155), 17-28.

[47] Clapp, J. (2021). The problem with growing corporate concentration and power in the global food system. *Nature Food*, published on line https://doi.org/10.1038/s43016-021-00297-7.

[48] Brouwer, H., Woodhill, J., Hemmati, M., Verhoosel, K., & van Vugt, S. (2019). The MSP guide: how to design and facilitate multi-stakeholder partnerships. (3rd ed.) WUR/Practical Action Publishing. https://edepot.wur.nl/543151

[49] Termeer, C.J.A.M., Drimie, S., Ingram, J., Pereira, L., Whittingham, M.J. (2018). A diagnostic framework for food system governance arrangements: The case of South Africa. NJAS/Wageningen Journal of Life Sciences, 84, 85-93.

[50] Candel, J.J.L., Pereira, L. (2017). Towards integrated food policy: Main challenges and steps ahead. Environmental Science and Policy, 73, 89-92.

[51] Klerkx, L., Begemann, S. (2020). Supporting food systems transformation: The what, why, who, where and how of mission-oriented agricultural innovation systems. Agricultural Systems, 184, 102901.

[52] Kalibata, A. (2021) Transforming food systems is within reach. NatureFood, Vol 2 May 2021, 313-314. https://doi.org/10.1038/s43016-021-00291-z

Chapter 2

Global Food System Transformation for Resilience

Jasper Okoro Godwin Elechi, Ikechukwu U. Nwiyi and Cornelius Smah Adamu

Abstract

Our world is incredibly diverse and beautiful, everything we do has an impact on the environment, and our actions are intertwined. Recognizing how our actions affect the Earth on a global scale means, we need to change the way we do things. We must ensure that the value society derives from our actions comes at a low cost to the environment. A sustainable strategy to establish a resilient food system is to ensure that human demand for the Earth's resources for food is kept within the supply of these resources. While more than 800 million people worldwide suffer from chronic malnutrition, our food systems emit roughly a third of all greenhouse emissions. Also, over 80% of our biodiversity gets lost. Hence, scaling up food system is simply not an option to feed nine to ten billion people by 2050 as we will need to produce more food in the next four decades than all of history's farmers have harvested in the last eight thousand years. Therefore, rather than upscaling, the global food systems require transformation. Four critical aspects of this transformation include: "Boosting the small; Transforming the Big; Losing Less; and Eating Smarter." Examining these four areas more deeply, it becomes evident that, while new technology will be critical to the transformation, government involvement, as well as better financial and behavioral change from residents and consumers, will be required. This chapter focuses on these four pillars that make up the global food system transformation for resilience.

Keywords: food system, resilience, livelihoods, global food system transformation, sustainable diet, boosting small, losing less, eating smarter

1. Introduction

Food, a crucial element of our everyday lives is essential to our health and well-being. It forms a part of our identity and culture, and a key component, if not the focal point, of many of our social activities. As a result, it is no surprise that food security (i.e., the availability of food for people) has shaped and continues to shape nations' economies, politics, and histories [1]. However, the current food production system and consumption create a variety of diseases, wreak havoc on the ecosystem, and obliterate the planet's safe operating zone. Transforming our food systems would help achieve a number of development objectives; including health, inclusion, safety, sustainability, efficiency, and resilience (HISSER) [2]. The existing food system is failing while also damaging the environment and jeopardizing human health [3]. Goals 2 (end hunger), 3 (improve health), 8 (decent work and economic growth), 12 (responsible consumption and production), 13 (climate action), 14 (life below water), and 15 (life on land) are all deeply intertwined with the global food system [3]. Global food system is made up of several types of structures, such as contemporary, mixed, and traditional food systems. To achieve long-term sustainability, deep transformations in food system design are required. Widespread adoptions of sustainable agricultural techniques, environmental conservation and regeneration, dietary adjustments, decrease of food loss and waste, and advances in economic and social justice along food supply chains are a few examples [4].

Food system encompasses all processes, players, and activities related to food production and consumption, from growing and harvesting to transporting and consuming [5]. According to the EC FOOD 2030 Expert Group [6]. Food systems "encompass the entire range of actors and their interconnected value-adding activities involved in the production, aggregation, processing, distribution, consumption, and disposal of food products that originate from agriculture, forestry, or fisheries, as well as parts of the broader economic, societal, and natural environments in which they are embedded, ". This includes the environment, comprehensive networks of people, processes, infrastructure, and institutions, as well as the consequences of their actions on our society, economy, landscape, and climate [7, 8]. (See **Figure 1**). Food environments shape consumers' capacity to obtain food and influence dietary preferences by forming the physical, economic, and social context of their interactions with the food system [10]. Food system structure is not static; rather, its components are influenced by a number of biophysical and socio-economic factors. Therefore, the importance of concentrating not only on individual elements but on all elements of a food system and the various feedback processes between them is crucial, especially in view of global environmental change [4].

According to Bart de Steenhuijsen et al. [11], the resilience of food systems is understood as the ability of food systems to achieve desired results in the face of shocks and

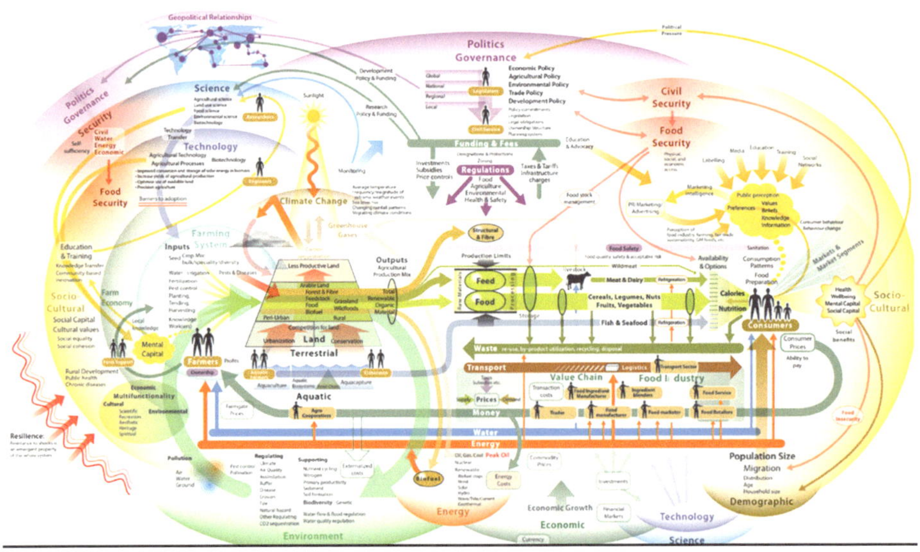

Figure 1.
Complexity of global food systems and multiple interactions source: ShiftN; Belchior., et al. (2016); [9].

stressors. The concept of resilience has its origins in ecological stability theory which explains the ability of ecosystems to return to their original state after a disturbance [12], as cited in [11]. Increasing resilience, as defined by the IPCC [13], is the ability of a system and its components to anticipate, cater, absorb, or recover from the effects of a dangerous event in a timely and efficient manner, including by ensuring the maintenance, restoration, or improvement of the system's essential structure and functions is a primary component of adaptation. With regard to food systems, resilience thinking has been applied to address the complex interactions between nature and society, with an emphasis on maintaining human wellbeing within planetary boundaries [14]. Sustainable food system is one that provides food security and nutrition for all in such a way that the economic, social and environmental foundations for creating food security and nutrition for future generations are not compromised. This means that a sustainable food system must be economically viable, have broad benefits for society and have positive or neutral effects on the natural environment. Itebinul, et al. (2021) viewed a sustainable food system as one that is capable of providing adequate, healthy, safe and affordable nutrition, which is the basis for a healthy life and the prerequisite for every individual's successful participation in society and, at the same time, a clean and healthy planet that recognizes it as the basis of all life on earth.

A food system must be viewed in the context of rapid population growth, urbanization, growing prosperity, changing consumer habits and globalization, as well as climate change and the depletion of natural resources. To achieve the SDGs, the global food system must be transformed so that it is more productive, more inclusive of poor and marginalized populations, environmentally sound and resilient, and is able to provide healthy and nutritious food to all. The focus on increasing food production is now deeply anchored in food policy. However, food security and sustainability are more than just the production, provision and consumption of food. Environmental sustainability and resilience of food systems are essential to ensure food security for all by 2050. Developments in food systems have produced many positive results, especially over the past three decades in developing countries. These outcomes include expanding non-farm employment opportunities as the food industry evolves and expanding food choices beyond local staples, thereby satisfying consumer preferences for taste, shape and quality. However, the associated rapid structural change has also led to increasing and considerable challenges, with potentially far-reaching consequences for food security and nutrition. These include the many highly processed, high calorie, and low nutrient foods that are widely available and consumed today; limited access of small producers and agribusinesses to viable markets; high levels of food loss and waste; increased cases of food safety and health problems in animals and humans; and increased energy intensity and ecological footprint associated with the elongation and industrialization of food supply chains. Hence, a better understanding of how different food systems work is critical to ensure that these systems evolve in such a way that their negative effects are minimized and their positive contributions are maximized. A food systems approach is a way of thinking and acting that looks at the food system in its entirety, taking into account all of the elements, their relationships, and their implications. It takes into account all relevant causal variables of a problem and all social, environmental and economic effects of the solutions in order to achieve transformative systemic changes.

However, there is growing recognition that long-term food security cannot be achieved without improving the resilience of food systems [15]. This requires producers and consumers to be able to adapt to unexpected changes in the (natural and political) environment through diversification strategies for livelihoods, nutrition and markets, which enable flexible and timely responses to global change [16]. In order to ensure resilience and a functional link with the circular economy, these strategies must also contribute to the long-term satisfactory functioning of the food systems by providing nutritional, environmental and livelihood benefits in the production, provision, consumption and disposal/recycling of food provide different levels and across different types of food systems [16]. The main reason for the growing interest in the transformation of the food system has to do with the recognition that the multiple problems of poverty, malnutrition, environmental degradation and climate change are combined and cannot be remedied with individual interventions, but instead a fundamental change in the dynamics of food systems [17, 18]. In response to the triple challenge of malnutrition, hunger, micronutrient deficiency and obesity, comprehensive strategies must be defined to support the availability, access, safety, affordability and attractiveness of food.

Food systems transformation occurs when significant and intentional changes are made to any of the food system's components [19], resulting in increased resilience to causes of food insecurity and malnutrition, as well as higher affordability of healthy diets [7]. The urgent need for this transition has become a focal point of a worldwide discussion aimed at tackling some of the most pressing issues facing sustainable development, particularly the challenge of eradicating hunger, food insecurity, and malnutrition in all forms by 2030. A number of significant drivers have had progressively detrimental consequences on food security and nutrition outcomes throughout the world as a result of their impact on food systems. Conflict, climatic variability and extremes, and economic slowdowns and downturns, which are exacerbated by poverty and inequality, are all major factors. Despite these obstacles, if food systems are transformed to be more resilient to the identified drivers, and incentives are put in place to encourage food systems to provide affordable healthy diets in a sustainable and inclusive manner, they can become a powerful driving force in ending hunger, food insecurity, and malnutrition in all forms – and put us on track to achieve SDG 2, while also triggering important synergies for other SDGs [7]. This transformation of food systems necessitates innovative systemic changes, which must be accompanied by an enabling environment of institutions, policies, laws, regulations, and investments that are aligned and complementary across sectors [20]. In addition, to achieve the necessary transformation, small-scale gradual transitions and larger-scale structural changes to institutions, laws, and standards are required – all in a coordinated and integrated manner [21].

The World Research Institute's (WRI) study on how to create a sustainable food future identified 22 solutions that are divided into five broad categories: (1) reduce demand for food and other agricultural products; (2) increase food production without expanding agricultural land; (3) protect and restore natural ecosystems; (4) increase fish supply; and (5) reduce GHG emissions from agricultural production [22]. All of these measures must be implemented simultaneously to close these gaps [22]. Similarly, FAO et al., [7] identified six pathways to global food system transformation, including integrating humanitarian development and peace building policies in conflict-affected areas; scaling up climate resilience across food systems, strengthening the resilience of the most vulnerable to economic adversity; intervening along food supply chains to lower the cost of nutritious foods; tackling poverty and structural inequalities, ensuring interventions are pro-poor and inclusive; improving the food environment and influencing consumer behavior to encourage eating patterns that are good for human health and the environment. However, Richardson, Christensen, and the Sustainability Science Center [23] identified four crucial parts of this transformation: Boosting the small; Transforming the big; Losing less; and Eating smarter, all of which require new technology, government intervention, and behavioral change from citizens and consumers. It is these four pillars of global food system transformation that are discussed in this chapter.

1.1 A brief overview of our food System's history

Historically, Lynda [24] identified six food systems, namely: Food System 1 (hunter-gatherer approach to food); Food System 2 (transition from nomadic life to settlement and development of agriculture); Food System 3 (selection of desirable traits in plants and animals and optimizing of food production for taste, climate, and pest protection); and Food System 4 (agricultural adaptation based on automation, fertilizer, and pesticides, with the selection of higher yielding and pest resistant plants); Food System 5 (convenience, shelf life stability, logistics, and economic optimization). Food system 5 has posed numerous challenges, including marginalization of primary growers, producers, and ranchers, limiting consumer purchasing decisions, increased inequity and lack of parity for critical stakeholders, and, most importantly, the production of processed foods lacking essential nutrients for human health [24]. "As a result, the time has come to rethink our existing food system and usher in humanity's sixth Food System - one that is optimized for the integrated and comprehensive priority of planetary and human health." This system will need to take into account the interrelationships between all stakeholders in the food system, as well as a holistic view of farm viability, sustainable ecosystems, healthy communities, and justice, and equity - features and parts of food production that have been overlooked by food systems 5″ [24].

1.2 The need for change in the food system

Despite the global efforts toward ending food insecurity and all forms of malnutrition by 2030, food insecurity is on the rise [25] because there has been no progress toward achieving either the SDGs target of "ensuring access to safe, nutritious, and sufficient food for all people all year round or eradicating all forms of malnutrition" [7]. "720-811 million people in the globe suffered hunger in 2020, up to 161 million higher than in 2019," according to the 2021 issues of the state of food security and nutrition in the world study. In 2020, about 2.37 billion people lacked appropriate food, an increase of 220 million individuals in only one year" [7]. Hence, considerable efforts and attention on increasing food production at both the global and regional levels notwithstanding, around 3 billion people in every part of the globe lack access to a good diet due to the high cost of a healthy diet, chronic poverty, and widening inequalities [7]. These factors place the entire world at a "critical juncture," not only in terms of overcoming the enormous challenge of food insecurity, ending hunger, and eliminating all forms of malnutrition, but also in terms of exposing the global food system's fragility and the need to build food system resilience through transformation [7]. "The current covid-19 epidemic and other zoonotic illnesses, the negative effects of climate change (e.g. frequent and severe floods, droughts, storms), pests and plant disease (e.g. locusts), conflicts and wars illustrate how vulnerable food systems are," according to LEAP4FNSSA [26]. These call for urgent need for transformation to systems that can adapt to future shocks, such as pandemics and natural disasters [27].

Similarly, the current status of agricultural and food systems has been dubbed a "triple catastrophe," in which climate change, undernutrition, and obesity are wreaking havoc on human and planetary health [25]. Unhealthy eating habits have made dietary hazards the third greatest cause of mortality worldwide, and malnutrition a prominent cause of healthy life years lost [28]. Non-communicable diseases (NCDs) caused by poor diet, such as cardiovascular disease, diabetes, and certain malignancies, are on the rise worldwide, with an estimated 40 million deaths per year [29]. These trends are compounded by the fact that when people become wealthier, their diets move substantially toward more sugar, animal, and fat products, at the expense of traditional and often more sustainable diets.

The global food system, particularly food production, is a key driver of global environmental change, causing huge changes in terrestrial and marine ecosystems. More than 70% of the world's ice-free land is directly affected by human activity, and estimates suggest that up to one-third of terrestrial net primary production is consumed for food, feed, wood, and energy ([30] a). More terrestrial, coastal, and offshore area is being taken up by aquaculture [31], and forecasts suggest that without substantial fisheries reforms, over 80% of world fish stocks would be overfished and below critical biomass by 2050 [31]. Industrialized agriculture is highly reliant on external inputs, contributes to chemical pollution through the use of pesticides and herbicides, alters nitrogen and phosphorous cycles through synthetic fertilizer additions, and has an impact on freshwater stocks through irrigation [32]. It is also energy demanding, contributing to climate change by producing about one-third of all greenhouse gases, including methane [33].

To secure a more equitable and sustainable future, it is clear that a significant structural transformation in food production and use is required [3]. The nature of the sustainability challenge necessitates a reconsideration of previously dominant ways of doing things and understanding the world [3] in order to make room for knowledge systems that can deal with accelerating change, increasing complexity, contested perspectives, and inevitable uncertainty.

1.3 Food systems transformation: Drivers and barriers

The current spike in hunger and halting progress in eliminating all types of malnutrition is due to conflict, climatic variability and extremes, and economic slowdowns and downturns (exacerbated by the COVID-19 pandemic). These key drivers are distinct, but not mutually exclusive, in that they wreak havoc on food security and nutrition by causing many, worsening effects across our food system [7]. Conflicts, for example, have a detrimental impact on nearly every part of the food system, from production, harvesting, processing, and transportation to raw material availability, finance, marketing, and consumption. Direct repercussions can include the loss of agricultural commodities and livelihoods, as well as major disruption and restriction of commerce, goods, and services, with severe implications for food supply and costs, especially healthful foods. Similarly, climate fluctuations and extremes have a wide range of repercussions on food systems, which are becoming more pronounced. They have a detrimental impact on agricultural productivity as well as food imports as countries strive to compensate for lost local output. Climate-related disasters have the potential to disrupt the whole food value chain, resulting in severe effects for sector growth and the food and non-food businesses [7].

Economic slowdowns and downturns, on the other hand, largely influence food systems by reducing people's access to food, including the cost of healthy eating, since they result in increased unemployment and lower salaries and incomes. This is true whether market fluctuations, trade conflicts, political turmoil, or a worldwide epidemic like COVID-19 are to blame. These significant global drivers and underlying structural variables impair food security and nutrition through interrelated and cyclical impacts on other systems, including environmental and health systems, in addition to their direct effects on food systems [7].

When the food system is transformed by making it more resilient to climatic variations and extremes, war, and economic lag and downturns, it becomes a major driving force in the elimination of hunger, food insecurity, and malnutrition in all forms for all people [7]. Therefore, objective of food system transformation is to create a future in which everyone has access to a healthy diet that is produced in a sustainable and resilient way, restores nature, and produces just and equitable livelihoods [34]. Considering the diverse perspectives and arguments toward achieving food system transformation ([35], 202; [36–38]), in the following sections we discuss global food system transformation for resilience based on the concept of the four pillars of food system transformation of "Boosting the Small; Transforming the Big; Losing Less; and Eating Smarter" developed by Richardson, Christensen and Sustainability Science Center, University of Copenhagen, Denmark.

2. Boosting the small

There is a risk that two constituencies may be left behind as food systems change. On the one hand, there are approximately half a billion self-employed smallholders in rural areas, including farmers, shepherds, and fishermen [39], and approximately two billion men and women who work in the informal economy and are currently unable to secure economic access to basic food supplies [40, 41]. Healthy nutrition, on the other hand, is out of reach for at least three billion people in both the global north and the global south [42, 43]. This number has risen dramatically as a result of the COVID-19 problem [44]. In the future decades, resolving the contradiction between enhancing smallholder livelihoods and guaranteeing an adequate and healthy food supply will be critical to boosting the food system's overall resilience [16].

2.1 Increasing know-how

By 2050, the globe will need to feed an extra 2 billion people, with Africa hosting the majority of them. Despite the fact that Africa possesses over 200 million hectares of uncultivated land, yearly food imports are predicted to rise from $35 billion to $ 110 billion by 2025 [23]. To strengthen the resilient of the people living there to the effects of climate change, the continent has huge food production potential that needs to be harnessed. Farmers with only a few hectares of land are critical to feeding the future population. There are anticipated to be 750 million smallholders in the globe by 2030. To begin with, these farmers require better understanding about best practices, both in terms of increasing productivity and in terms of improving soil quality. According to FAO et al., [7], a best practice is one that has been demonstrated to work, has produced positive outcomes after a thorough examination, and is thus suggested as a model for scaling. This entire compendium, or all of these "best practices," allows farmers to reap a bumper crop [23].

2.2 Better financial access and livelihood adaptation

Inequality affects access to food. Around 80% of the world's poorest people reside in rural regions, where poverty rates are three times greater than in cities [7]. Policies, investments, and legislation are needed to address the underlying structural inequities that disadvantaged communities in rural and urban regions face, while also boosting their access to productive resources and new technology can help to alleviate severe poverty and structural inequalities by hastening the transformation of pro-poor and inclusive food systems. Lack of access to productive resources and inadequate market integration worsen rural poverty among smallholders in Southeast Asia, which is compounded by climate-related and economic shocks, as well as frequent outbreaks of plant and animal diseases [45]. In this region, public-private producer partnerships (PPPPs) have aided the integration of poor smallholders into the food value chain, which offer opportunities to alleviate poverty and structural inequalities, especially when bolstered by improved governance mechanisms and multi-stakeholder platforms [7].

The adaptation process, which the IPCC describes as "the adaptation to the present or predicted climate and its impacts," is the primary way of mitigating the danger of climate change to rural livelihoods. Adaptation in human systems aims to reduce or eliminate damage while also taking advantage of possibilities. The skills, assets, and activities required for a livelihood that allows individuals to reach a minimal degree of wellbeing are referred to as livelihood. Climate change poses a danger to these livelihoods, necessitating systematic and transformational adaptation, which in turn need more and inventive funding. As the food system transforms, adequate finance is vital to achieving successful transformational adaptation for resilient livelihoods in the agri-food industry. This entails not just increasing the availability of financial resources, but also ensuring that those resources are available to individuals who need them and that suitable finance channels are employed to make them available.

Hence, "dismantling barriers to just and equitable livelihoods, such as lack of access to productive resources requires institutional changes, policy support and investment to empower those whose livelihoods are tied to food systems" [34]. As a result, policy solutions should consider the role of women in agri-food systems and guarantee that their unique requirements as household food security keepers, food producers, farm managers, processors, merchants, wage employees, and entrepreneurs are effectively met [7]. More so, Youth, especially in less developed countries, where more than 80% of youth reside [46], provide a significant potential for revolutionary change in food systems [47]. Young people (aged 15-24) account for around 16 percent (1.2 billion) of the world's population, and as prospective young entrepreneurs, they represent the future agents of change. Unlocking their entrepreneurial and creative potential requires strengthening their skills and agency through training, positive role models, and mentorship [48]. As a result, particular initiatives to increase young people's access to productive resources, financing, markets, and connections, as well as decision-making, are required as part of larger efforts to encourage responsible investing. Social conventions that may inhibit rural young people, particularly vulnerable groups such as young women and indigenous youth, from taking advantage of new possibilities must also be addressed [49].

2.3 Sharing economy

The sharing economy has long existed in many regions of the world, but the widespread availability of low-cost Android devices has created new possibilities for small farmers to hire a tractor for a certain period of time, giving them access to automation that would otherwise be prohibitively expensive. In the crop production cycle, mechanization is crucial for farmers. It has the potential to boost and affect farmer yields and profits in a variety of ways [23].

2.4 A more fair trade system through good governance

Many innovative strategies can help smallholder farmers enhance their agricultural output. However, reforms to the trade mechanisms are also essential to truly overhaul the food systems. Farmers in developing nations compete with industrialized countries' subsidized produce. Subsidies from wealthier countries lower prices in poorer countries, discouraging domestic manufacturing. At the same time, agricultural products are subject to high tariffs of up to 50% in both north–south and south–south commerce. This complicates things even further. It will be significantly more difficult for developing nations to disrupt trade patterns as a result of this [23]. Smallholders require more knowledge and green expenditures in order to enhance their output in a sustainable manner. As a result, maintaining excellent governance through a fair trade system is critical to achieving a beneficial food system transformation. Fanzo et al. [34] "proposed a working definition of governance for positive food system transformation as the mode of interaction among the public sector, private sector, civil society and consumers to identify, implement resource and monitor solutions for achieving healthy sustainable, resilient, just and equitable food system without leaving anyone behind".

2.5 Boosting innovative and transformative entrepreneurs

Given that the current industrial food system is responsible for greenhouse gas emissions, environmental and soil degradation, animal welfare abuses, public health, and labour crises, a wide range of business efforts are required to assist in the resolution of the various problems that the food system faces. Training, promoting, and engaging young innovative and transformational youth and women to take advantage of more mindful and holistic food chain management that considers the connections between people and parts at every level and how they cannot be improved but can be transformed [24]. The rising emphasis on food system transformation by academic institutions and corporate organizations' evaluation of the influence of stakeholders on their business has resulted in a massive rush of innovation and entrepreneurs into the food system [24, 50].

As a result, these new business groups will require assistance in developing and scaling solutions that challenge / distort existing conventional practices and legacy players throughout the food and agriculture value chain, thereby creating value that is based on both the planet's capacities and consumer needs. These revolutionary technologies and entrepreneurs encounter hurdles in their attempts to disrupt the existing actors in the food and agricultural systems, but their novel solutions are more sustainable for planetary resources and have high customer preference and demand. Lynda, [24] also advocated for productive collaboration between bigger incumbents and smaller businesses that does not dilute or eliminate the fundamental value created by innovators. Huge sums of money have been invested in these entrepreneurs all across the world, and they are projected to increase as the new food system matures and iterates.

3. Transforming the big

Large, multinational food firms confront sustainability difficulties that are vastly different from those encountered by smallholder farmers. They must, figure out how to develop in a sustainable manner. However, they are also confronted with the task of revamping an existing production plant that has a significant environmental impact. Agriculture, along with transportation, was one of the most essential activities not included in the Kyoto Protocol's quota system. As a result, agriculture has been overlooked in many efforts to reduce greenhouse gas emissions [23].

3.1 Goal-based planning and shared vision

In order to determine priority guidelines and desired objectives in all subject areas of the food system transformation, a shared vision refers to integrative, participative procedures [7]. The agriculture industry in Denmark is responsible for around 20% of total Danish greenhouse gas emissions. The majority of these emissions originate from livestock, with cows accounting for 63% and pig production accounting for 32%. These astounding figures are mostly attributable to two additional greenhouse gases: nitrous oxide (laughing gas) and methane, rather than CO_2 emissions from equipment. Nitrous oxide (laughing gas), which is mostly emitted by liquid manure and fertilizers, has a greenhouse impact over 300 times larger than CO_2. Methane has a 25-fold greater warming effect than CO_2, and it is also released by manure. Burps from ruminants like cows and sheep also release methane into the atmosphere. It is critical to address these various emissions in order to meet both the Paris Agreement and the SDGs [23].

Therefore, Denmark's cattle industry has set lofty ambitions for the future: Danish Crown, Europe's largest pork producer, plans to cut greenhouse gas emissions in half by 2030 and achieve CO2 neutrality by 2050 [23]. This might be accomplished by implementing mixed agriculture, biogas usage, sustainable slaughterhouse management, and individual animal treatment, all of which are necessary for reducing environmental and climate consequences. Individualizing treatment for each animal not only extends the animal's life expectancy, but it also allows for more sustainable antibiotic use [23].

3.2 Sustainable soils

Another issue that plagues industrial agriculture is soil deterioration. Land use, climate, water usage, biosphere intensity, and pollution are the key environmental systems and processes that interact with the food system, and they all alter and are impacted by the Earth system [34]. Agriculture dominates global land usage, with 14.5 billion hectares of arable land used for cultivation and 3.5 billion hectares used for grazing ([34]; Mboro et al., 2019). Around 12.5 percent of agriculture in Europe is thought to be subjected to moderate to severe erosion. This amounts to an area greater than Greece's whole territory [23]. According to FAO and ITPS [51], a third of the world's peaks have been degraded due to highly chemical-induced agriculture, global warming, and deforestation, leaving just sixty years of topsoil on the planet. As a result, the present food and farming system has damaged the topsoil where 95% of our food is grown, necessitating quick action to transform the industrial agricultural production paradigm into regenerative agriculture [24].

Regenerative agriculture, according to Lynda [24], is a farm and food system rehabilitation and conservation approach that focuses on regenerating the topsoil, strengthening the health and vitality of agricultural soil, increasing biodiversity, improving ecosystem services, improving the water cycle, increasing the focus on climate change resilience, and supporting bioequestration. Composted manure created from biodegradable waste is used in regenerative agriculture, as is reusing as much agricultural waste as feasible. Deforestation and land conversion must be stopped in order to minimize greenhouse gas emissions, enhance water cycles, and safeguard biodiversity. This operation has the ability to dissolve between 200 and 300 gigatons of carbon dioxide [30, 34].

3.3 Closed-system farming

Precision farming under controlled conditions allows for a more personalized approach to plant care. Precision farming is not just for indoor farming anymore, as new types of sensors and data processing are being developed. As a result, digital agriculture and precision agriculture are two of the most essential strategic future themes. Machine learning in crop production is another example of how current innovations will influence future food systems. To manage pests in these crops, greenhouses and precise engineering in water usage, fertilizer use, and the application of numerous biological control agents. One part of this diverse agricultural method in the Netherlands is the use of LED lights to impact not only plant growth but also, for example, insect resistance and hence pesticide use in plant production in the greenhouse is lowered thereby affecting the product's quality [23].

Plants having helpful traits have been selected for further breeding by humans for as long as they have grown plants. These features represent naturally existing genetic variants and may lead to higher yield, disease resistance, or resilience to environmental stress, among other things. Plants that have been genetically modified (GMOs) are those that have had their genomes altered in a laboratory rather than via breeding. Plant genetic alterations have mostly been used to improve pest resistance and herbicide tolerance. As a result, the use of genetically modified organisms (GMOs) in agriculture has been linked to unsustainable, highly industrialized monoculture agricultural methods. More than 93 percent of maize and soy farmed in the United States has been genetically engineered in some form.

Vertical farming is another specialty in greenhouse production. It is seen as a solution to the urbanization problem: People are increasingly relocating to large cities, and there are now numerous cities in the globe with populations exceeding 10 million. They live in a limited region, and their food is imported from all over the world, but an increasing number of people demand fresh, locally produced food. Vertical farming is frequently based on hydroponics, aquaponics, or aeroponics, which are soilless techniques of growing plants. The advantages of vertical agriculture include a high production rate, the use of less area for food production, the use of very little water, the use of very few nutrients, and the use of fewer pesticides, all of which result in extremely high scores on many sustainability criteria. On the other hand, it is pricey, and consumes a lot of energy – lighting, which contributes to the price. As a new technology, there is still much to be improved and refined in future to reduce costs [23].

3.4 Food system synergy and policy monitoring

Existing national, regional, and global policies, plans, legislation, and investments are divided out into multiple conversations, which is a major barrier to sustainable food system transformation. These issues may be addressed by developing and implementing cross-sectorial policy, investment, and legislative portfolios that fully address the negative effects of diverse elements impacting agricultural systems on food security and nutrition [7]. Given that most food systems are impacted by several factors, each of which has a varied impact on food security and results, broad portfolios of policies, investments, and laws can be developed in multiple ways at the same time. This will allow them to maximize their collective effect on food system reform, take advantage of win-win solutions, and avoid undesirable tradeoffs. Coherence in the formulation and implementation of policies and investments in the food, health, social protection, and environmental systems is also required to create synergies that lead to more efficient and effective food system solutions that ensure affordable, healthy nutrition in a sustainable and inclusive manner [7].

Fanzo et al. [34] presented a science-based surveillance framework / method to measure and monitor the performance of food system operations globally, which might help achieve real progress, establish priorities, set clear targets for action, and align food system players make a list of trade-offs. According to the authors, such a mechanism can assist "food system actors and other stakeholders (e.g. civil society, governments and international organization) actionable evidence to hold government, consumers and other private sector accountable for food system transformation". The authors have used various food systems frameworks to illustrate the confluence and interrelationships between the components of the food system (see **Figure 2**), in order to address five thematic areas for the food system monitoring mechanism that comprises of (1) nutrition, nutrition and health (2) environment and climate (3) livelihoods, poverty, and justice (4) governance and (5) resilience and sustainability with indicators, domains and tables.

Similarly, Hebirick et al. [52] developed a sustainability compass for political navigation in the transformation of food systems, based on four interrelated, desirable societal perspectives: healthy, adequate, and safe nourishment for all; a clean and healthy world; and a fair, ethical, and fair food system. The compass (see **Figure 3**) provides an all-encompassing framework for assessing sustainability that allows for an integrative and transparent political discussion and can deliver practical findings. The compass may be utilized at many levels of policy development to promote inclusive multi-stakeholder discussions and assure reflective and thorough evaluations, setting the framework for building integrated policies that deal with trade-offs in a reflexive manner [52].

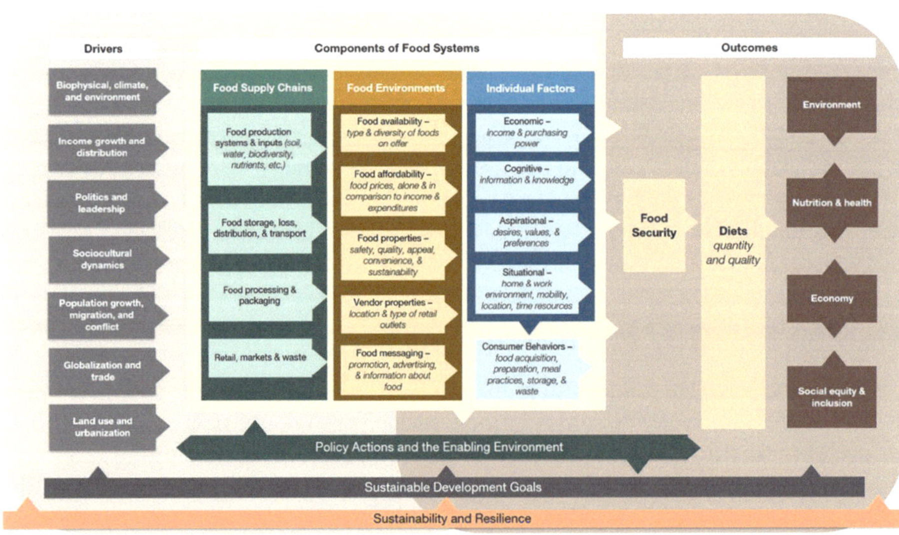

Figure 2.
Food system components, drivers, and outcomes. Source: Fanzo et al., [34].

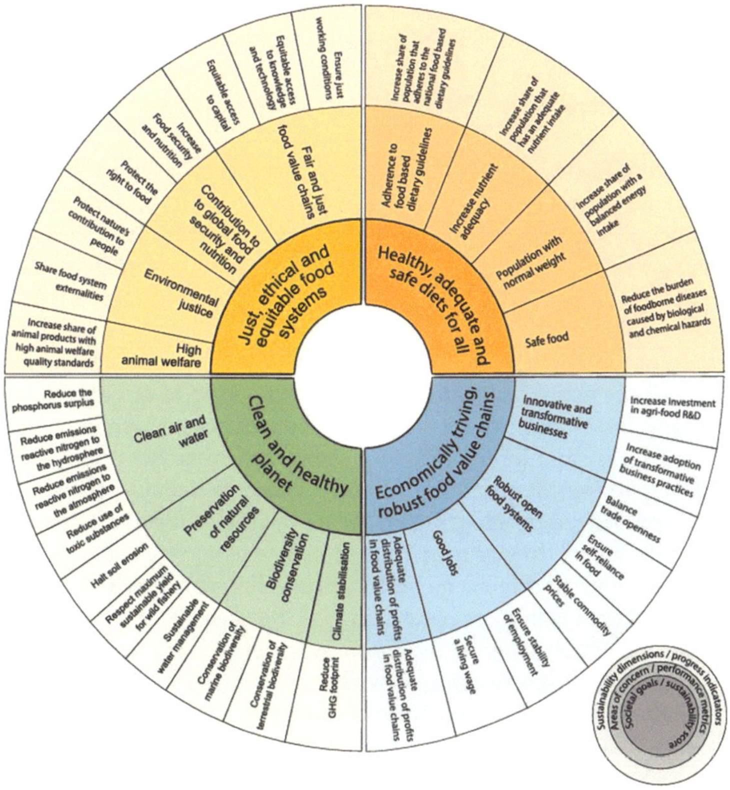

Figure 3.
A sustainability compass for policy navigation to sustainable food systems. Source: Hebinck et al.,[52].

4. Losing less

While the problem is obvious, the narrative that we must feed the globe legitimizes present production systems erroneously [23]. Even though food production is already high, a third of it is lost or wasted. Inevitably, this implies that a large portion of the resources utilized in food production are squandered, as are the greenhouse gas emissions associated with producing food that is lost or wasted. These losses occur at several points along the food supply chain, including harvesting, processing, shipping, marketing, and consumption, and they could feed 2 billion hungry people each year. Food loss and waste costs the economy $940 billion each year.

Losing less therefore, is critical to fulfilling the needs of an expanding population while also driving production in a more sustainable path. Food losses are defined as a reduction in the mass of edible food in the segment of the supply chain that leads to edible food for human consumption. Food losses occur in the food supply chain during the production, post-harvest, and processing phases [53]. Food losses at the end of the food chain (retail and final consumption) are more likely to be labeled as waste, which has to do with retailer and consumer behavior [53].

Food is obviously wasted more at the consumption level in industrialized nations, that is, it is thrown away even while it is still fit for human consumption. Developing countries have higher post-harvest agricultural losses, which mean that considerably less food is wasted at the consumer level. One-sided investments in agricultural resources are to blame for the substantial post-harvest losses in underdeveloped nations.

4.1 Circular food systems

Food system transformations are interactive processes that need adaptive skills in order to respond properly to unanticipated obstacles. Food system development is not a linear process, and various trends occur at the same time [16]. Diverse sorts of food systems have different and unique means of delivering nutritious, economical, safe, and long-term nourishment, necessitating customized solutions. The move to circular systems based on resource recycling, on the other hand, benefits all types of food systems by enhancing resource responsiveness and efficiency. A thorough understanding of the major leaks underpins the promotion of circular food systems [16]. Post-harvest losses and waste (PHL) must be reduced, which necessitates physical infrastructure and food management expenditures. Recycling and reusing materials can help to improve material balances. Many perishable items can have their shelf lives prolonged by adopting upstream drying or fermentation techniques to improve food integrity downstream in the food system [54]. Local indigenous food improvement strategies that focus on resource recycling can also help foster youth employment and women's entrepreneurship [54]. Because global food production is the leading cause of environmental deterioration, methods for making the best use of biomass from plant-based systems, as well as approaches for reducing pressure on forests and biodiversity, and opportunities to improve feed conversion and circularity within animal husbandry systems are all given special attention.

4.2 Transport and storage

Food loss and waste is a worldwide issue, yet while it affects people everywhere, the issues are different in each country [55]. Several studies suggest that investment in rural transportation and communication infrastructure helps farmers and merchants minimize transaction costs, improve the quality and freshness of local products, and boost output [56]. Dorosh et al. [57] show that in Sub-Saharan Africa, agricultural yield and adoption of high-input technologies are greater when farmers reside closer to metropolitan areas, emphasizing the relevance of accessibility.

Both pre-harvest and post-harvest infrastructure, such as collecting centres, (refrigerated) storage, distribution, or processing centres, are critical. Farmers who have access to storage space might boost their revenue by taking advantage of seasonal price changes if they can wait [58].

4.3 Connectivity: Connecting producers and consumers

The type and strength of the interactions between the various components of any system is referred to as Connectivity. Connectivity at the neighborhood, business, and national levels helps people build resilience and protect themselves from negative repercussions. The food system's resilience may be improved by tying rural and urban populations together [55] and expanding agricultural and non-agricultural job options to absorb surplus labour. Investing in small and medium-sized businesses for local processing, storage, and retailing produces crucial new job possibilities, encourages value creation, and allows for cyclical resource usage [59]. Connecting farmers and consumers to dependable and transparent informal and formal markets has the potential to improve access to inexpensive and good nourishment, as well as boost nutrition, inclusiveness, and sustainability, as well as increase food supply stability [60].

Therefore, improved agricultural value chain connectivity increases a food system's ability to respond to shocks and stresses, as well as its adaptive and transformation capacities. As a result, food waste is not only a technological issue, but also a question of enhancing the interaction between producers and consumers [23]. Prices in European supermarkets and businesses do not frequently change during the day. Too Good To Go is an app that helps consumers avoid wasting food by linking them with establishments that have leftover foods at the end of the day. This allows these customers to reserve food at the store at the end of the day, and after the store closes, the customer will pick up those items and take them home to eat instead of the business throwing them away. There are several benefits to this, the most notable of which is that the shop does not have to waste out food, and the consumer receives a wonderful dinner at a reasonable price [23].

The problem of date marking is one of the political concerns that the app handles with similar success in both Denmark and France. According to research conducted by the European Union, up to ten percent of all food thrown out in Europe each year is due to a misinterpretation of the date marking on everyday items like breakfast cereals or rice. Basically, people get the two date labels 'best before' and 'use by' mixed up ahead of time and use them interchangeably [23]. That is, when food passes its best before date, consumers just toss it away. Consumers who frequently use the app to assist in the battle against food waste will be able to understand this in a very relevant way. Additionally, food makers can frequently add 'often good after' to their best-before date, indicating that the product has passed its best-before date but is still edible days or weeks afterwards [23].

4.4 Decreasing food miles

By 2050, emerging nations will account for 97 percent of the world's increase population with 70 percent of the new population settling in cities. As a result, there is a significant gap between where food is produced and where it is consumed. Farmers must relocate further from cities in order to feed this rising population, while rural residents must relocate further from farms to cities thereby increasing food miles. As a result, real food markets are critical for connecting rural production with urban demand. Cities in Sub-Saharan Africa are planning and constructing markets, or retrofitting existing ones with proper sanitation, storage, and lighting [61]. Investing in informal market infrastructure and spatial design is thus at least as essential as investing in official markets. Understanding how to effectively preserve these informal market connections is also important, yet this information is frequently absent [62].

4.5 Food wastage resilience through agroecology, insurance, and agroforestry

Strategies which guarantee that less food is lost in the food chain, is critical to build resilience. Building resilience to ensure higher food production and reduced loss necessitates the implementation of a food production system that respects the natural environment by making the best use of the limited land area available, particularly for animal production. The adoption of agrocology, agroforestry, and insurance is a sustainable strategy to buffer shocks and stressors in the food production and supply chain, preventing post-harvest losses and securing the livelihood of food system operators [23].

Agroecology is an alternative that advocates a variety of ecosystem-based ideas that encourage natural processes to minimize dependency on chemical inputs and cut production costs [63]. Anderson et al. [64] highlighted six key areas in agroecological transformation that must be considered: (1) access to natural ecosystems; (2) knowledge and culture; (3) trade systems; (4) networks; (5) equality; and (6) discourse.

It is not enough to adjust agricultural methods to climate change to boost the overall resilience of food production. Farmers should be insured not only for the food they have already produced, but also for their whole operation. Steps to better adapt to climate change for farmers go hand in hand with insurance preparation for extreme weather events, as on-farm activities come with premiums. In this approach, decreasing food waste and loss is about strengthening farmers' resilience as well as enhancing storage, transportation, and the relationship between producers, sellers, and consumers [23].

4.6 Diversity

While efficient, dependable, and sustainable food production is still critical, focusing only on agricultural output has resulted in certain unforeseen and unpleasant consequences that are not all insufficient [16]. Furthermore, the manner in which the intensification was carried out has generated environmental issues [17], and the food system's 37 percent contribution to greenhouse gas emissions necessitates a significant decrease to satisfy the Paris Agreement and mitigation demands [15]. Diversification is important for strengthening the food system's resilience. Diverse diets will only benefit nutrition and health if they are supported by greater affordability and accessibility to nutrient-dense foods [65]. Diversification of food production can enhance rural livelihoods while also promoting biodiversity and natural resource landscape management.

Diverse systems make up resilient systems. The loss of one resource can be compensated for by another. An excess elsewhere can compensate for a shortfall. According to studies on environmental resilience, biodiversity contributes significantly to system stability and continuity [66]. More varied agricultural systems have a better capacity to absorb the effects of shocks and stresses, which helps to stabilize food supply as they travel through value chains to consumer markets [67].

4.7 Peace building

During times of violent conflict, entire food systems are frequently disrupted, making it difficult for people to get nourishing meals. Food security, as defined by FAO [68] and WHO (1996), is all people having physical and economic access to safe and nutritious food that meets their dietary preferences at all times for an active and healthy lifestyle. Economic growth and social progress, as well as political stability and peace, are all linked to food security [69]. Wars, political unrest, insecurity, insurgency, banditry, and terrorism limit access to food, resulting in increased hunger, malnutrition, and loss of livelihood, all of which wreak havoc on the food system's resilience. Conflicts are causing a rise in the number of displaced people in many regions of the world, who are living in risky situations and unable to satisfy their food and nutritional demands. In Africa, the number of wars grew by 90% in the fourth quarter of 2020 compared to the fourth quarter of 2019, causing more economic disruption [70].

In addition, ending wars and promoting peace should be a regional and global priority. The combination of humanitarian, development, and peace building initiatives in conflict zones, according to FAO et al., [7], is critical. It is vital to remember that the majority of chronically hungry people, as well as many undernourished people, live in nations plagued by insecurity and violence. As a result, conflict-sensitive policies, investments, and actions to alleviate acute food insecurity and malnutrition must be implemented concurrently with conflict-reduction measures and reconciled with long-term socio-economic development and peace initiatives [67]. Policy actions backed by institutional and legislative changes should strive to minimize and, if feasible, avoid these underlying causes' consequences on food systems, food security and nutrition, and the economy as a whole [7].

4.8 Sustainable food safety practices and management

Inadequate food safety and quality endangers food production, distribution, and consumption [71]. Foodborne illness lowers the quality and amount of agricultural produce, lowering food availability and access for communities whose livelihoods are dependent on its sale [72]. When people are on the verge of starving, they will eat whatever food is available, even if it is dangerous. Food safety is a critical component of successfully transforming food systems, strengthening supply networks, diversifying value chains, and fostering the circular economy. As a result, there is no food security without food safety, and food that is not safe is not food [73–77]. Climate change and extremes, agricultural intensification, and the evolution of antibiotic resistance are all issues that can impact food safety at the production level. Changes in food processing, value creation, and packaging are being driven by technological advancements, research, and creativity, all of which necessitate careful attention to food safety. Furthermore, if not carefully handled, globalization, new digital distribution networks, e-commerce, and informal markets might have an impact on food safety [73–77]. Food safety, as a component of food security, is also a key component of the Sustainable Development Goals (SDGs), since the FAO/WHO estimates that over 600 million instances of foodborne illness and 420,000 fatalities result from contaminated food intake each year [36, 69, 73–77]. Apart from the fact that SDG2, which covers a wide range of themes such as eliminating hunger, establishing food security, enhancing nutrition, and supporting sustainable agriculture, can only be realized if food is available and safe to eat [69]. Similarly, Nwiyi and Elechi [72] argued that in order to safeguard a people's food, the food system's safety and nutritional-physiological characteristics must be assured at all times, regardless of how primitive, cultural, indigenous, traditional, contemporary, or technically sophisticated it is.

Strengthening high-level political involvement for food safety, prioritizing sustainable investments in effective national food control systems, and mobilizing enough public and private resources within dynamic systemic change are all important, according to FAO [73–77]. With the declaration of June 8 as World Food Safety Day and the recent establishment of a dedicated food safety and quality department by FAO in recognition of the urgent need for sustainable food safety management, with the mission of supporting science-based governance and food safety decisions, improving food safety management along the food chain to reduce disease and trade disruption, and evaluating new technologies to improve food safety and protect public health [69, 73–77].

4.9 Reducing global postharvest skill technology gaps

There are technological deficits, particularly in poor countries, as a result of the loss of post-harvest investment. To overcome this problem, we urgently require more sustainable post-harvest initiatives as well as new technologies. The "World Food Preservation Centre" meets this need by training young post-harvest scientists from developing countries in advanced food preservation technologies that are appropriate for their countries, as well as conducting research and developing innovative food preservation technologies that are suitable for developing countries.

4.10 Building food systems climate resilience

Humans and environment can survive and prosper in a climate-positive future if we change the way we produce food and utilize natural resources [78]. This is significant not just because environmental degradation and climatic events have an impact on food systems, but also because food systems influence the status of the environment and are key drivers of climate change. These initiatives are centered on protecting the environment, managing current food production and supply systems sustainably, and restoring and rehabilitating natural habitats [7]. Stronger partnerships and multi-year, substantial funding are needed to support (among other things) integrated disaster risk reduction and response programs, climate change adaptation strategies, and short-, medium-, and long-term practices [19] to mitigate the effects of climate variability and extremes, such as persistent poverty and inequality. The adaptation and upgrading of instruments and interventions such as risk monitoring and early warning systems, emergency preparedness and response, measures to reduce vulnerability and measures to build resilience, shock-active social protection mechanisms, risk transfers (including climate risk insurance), and forecast-based funding, as well as strong risk governance structures in the environment, are all required for the implementation of climate resilience policies and programs. Climate-Smart Agriculture (CSA), has shown triple success in the transformation of food systems, is a proven approach to building climate resilience. CSA builds resilience in a variety of ways through climate-sensitive and socio-economically advantageous approaches that boost agricultural production and incomes while also strengthening climate change resilience and reducing greenhouse gas emissions [79].

5. Eating smarter

It is not only a question of cost and affordability to have access to nutritious meals and a balanced diet. Culture, language, culinary traditions, patterns of knowledge and consumption, food preferences, attitudes, and values all have an impact on how food is sourced, produced, and consumed [7]. Dietary habits have shifted, with both beneficial and harmful consequences for human health and the environment [8]. Most food systems today neglect the hidden costs to human health and the environment. Because they are not frequently quantified, they are not taken into consideration and are not included into food pricing, putting the sustainability of food systems in jeopardy. As a result, action, legislation, and investment are required, depending on the specific country context and current consumption patterns, to create a healthier food environment and empower consumers to follow nutritious, healthy, and safe eating patterns with a lower nutritional impact on the environment [74].

5.1 Ensuring diet biodiversity through local foods

Many family recipes have been passed down for centuries. According to McCouch et al., [80], 80 percent of human caloric intake is reliant on less than a dozen of the world's 300,000 flowering plant species. As a result, the vast genetic variety that each of these 300,000 species contains is largely untapped. According to McCouch et al., [80], a more concentrated worldwide effort is needed to better use agrobiodiversity in the global food supply.

Local foods, defined as foods produced and/or processed in close proximity to where they are consumed [81], are an important part of the food system: rural and urban communities in many developing countries are reliant on endogenous, locally available vegetable and food products as well as animal resources [82]. There is evidence that improving urban inhabitants' awareness of the economic and health benefits of buying locally grown vegetables, fruits, and grains may aid rural communities by increasing demand for these items [55, 83].

5.2 Using unconventional food

When it comes to environmental sustainability, adding local wild plants in the diet not only serves to diversity the plate, but it also helps to promote environmental sustainability by lowering dependency on commercially farmed veggies and connecting people to nature. On farms, in urban parks, and even in backyards, wild edible plants abound. On agricultural ground, these plants can be found growing along the borders of fields, in hedges, or in small woods. Even in the lean months leading up to the yearly harvest, they can supplement food and nutritional needs and provide seasonal alternatives, especially in low-income nations where agriculture is dependent on rainfall and seasons influence. It is critical that arable land maintains biodiversity in many low-income nations where people still rely on edible wild plants for subsistence [84]. Wild edible plants, on the other hand, are prevalent in the British countryside. Some of these unusual food sources include algae, fungus, insects, invading species, and weeds. These resources can assist in achieving long-term nutrition and meeting the 2050 target of feeding 9-10 billion people.

5.3 Replacing meat

Despite the advantages of meat eating and livestock production in poorer nations, farm animal food contributes significantly to climate change, habitat damage, and biodiversity loss [30]. Non-communicable illnesses claim the lives of 41 million people each year, accounting for 71% of all fatalities globally. 18 million of these fatalities are caused by cardiovascular disease, which is linked to our food in many cases [23].

Artificial meat or meat derived from the culture of animal cells, has attracted a lot of research investment and has the potential to drastically reduce the cost of meat. However, because this process consumes a lot of energy right now, it's unknown how essential such items will be in the shift to more sustainable food systems.

In several European nations, plant-based meat replacements are already available in supermarkets. Consumers accept plant-based meat replacements easily; however they lack nutritional value when compared to actual meat. Insects, on the other hand, have sparked widespread attention as a food source due to their high protein content and fatty acid composition present in many insects. Up to 2 billion people worldwide are estimated to eat insects in some form or another [23]. Insects are a rich source of vitamins that are otherwise difficult to receive through a vegetarian diet and can only be gained in adequate quantities through a carnivorous diet. In recent years, various ecological arguments have been made for eating insects, claiming that insects have an extraordinarily efficient nutritional turnover compared to cows and pigs. Insects are also better at turning food into weight than humans. That implies we will use less land and resources to generate the same amount of food energy, which is a good thing [23].

Insect output must be enhanced if insects are to become a viable source of food on a global scale. This necessitates ethical, economic, and health considerations: one of the most difficult challenges in developing a food system that can produce insects, is to increase production; and for that, we need some knowledge; it is said that many insects thrive particularly close to one another, and mealworms thrive in dark and narrow spaces; thus, having many of them in one place in the production system is beneficial. We also need to figure out how to automate the process because this would be a costly production. Some argue that one of the benefits of insects is that they are significantly different from humans, implying that they have a lesser risk of spreading diseases known as zoonoses when consumed. In addition, the EU has decided to legalize the consumption of insects, as well as the production of insects as animal feed in all EU nations [23].

5.4 Changing habits

Brouwer et al. [65] argues that influencing eating habits requires the application of social norms to promote a healthy diet. Social norms around healthy eating, as defined by culture and circumstance, might impact a person's food choices, implying that a code of suitable conduct exists [65]. In low- and middle-income countries, there are well-established societal norms and taboos, such as those around the feeding of young children (e.g., avoiding eggs) and the treatment of pregnant and nursing mothers. Understanding individual behavior and community reactions is critical for a system's overall resilience. Government policies may have a significant impact on a country's dietary patterns. Institutions that encourage sustainable consumption and nutrition are required. Dietary guidance is a fantastic illustration of how politics may play a role in this whole puzzle in the Nordic nations. Nudging is a psychological phenomena that may be utilized to alter eating habits on a personal and societal level. It can be used to get someone to consume something else in a tiny situation and foster healthy eating habits in a wider context, such as lowering in certain areas while growing in others. Another idea is to use smaller dishes in the cafeteria to prevent food waste [23].

5.5 Citizen-driven transformation

Nutrition democracy, according to Baldy and Kruse [85], is a notion that is gaining traction in nutrition policy research. It is about citizens reclaiming democratic control over the food system and allowing long-term change. Nutrition democracy research has thus far overlooked the potential of state-driven nutrition-related participatory procedures due to its concentration on civil society efforts. The authors looked at how local actors shape state-driven participation processes for long-term food system transformation along eight key dimensions of food democracy: mutual knowledge exchange, legitimacy and credibility of knowledge claims, transparent processes for generating ideas, common language for exchanging ideas, expectations and experiences with effectiveness, and role model.

5.6 Improving aquaculture

Today, fish remains a nutritious alternative to red meat. Between 1961 and 2016, the average yearly rise in worldwide fish consumption was 3.2 percent per year, out-pacing population growth. Fish contributes over 20% of the average per capita animal protein consumption for more than 3 billion people. Whereas average per capita consumption in Central Asia is roughly 2 kg per year, it is around 50 kg per person in the Small Island Developing States (SIDS) [23]. Blue proteins would play a critical role in protein shifting. They are not spoken about as often as green ones, but they have a far less ecological imprint than red ones and come in a variety of sustainability levels [23]. In poor nations where red meat is not as readily available as it is in Europe, for example, Blue proteins are even more significant, as they have been connected to a slew of positive health benefits. Fish are high in vital nutrients, thus they should be included more in the protein shift discussion [23].

5.7 Lowering the cost of nutritious foods

Food supply chain interventions are needed to boost the availability and affordability of safe and nutritious food, particularly to make healthy eating more affordable. To accomplish these targets, this approach necessitates coordinated effort and investment from production to consumption focused at increasing efficiency and lowering food losses and waste [86]. Incentives should encourage, among other things, diversification of production in the food and agriculture sectors toward nutritious foods such as fruits, vegetables, pulses, and seeds, as well as foods of animal origin and bio-enriched plants, as well as investments in innovation, research, and expansion, and productivity increases. The nutritional content of food and drinks can be increased at various points in the supply chain by fortifying staple foods after harvest in accordance with international norms. Fortification and biofortification have been used to address micronutrient shortages while simultaneously improving the availability and affordability of healthy meals (WHO. 2016).

6. Case examples of global food system transformations

The facts and examples that illustrate that transformation of food systems is conceivable and is currently occurring are far more compelling. This section exemplifies efforts of global transformation for resilience as reviewed by FAO *et al.*, [7].

When the structural roots of conflict are connected to competition for natural resources, such as fertile land, forests, fisheries, and water supplies, deep economic crises can occur. The following scenario is for Somalia, where people have suffered from chronic food insecurity and hunger for three decades (including famine in 2011) as well as numerous harsh weather occurrences (mainly droughts and floods) [7]. Drought-related severe food insecurity and malnutrition affected up to 6 million people in 2017-2019, including acute malnutrition in 900,000 children (FEWS Net, 2019). Appropriate measures were taken in recent years to respond, for example, to the severe food insecurity and malnutrition caused by drought. In 2018, the FAO launched the Cash + nutrition-sensitive program, which combines unconditional long-term cash transfers with livelihood support to increase resilience to future shocks while sustaining production capacity and food supply networks [73–77]. Seeds and tools for home gardening were sent to farming households, and shepherds were given assistance in raising livestock, which boosted animal health and milk output. The initiative has increased access to food for families in need, improved the quality and diversity of their meals, and enhanced program members' nutritional awareness via nutrition and food safety education.

A landscape restoration initiative in Ethiopia from 2015 to 2020 not only increased agricultural output by protecting soil and water, but also effectively linked farmers to markets, improving their economic potential. Food security improved for households, average family income increased considerably, and minimum nutritional diversity levels increased [45]. In India, a 2012-2016 project to restore land and intensify crops combined traditional water storage systems with infrastructure investments and technology transfers, resulting in positive effects on degraded and rain-harvested soils: crop yields increased by 10 to 70% and average household income increased by 170 percent [7]. This method also allowed for groundwater recharging, which improved the long-term sustainability of water consumption.

Interventions that remove some of the age-specific limits on young people's capacity to be productive in agricultural and food systems can also benefit them [7]. Professional and life skills training significantly increased the likelihood of adolescent girls of working age participating in safe income-generating activities (by 48 percent), while also reducing teenage pregnancies (by 34 percent) and the likelihood of marrying or living together prematurely (by 62 percent) according to evidence from a youth empowerment and livelihood program in Uganda [87].

7. Conclusion

A transition is neither a gradual enhancement of an existing system nor a complete revolution. A transformation is the outcome of a large number of little changes occurring at the same time in various regions of the system. These desired changes or initiatives are self-contained, but they are all linked because they are all measured against the same challenge: How can 8 billion people coexist with the planet's natural resources while also making room for 2 billion more? We begin to believe that a transformation of the global food system is possible when we combine all of the elements we have examined, all of the actions, large and small, of people changing their habits, work, and way of thinking. According to the World Resources Institute's baseline scenario, with 10 billion people on the planet in 2050, greenhouse gas emissions from food systems will be 15 gigatons per year, measured in CO_2 equivalents.

These emissions only need to be 4 gigatons per year to keep global warming below 2 degrees Celsius. As a result, the change will need to save 11 gigatons of CO_2 from our food systems. In 2050, we can save 5 gigatons of CO_2 emissions by lowering the demand for food and other agricultural goods. This is accomplished mostly by lowering food losses and waste by 50% and consuming 30% less ruminant meat than in the baseline scenario. We can save an additional 2 gigatons of CO_2 per year by improving food production on current agricultural regions using new technology. This, however, necessitates a 25% increase in productivity over the original condition. In addition, agricultural yields have improved by 56% since 2010. The next minor step is to boost fish supply by improving wild fisheries management and increasing productivity aquaculture. Cutting greenhouse gas emissions from agricultural output has a higher impact, such as reducing methane emissions from ruminants by 30%. Wet manure emissions are cut in half, reducing greenhouse gas emissions by 80%. A 50% decrease in energy emissions per agricultural unit and a reduction in nitrogen fertilizer consumption. All of these advances in agricultural productivity might result in CO_2 reductions of about 3 gigatons per year. In the end, 80 million hectares of previously unforested land will be totally reforested, resulting in significant CO_2 reductions when combined with an ambitious moor renaturation program.

Overall, improvements will cover an increase of 15 gigatons of CO_2 emissions from global food systems to a shocking 6 gigatons of the shortfall, allowing for land use changes. This entails altering the planet's appearance. And it demonstrates that transformation is not only essential, but also beautiful. In the countryside, there is less manure smell, whereas in the metropolis, there is more vertical green. A better quality of life with a healthier diet. And a world that is teeming with life. People with a variety of abilities from all over the world must adapt to this transformation. Political action, technical innovation, improved financial institutions, and behavioral improvements are all required. So let us get started on this transformation right now!

Acknowledgements

This chapter discusses the four pillars of global food system transformation developed by Katherine Richardson, Jakob Fritzbøger Christensen and the Sustainability Science Center. Grateful acknowledgement and credit is thereby made to Katherine Richardson, Jakob Fritzbøger Christensen and the entire Sustainability Science Center of the University of Copenhagen, Denmark, for permission to reproduce their materials. The authors equally acknowledge **Ana I. Ribeiro-Barros Ph.D**, the Academic Editor of this book for providing access to huge scientific literature that significantly improved this chapter.

Conflict of interest

The author declares no conflict of interest.

Thanks

The authors appreciate Ms. Eno-Obong Abia Sampson for typing the draft manuscript.

Author details

Jasper Okoro Godwin Elechi[1*], Ikechukwu U. Nwiyi[2] and Cornelius Smah Adamu[3]

1 Department of Food Science and Technology, College of Food Technology and Human Ecology, University of Agriculture, Makurdi, Nigeria

2 Faculty of Biosciences, Department of Applied Microbiology and Brewing, Nnmadi Azikwe University, Awka, Nigeria

3 Department of Agricultural and Environmental Engineering, College of Engineering, University of Agriculture, Makurdi, Nigeria

*Address all correspondence to: helloeljasper@gmail.com

References

[1] Elissavet G. Food Safety Management Strategies Based on Acceptable Risk and Risk Acceptance [PhD Thesis]. Wageningen, The Netherlands: submitted to Wageningen University; 2019. DOI: 10.18174/496132

[2] Cees L, Boogaard BK, Atta-Krah K. How food systems change (or not): Governance implications for system transformation processes. Food Security. 2021;**13**:761-780. DOI: 10.1007/s12571-021-01178-4

[3] Pereira LM, Drimie S, Maciejewski K, Tonissen PB, Biggs RO. Food system transformation: Integrating a political–economy and social–ecological approach to regime shifts. International Journal of Environmental Research and Public Health. 2020;**17**:1313. DOI: 10.3390/ijerph17041313

[4] Sperling F, Havlík P, Denis M, Valin H, Palazzo A, Gaupp F, et al. IIASA–ISC Consultative Science Platform: Resilient Food Systems. Paris: Thematic Report of the International Institute for Applied Systems Analysis (IIASA), Laxenburg, and the International Science Council (ISC); 2020

[5] Van Berkum S, Dengerink J, Ruben R. The Food Systems Approach: Sustainable Solutions for a Sufficient Supply of Healthy Food. The Hague: Wageningen Economic Research; 2018

[6] EC FOOD 2030 Expert Group. A Recipe for Change. An Agenda for a Climate-Smart and Sustainable Food System for a Healthy Europe. Brussels, Belgium: European Commission; 2018

[7] FAO, IFAD, UNICEF, WFP and WHO. The State of Food Security and Nutrition in the World 2021. Transforming Food Systems for Food Security, Improved Nutrition and Affordable Healthy Diets for all. Rome: FAO; 2021. DOI: 10.4060/cb4474en

[8] High Level Panel of Experts on Food Security and Nutrition (HLPE). Food Security and Nutrition: Building a Global Narrative towards 2030. Rome; 2020. (also available at www.fao.org/3/ca9731en/ca9731en.pdf)

[9] SWAC/OECD (2021), Food system transformations in the Sahel and West Africa: Implications for people and policies, Maps & Facts, no. 4, 2021

[10] HLPE (High Level Panel of Experts on Food Security and Nutrition). Nutrition and Food Systems: A Report by the High Level Panel of Experts on Food Security and Nutrition of the Committee on World Food Security. Rome, Italy: HPLE; 2017. Available from: http://www.fao.org/3/a-i7846e.pdf [Accessed 9 December 2021]

[11] de Steenhuijsen Piters B, Termeer E, Bakker D, Fonteijn H, Brouwer H. Food system resilience towards a joint understanding and implications for policy. Wageningen Economic Research. 2021 | Policy paper June 2021

[12] Holling CS. Resilience and stability of ecological systems. Annual Review of Ecology and Systematics. 1973;**4**(1):1-23

[13] IPCC. In: Field CB, Barros V, Stocker TF, Qin D, Dokken DJ, Ebi KL, Mastrandrea MD, Mach KJ, Plattner G-K, Allen SK, Tignor M, Midgley PM, editors. Managing the Risks of Extreme Events and Disasters to Advance Climate Change Adaptation. The Edinburgh Building, Shaftesbury Road, Cambridge CB2 8RU

ENGLAND: Cambridge University Press; 2012, 582 pp

[14] World Bank. Four Steps to Feeding the World in 2050 (Online). 2012. Available at: http://www.worldbank.org/en/news/feature/2012/10/16/four-steps-feed-world-2050 [Accessed 15 October, 2021]

[15] Leslie L, Cavatassi R, Symons R, Gordes A, Page O. Financing adaptation for resilient livelihoods under food system transformation: The role of multilateral development banks. Food Security. 2021. DOI: 10.1007/s12571-021-01210-7

[16] Ruerd R, Cavatassi R, Lipper L, Smaling E, Winters P. Towards food systems transformation—Five paradigm shifts for healthy, inclusive and sustainable food systems. Food Security. 2021. DOI: 10.1007/s12571-021-01221-4

[17] Giller K et al. Farming for food, for income, or for lack of better options? Small farms, sustained food insecurity and poverty in sub-Saharan Africa. Food Security. 2021a (In Press)

[18] Giller K et al. The future of farming: Who will produce our food? Food Security. 2021b (In Press)

[19] FAO, IFAD, UNICEF, WFP & WHO. The State of Food Security and Nutrition in the World 2018. Building Climate Resilience for Food Security and Nutrition. Rome: FAO; 2018. (also available at www.fao.org/3/I9553EN/i9553en.pdf)

[20] EAT-Lancet Commission. Food, Planet, Health: Healthy Diets from Sustainable Food Systems. London, The Lancet: Summary Report of the EAT-Lancet Commission; 2019

[21] HLPE. Agroecological and Other Innovative Approaches for Sustainable Agriculture and Food Systems That Enhance Food Security and Nutrition. A Report by the High Level Panel of Experts on Food Security and Nutrition of the Committee on World Food Security. Rome; 2019

[22] Janet R, Waite R, Searchinger T, Hanson C. How to Sustainably Feed 10 Billion People by 2050, in 21 Charts December 5, 2018. World Resources Institute; 2018. Available from: https://www.wri.org/insights/how-sustainably-feed-10-billion-people-2050-21-charts

[23] Katherine R, Christensen JF, The Sustainability Science Center. Transformation of the Global Food System. The Sustainability Science Center, the University of Copenhagen; 2021. Available at: https://www.coursera.org/learn/transformation-global-food-system [Accessed 22 October, 2020]

[24] Renske L. Innovation & entrepreneurship driving food system transformation. Physiology & Behavior. 2020;**220**(2020):112866. DOI: 10.1016/j.physbeh.2020.112866

[25] Canfield M, Anderson MD, McMichael P. UN food systems summit 2021: Dismantling democracy and resetting corporate control of food systems. Front. Sustain. Food Syst. 2021;**5**:661552. DOI: 10.3389/fsufs.2021.661552

[26] LEAP4FNSSA Europe-Africa Partnership for Food and Nutrition Security and Sustainable Agriculture (LEAP4FNSSA). FOOD SYSTEM RESILIENCE: Recommendations for the EUR-Africa R&I Partnership on FNSSA a Report Submitted to the LEAP4FNSSA Project in June 2021. 2021

[27] European Commission. Farm to Fork Strategy. For a Fair, Healthy and Environmentally- Friendly Food System. 2020a. Available at: https://ec.europa.eu/food/sites/food/files/safety/docs/f2f_action-plan_2020_strategy-info_en.pdf [Accessed: 1st October 2020]

[28] GBD (Global Burden of Disease Study). Global burden of 369 diseases and injuries in 204 countries and territories, 1990– 2019: A systematic analysis for the global burden of disease study 2019. The Lancet. 2020;**396**: 1204-1222

[29] WHO. Guideline: Fortification of Rice with Vitamins and Minerals as a Public Health Strategy. Geneva, Switzerland; 2018

[30] IPCC. In: Shukla PR et al., editors. Climate Change and Land: An IPCC Special Report on Climate Change, Desertification, Land Degradation, Sustainable Land Management, Food Security, and Greenhouse Gas Fluxes in Terrestrial Ecosystems. Geneva: Intergovernmental Panel on Climate Change (IPCC); 2019. Available from: https://spiral.imperial. ac.uk/bitstream/10044/1/76618/2/SRCCL-Full-Report-Compiled-191128.pdf

[31] Lester SE, Stevens JM, Gentry RR, Kappel CV, Bell TW, Costello CJ, et al. Marine spatial planning makes room for offshore aquaculture in crowded coastal waters. Nature Communications. 2018;**9**:945. (CrossRef)

[32] IPES-Food. From Uniformity to Diversity: A Paradigm Shift from Industrial Agriculture to Diversified Acroecological Systems. International Panel of Experts on Sustainable Food Systems; 2016. Retrieved from: http://www.ipes-food.org/_img/upload/files/UniformityToDiversity_FULL.pdf

[33] Vermeulen SJ, Campbell BM, Ingram JSI. Climate change and food systems. Annual Review of Environment and Resources. 2012;**37**:195-222. (CrossRef)

[34] Jessica F, Haddad L, Schneider KR, et al. (2021) viewpoint: Rigorous monitoring is necessary to guide food system transformation in the countdown to the 2030 global goals. Food Policy. 2021;**104**:102163. DOI: 10.1016/j.foodpol.2021.102163

[35] Herrero M, Thornton PK, Mason-D'Croz D, et al. Innovation can accelerate the transition towards a sustainable food system. Nat. Food. 2020;**1**:266-272. DOI: 10.1038/s43016-020-0074-1

[36] FAO. The State of Food Security and Nutrition in the World 2019. 2019b. Available through http://www.fao.org/publications/sofi/en/ 20

[37] FAO. The Future of Food Safety, First FAO/WHO/AU International Food Safety Conference, Addis, 12-13 February. 2019a. Available through: http://www.fao.org/3/CA3247EN/ca3247en.pdf [Accessed: 21 November 2019] 19

[38] Loboguerrero AM, Thornton P, Wadsworth J, Campbell BM, Herrero M, Mason- D'Croz D, et al. Perspective article: Actions to reconfigure food systems. Global Food Security. 2020;**26**:100432. DOI: 10.1016/j.gfs.2020.100432

[39] Woodhill J, Hasnain S, Griffith A. Farmers and Food Systems: What Future for Smallscale Agriculture? Oxford: University of Oxford; 2020

[40] Global Nutrition Report. Global Nutrition Report: Action on Equity to End Malnutrition. Bristol: Development Initiatives Poverty Research Ltd; 2020

[41] International Labour Office. Women and Men in the Informal Economy: A Statistical Picture. 3rd ed. International Labour Organization ILO; 2018

[42] Herforth A, Masters W, Bai Y, Sarpong D. The cost of recommended diets: Development and application a food Price index based on food-based dietary guidelines (P10-033-19). Current Developments in Nutrition. 2019;**3**. DOI: 10.1093/cdn/nzz034.P10033-19

[43] Hirvonen K, Bai Y, Headey D, Masters WA. Affordability of the EAT–lancet reference diet: A global analysis. The Lancet Global Health. 2020;**8**(1): e59-e66. DOI: 10.1016/S2214-109X(19) 30447-4), 10.1016/S2214-109X(19) 30447-4)

[44] Swinnen J, McDermott J, editors. COVID-19 and Global Food Security. Washington, DC: International Food Policy Research Institute (IFPRI); 2020. DOI: 10.2499/p15738coll2.133762

[45] FAO. Making Climate-Sensitive Investments in Agriculture – Approaches, Tools and Selected Experiences. Rome; 2021. (also available at doi:10.4060/cb1067en)

[46] United Nations Population Fund (UNFPA). 2014. The State of World Population 2014. The power of 1.8 billion adolescents, youth and the transformation of the future. New York, USA. Also Available at: www.unfpa.org/sites/default/files/pub-pdf/EN-SWOP14-Report_FINAL-web.pdf

[47] United Nations Department of Economic and Social Affairs (UNDESA). World Population Prospects. New York, USA: UNDESA (online); 2019. (Cited 25 May 2021). https://population.un.org/wpp

[48] Betcherman G, Khan T. Youth Employment in Sub-Saharan Africa: Taking Stock of the Evidence and Knowledge Gaps. Ottawa: International Development Research Centre (IDRC); 2015

[49] IFAD. IFAD RDR 2021 – Framework for the Analysis and Assessment of Food Systems Transformations Background Paper IFAD Rural Development Report 2021. 2019

[50] Hartle JC, Cole S, Chrisinger BW, Gardner CD. Interdisciplinary food-related academic programs: A 2015 snapshot of the United States landscape. J. Agric. Food Syst. Commun. Dev. 2017;**7**(4):35-49. DOI: 10.5304/jafscd.2017.074.006

[51] FAO and ITPS, Status of the World's Soil Resources (SWSR) – Main Report, Food and Agriculture Organization of the United Nations and Intergovernmental Technical Panel on Soils, Rome, Italy. 2015. Available online at: http://www.fao.org/3/ai5199e.pdf

[52] Aniek H, Kuiper M, Zurek M, Nørrung B, Achterbosch T, van't Veer P, et al. A sustainability compass for policy navigation to sustainable food systems. Global Food Security. 2021;**29**(2021): 100546. DOI: 10.1016/j.gfs.2021.100546

[53] Parfitt J, Barthel M, Macnaughton S. Food waste within food supply chains: Quantification and potential for change to 2050. Philosophical Transactions of the Royal Society. 2010;**365**:3065-3081

[54] Schoustra S, Materia V, et al. Empowering actors in the value chain of local foods: Traditional fermented foods in Africa. Food Security. 2021 (In Press)

[55] Sophie d B, Dengerink J, van Vliet J. Urbanisation as driver of food system transformation and opportunities for rural livelihoods. Food Security. 2021;**13**:781-798. DOI: 10.1007/s12571-021-01182-8

[56] Torero M. Infrastructure challenges and potential for Africa south of the Sahara. In: Badiane O, Makombe T, editors. Beyond a Middle Income Africa: Transforming African Economies for Sustained Growth with Rising Employment Incomes (pp. 157179): Resakss Annual Trends Outlook Report. 2014

[57] Dorosh P, Wang HG, You L, Schmidt E. Road connectivity, population, and crop production in sub-Saharan Africa. Agricultural Economics. 2012;**43**(1):89-103. DOI: 10.1111/j.1574-0862.2011.00567.x

[58] Sheahan M, Barrett CB. Food loss and waste in sub-Saharan Africa: A critical review. Food Policy. 2017;**70**:1-12

[59] Reardon T et al. The SMEs' Quiet Revolution in the hidden middle of food systems in developing regions. Food Security (Submitted). 2021

[60] Van Berkum S, Ruben R. Exploring a food system index for understanding food system transformation processes. Food Security. 2021 (in press)

[61] Minten BR, Thomas, Chen KZ. Agricultural value chains: How cities reshape food systems. In: 2017 Global Food Policy Report. Washington, DC: International Food Policy Research Institute (IFPRI); 2017. pp. 42-49

[62] Resnick D. Governance: Informal food markets in Africa's cities. In: IFPRI Book Chapters. 2017. pp. 50-57

[63] Dumont B, Groot JCJ, Tichit M. Review: Make ruminants green again – How can sustainable intensification and agroecology converge for a better future? Animal. 2018;**12**(S2):s210-s219

[64] Ray AC, Bruil J, Chappell MJ, Kiss C, Pimbert MP. From transition to domains of transformation: Getting to sustainable and just food systems through agroecology. Sustainability. 2019;**2019**(11):5272. DOI: 10.3390/su11195272

[65] Brouwer ID, Lachat C, van Liere MJ, Omosa EB, de Brauw A, Talsma EF, et al. Reverse thinking: Taking a healthy diet perspective towards food systems transformations. Food Security. 2021. DOI: 10.1007/s12571-021-01204-5

[66] Oliver TH. Biodiversity and resilience of ecosystem functions. Trends in Ecology & Evolution. 2015;**30**:673-684

[67] FAO, IFAD, UNICEF, WFP and WHO. The State of Food Security and Nutrition in the World 2017. Building Resilience for Peace and Food Security (Online). Rome: FAO; 2017. Available at: http://www.fao.org/3/a-I7695e.pdf [Accessed: 15 October, 2021]

[68] FAO & Famine Early Warning Systems Network (FEWS Net). More than 1.5 million people in Somalia still facing acute food security crisis or worse outcomes. Mogadishu and Washington, DC, FAO and FEWS Net. 2019. Also Available at: www.ipcinfo.org/ fileadmin/user_upload/ipcinfo/docs/FSNAU-FEWSNET_Somalia_Post-Deyr-Technical-Release_2019FebJune.pdf

[69] Corina E. Food security and food safety: Meanings and connections. Economic Insights – Trends and Challenges. 2020;IX(LXXII) No. 1/2020:59-68

[70] Herforth A, Bai Y, Venkat A, Mahrt K, Ebel A, Masters WA. Cost and affordability of healthy diets across and within countries. Background paper for the state of food security and nutrition in the world 2020. In: FAO Agricultural Development Economics Technical Study No. 9. Rome: FAO; 2020. (also available at doi:10.4060/cb2431en)

[71] Eke MO, Elechi JO. Food safety and quality evaluation of street vended meat pies sold in Lafia Metropolis, Nasarawa state, Nigeria. Int. J. Sci. Res. in Biological Sciences. 2021;**8**(1)

[72] Ikechukwu NU, Elechi JOG. Evaluation of food safety and nutritional quality of indigenous beverages vended in informal market of Nasarawa state, north central, Nigeria. Ukrainian Food Journal. 2021. Submitted

[73] FAO. Rationale for a new FAO food safety strategy. Committee on Agriculture. 2020a

[74] FAO. COVID-19 and its Impact on Agri-Food Systems, Food Security and Nutrition: Implications and Priorities for the Africa Region. Rome: FAO Regional Conference for Africa, thirty-first session, 26-28 October 2020; 2020b. (also available at: www.fao.org/3/ne079en/ne079en.pdf)

[75] FAO. Nutrition-Sensitive Cash+ in Somalia. Rome; 2020c. (also available at www.fao.org/3/ca9824en/ca9824en.pdf)

[76] FAO. FAO COVID-19 Response and Recovery Programme: Economic Inclusion and Social Protection to Reduce Poverty: Pro-Poor COVID-19 Responses for an Inclusive Postpandemic Economic Recovery. Rome; 2020d. (also available at: DOI:10.4060/cb0282en)

[77] FAO. Gendered Impacts of COVID-19 and Equitable Policy Responses in Agriculture, Food Security and Nutrition. Rome: FAO; 2020e. (also available at doi:10.4060/ca9198en)

[78] UN. Discussion Starter Action Track 3: Boost Nature-Positive Food Production at Scale. New York, USA; 2020. (also available at: www.un.org/sites/un2.un.org/files/unfss-at3-discussion_starter-dec2020.pdf)

[79] Lipper L, Thornton P, Campbell BM, Baedeker T, Braimoh A, Bwalya M, et al. Climate-smart agriculture for food security. Nature Climate Change. 2014;**4**(12):1068-1072

[80] McCouch S, Baute GJ, Bradeen J, Bramel P, et al. Agriculture: Feeding the future. Nature. 2013;**499**(7456):23-24

[81] Waltz CL. Local Food Systems: Background and Issues. Incorporated: Nova Science Publishers; 2010

[82] Chadare FJ, Fanou Fogny N, Madode YE, Ayosso JOG, Honfo SH, Kayodé FPP, et al. Local agro-ecological condition-based food resources to promote infant food security: A case study from Benin. Food Security. 2018;**10**:1013-1031

[83] Bizzotto-Molina P, D'Alessandro C, Dekeyser K, Marson M. Sustainable Food Systems through Diversification and Indigenous Vegetables: An Analysis of the Arusha Area. ECDPM; 2020

[84] Shumsky SA, Hickey GM, Pelletier B, Johns T. Understanding the contribution of wild edible plants to rural social-ecological resilience in semi-arid Kenya. Ecology and Society. 2014;**19**(4):34. DOI: 10.5751/ES-06924-190434. [Accessed 22 October 2017]

[85] Jana B, Kruse S. Food democracy from the top down? State-driven participation processes for local food system transformation towards sustainability. Politics and Governance. 2019;7(4):68-80

[86] FAO, IFAD, UNICEF, WFP & WHO. The State of Food Security and Nutrition in the World 2020. Transforming Food Systems for Affordable Healthy Diets. Rome: FAO; 2020. (also available at: 10.4060/ca9692en)

[87] Bandiera O, Buehren N, Burgess R, Goldstein M, Gulesci S, Rasul I, et al. Women's Empowerment in Action: Evidence from a Randomized Control Trial in Africa. Washington, DC: World Bank; 2018. (also available at: https://openknowledge.worldbank.org/handle/10986/28282)

Chapter 3

Bundling Weather Index Insurance with Microfinance: Trekking the Long Road between Expectations and Reality – A Study on Sub-Saharan Africa

Dorcas Stella Shumba

Abstract

Food production in sub-Saharan Africa (SSA) is exposed to climatic variations and weather-related shocks which affect agricultural output beyond the manageable limits of smallholder farmers. To manage food production uncertainties, weather index insurance (WII) pilot projects have been launched across SSA since the early 2000s. Due to low adoption rates among smallholder farmers, insurance providers have partnered with risk aggregators such as microfinance institutions to foster the demand for and uptake of WII. Despite this, demand for WWI remains low. This chapter seeks to explore the gap between the assertion, that WII is a promising risk transfer mechanism for smallholder farmers in SSA and the realisation that, even where microfinance is made available, subscription rates among smallholder farmers rarely rise. The practice of linking insurance with credit is considered to be important because, in principle, when smallholder farmers have access to insurance, they pose less risk to creditors. In this sense, insurance can crowd-in credit, the lack of which has long been identified as a major, if not the main, constraint for smallholders in developing countries.

Keywords: weather index insurance, microfinance, food systems resilience, climate change, risk transfer, smallholder farmers, sub-Saharan Africa

1. Introduction

Agriculture is a major source of food in Sub-Saharan Africa (SSA), and a primary source of livelihood [1]. The sector employs more than half of the total labour force and accounts for roughly a third of the gross domestic product (GDP) [2–4]. The share of agriculture in GDP varies significantly by country ranging from below 3% in Botswana to over 50% in Chad [5]. Due to the fragmentation of land caused by population pressure in most rural areas, farm sizes are typically less than 2 hectares each [6]. As a result, smallholder farms are dominant across the subcontinent [7]. They make up 80% of the farms, which translates to approximately 33 million smallholder farms [8]. Although the widely accepted view is that, smallholder farmers produce the majority of the food, because they farm land very intensively resulting in high levels of productivity per unit of land [9, 10], their farms are often too small to provide a sustainable income at the household level, let alone food security [7][1]. In addition, smallholder farmers are known to face several challenges associated with missing markets for credit, insurance, information including economies of scale in marketing and transportation [10]. Problematically, they are also reliant on non-drought tolerant crops and seed varieties[2], non-mechanised farming systems and subsistence rain-fed farming[3], factors which jointly contribute to the volatility of agriculture and the vulnerability of the smallholder farmers [13]. Having a full grasp of the character of risks that affect smallholder farmers is key to developing appropriate solutions to deal with risks. Similarly, it is important to understand how farmers respond to the solutions designed to ameliorate risk as this will help to establish the effectiveness and compatibility of the measures apropos the target market.

This chapter seeks to explore the gap between the assertion, that weather index insurance (WII) is a promising risk transfer mechanism for smallholder farmers in SSA and the realisation that, even where microfinance is made available, subscription rates among smallholder farmers rarely rise. The chapter pays attention to the risk response behaviour of smallholder farmers when presented with the option of purchasing WII that is bundled with microfinance. Weather index insurance is crucial because it potentially addresses welfare losses due to weather risk and complements existing informal risk management strategies [14]. The linkage between WII and credit has been discussed widely in theory but rarely investigated empirically, yet a lot of recommendations have been put forward by scholars for WII to be bundled with microfinance (see [15–19]). This is because, when smallholder farmers are believed to pose less risk to creditors when they have access to insurance [20]. In this sense, agriculture insurance can crowd-in credit, the lack of which has long been identified as a major, if not the main, constraint for smallholders in developing countries [21].

Access to agriculture insurance is crucial for smallholders because agriculture is generally prone to production failure due to the risk of catastrophic events such as those linked to extreme weather events [22]. Weather extremes have been repeatedly seen to have long-lasting impacts on farming livelihoods [23–26]. Sub-Saharan Africa is especially vulnerable to weather-related risks because of the strong reliance on climate-sensitive rainfed agriculture [27]. While extreme weather shocks are not new to this region, the frequency and intensity of the events have increased over the past few decades. Based on the Human Cost of Disasters 2000–2019 Report, there has been a sharp increase in weather-related disasters[4] over the past 20 years. Notably, disasters

---

[1] Smaller farms are generally thought to have an advantage over large farms in per capita productivity due to higher labour utilisation (e.g., using family labour) and intensive farming on smaller pieces of land [9].

[2] Gollin et al. [11] revealed for example that, in 2000, only 17% of the area planted for maize had modern maize varieties in sub-Saharan Africa compared to 57% in Latin America and the Caribbean.

[3] According to Demeke et al. [12] the irrigated area in this region which extends over six million hectares, makes up just 5 per cent of the total cultivated area, compared to 37 per cent in Asia 14 per cent in Latin America. Two-thirds of that area is in three countries: Madagascar, South Africa, and Sudan.

[4] To be recorded as a disaster in EM-DAT, one or all the following must take place: 10 or more people must be reported killed, 100 or more people must be reported affected, a state of emergency must be declared by the State, and a call for international assistance made. Based on this delineation, hazards only become disasters when human lives are lost, and livelihoods are equally damaged or destroyed [28].

including extreme weather events rose from 4212 in the period 1980 to 1999, to 7348 in the period 2000 to 2019 [28]. Weather events figure large among the recorded disasters[5].

Equally alarming are the rising patterns of loss and damage in the agricultural industry that are strongly correlated to the increasing catastrophic events [29]. For example, it is estimated that more than 75% of recent economic losses caused by natural hazards in Sub-Saharan Africa are attributable to climate change-induced weather events [30]. Outcomes linked to economic loss include livelihood insecurity, poverty, food insecurity and poor nutrition – cyclical patterns which can be ameliorated through adaptation financing [31]. What smallholders need therefore is access to perfect financial markets (savings, credit and insurance) and economic incentives to (re)invest in agriculture [7]. Reducing the economic impact of severe weather events is thus a crucial step towards supporting agricultural growth, sustainable livelihoods, poverty alleviation as well as bolstering food security and nutrition [32]. Given the foregoing, the vulnerability of smallholder farmers in lower-income countries is acute in part because they repeatedly lack access to financial mechanisms to efficiently manage production uncertainties [33]. In the absence of effective insurance and credit markets, households remain vulnerable to the financial consequences of high-magnitude loss events.

2. Understanding the nature of climate change risk in SSA

While SSA is not a single unit and challenges vary spatially and temporally, agriculture, and especially crop production in this region is predominantly rainfed and as such reliant on unpredictable climatic events [24, 31, 34, 35]. Under the current variable climate conditions, SSA already experiences a major deficit in food production especially in semi-arid and subhumid regions and areas [1]. This means a further drop in soil moisture due to mounting climate extremes will have devastating effects on agricultural production and will worsen food insecurity [26]. SSA is vulnerable to climate change also because the economies of most countries in this region are dominated by subsistence agriculture, the productivity of which is grossly susceptible to changing weather patterns [36]. Furthermore, the sub-continent is prone to complex natural climatic phenomena such as the El Nino-Southern Oscillation (ENSO), the West African Monsoon and the Indian Ocean Dipole [37], which influence climate variability (inter-annual and intra-seasonal rainfall), trends (upward or downward) and the persistence thereof [38]. The natural climatic phenomena give rise to regional climatic patterns which are impacted to some degree by climate change [37]. Because of the regional climatic phenomena, SSA has a long history of rainfall fluctuations of varying lengths and intensities (ibid) and is prone to cyclical drought patterns which are a frequent event in the semi-arid countries of the sub-continent [1]. The droughts in SSA have in recent times become more frequent and protracted, ostensibly due to climate change [39].

Climate forecasts have shown warming of approximately 0.71°C over much of the African continent in the twentieth Century [1], and an increase of over 1°C in the twenty-first Century [40]. Rather, average near-surface temperatures across parts of the continent have risen by more than twice the global rate of temperature increase

[5] For example, floods were the highest recorded disaster event – 3254, followed by storms – 2043 (ibid).

in the twenty-first Century [41]. According to WMO [40], the year 2019 was among the three warmest years on record for the continent. Recent decadal predictions encompassing a five-year period from 2020 to 2024, signify continued warming and decreasing rainfall markedly over North and Southern Africa (ibid). Further predictions by Woetzel et al. [42] suggest that, due to climate change, the number and intensity of extreme weather events in SSA are set to increase. This is consistent with findings submitted in the Human Cost of Disasters 2000–2019 Report, which revealed that 1192 extreme weather events were recorded in Africa over the last 20 years (see [28]).

An enquiry on climate change and its likely impacts on SSA cannot be achieved by examining long term weather changes alone [43], as most countries in SSA suffer from intersecting stressors that give rise to low resilience and limited adaptative capacity to climate-related shocks [1]. Incidentally, climate change acts to exacerbate pre-existing conditions and has thus been dubbed a threat multiplier [25]. As such, the effects of drought and other climate extremes in SSA are exacerbated by endemic poverty, complex governance and institutional dimensions; limited access to capital, including markets, infrastructure and technology; ecosystem degradation; and complex disasters and conflicts ([36], p. 435).

SSA accounts for more than half of the world's extreme poor, amounting to approximately 400 million people, most of which are smallholder farmers [37]. Poverty is among the key reasons why a lot of smallholder farmers in SSA are continuously exposed to inter-annual variations and occasional shocks caused by weather which affect agricultural output beyond their manageable limits [30]. As a result, at the 25th session of the Conference of the Parties (COP) to the United Nations Framework Convention on Climate Change (UNFCCC) that took place in Madrid in December 2019, it was revealed that 7 out of the 10 most climate-vulnerable nations in the world are located in Africa [44]. The figure is consistent with findings published in the Human Cost of Disasters 2000–2019 Report, which pointed out that, the top 10 list of countries with the highest share of affected populations by extreme weather shocks over the last 20 years is dominated by Sub-Saharan African countries, which make up 6 out of the 10 countries on the list [28].

3. Risk response mechanisms used by smallholder farmers in SSA

Risk is the aggregate of the likelihood or possibility of a shock event occurring, and the severity of loss or impact caused by the event [45]. Three aspects make up risk, namely, threat, uncertainty, and loss. Climate change poses significant risks for food systems and has thus emerged as one of the greatest challenges of the twenty-first Century. Climatic extremes affect the primary sources of farm income, such as crops and livestock, and can further destroy household assets such as farming equipment – investments accumulated over time that are needed to generate future income [46]. Loss and damage due to extreme weather events can push farming households into cycles of poverty. According to GlobalAgRisk [47], households that are just above the poverty line can be pushed instantly below the poverty line by a major weather event. In the absence of perfect financial markets, including savings, credit and insurance, smallholdings in SSA generally struggle to recover from loss and damage caused by extreme weather events [34].

In the absence of perfect financial markets, an array of behavioural responses often emerge to fill in the gaps created by market failures [48]. Despite having considerable experience dealing with weather extremes, smallholders are much less likely to plan for low probability, high consequence risks [49]. This is a result of a cognitive bias that causes people to ignore risks with low probability, except when the likelihood of occurrence is well-known [50]. This psychological phenomenon influences the willingness of poor households to spend their limited income to cover low probability risks. Be that as it may, from a risk perspective, behavioural responses to shocks consist of three types of choices, namely, risk mitigation, risk coping and risk transfer [51]. The behavioural responses are characterised as being *ex ante* or *ex post* based on chronology and functional objective [52]. *Ex ante* strategies are those measures taken before shocks occur to avoid, transfer or reduce risk exposure, while *ex post* strategies are measures taken after shocks occur to mitigate or insulate welfare impacts of the shocks [52–54]. According to Frankenberger et al. [54], *ex ante* strategies are about preparation, whereas *ex post* strategies are about coping and recovery.

Smallholder farmers in SSA are more susceptible to weather fluctuations than farmers in developed countries, who for instance, can more easily alter crop varieties, irrigate their fields, or secure crop insurance [42]. In more developed countries financial markets exist which allow farmers to insure against shocks *ex ante*, or to borrow *ex post* to achieve *quasi*-insurance through *ex post* loan repayment [55], increasing the options for recovery in the event of loss events. Because smallholder farmers in SSA are risk averse, they ordinarily choose to rely on traditional methods of risk management in the absence of ready access to savings, insurance and credit markets [21].

Faced with no savings, credit or insurance, they typically manage risk by smoothing consumption through choosing low-risk activities or technologies, which generally yield low to average returns [56]. Smallholder farmers in SSA also smooth consumption through asset attrition. According to Carter and Lybbert [57], since the rural poor have limited access to financial markets, consumption smoothing typically involves amassing assets in good times to use as a fallback in bad times. For example, a study on the impacts of drought on rural households in Burkina Faso showed that a good number of households that sell livestock do so to offset consumption shortfalls due to negative income shocks. Similar findings were observed in studies carried out in the rural Districts of Buhera and Nyanga in Zimbabwe where farmers mentioned the sale of livestock as a means of buffering income losses caused by production uncertainties [58]. Wealth for the rural poor is usually not in the form of cash or savings [47], but productive assets such as livestock [48]. Thus, when a severe weather event occurs, livestock is often sold off, often at a loss [59], because the distressed sale of large numbers of livestock at the same time flood the market, significantly reducing their value [60]. In contrast, insurance has been seen to positively influence households' behavioural responses to risk through enabling them to reduce the need to rely on costly coping strategies such as selling productive, as this undermines future productivity. Results from an index-based livestock insurance (IBLI) pilot in Marsabit District of northern Kenya, showed that insured households are less likely to sell livestock [61]. Nonetheless, because insurance is not readily available in most rural areas, and where available, demand for it is low, smallholders tend to rely more on on-farm risk mitigation strategies. Thus, to preserve assets, households may smooth consumption further by cutting back on meals and diverting children from school which undermines crucial investments in human capital, hampering current and future productivity (ibid). In terms of its functional objective, consumption smoothing involves creating a balance between spending and saving to achieve a higher overall standard of living and can for that reason be used as a welfare dimension to assess a household's preparedness to deal with climate change risk [62].

In addition to consumption smoothing, smallholder farmers in SSA also smooth income when dealing with climate change risk [44]. Income smoothing refers to the different strategies and approaches used by households to control the impact of extreme volatility in household income [48]. It is most often achieved *ex ante*, through diversifying economic activities and employment choices (ibid). Since most farming households in SSA lack access to savings, credit and insurance, they try as much as possible to prepare for loss events *ex ante* through income generation [63]. Thus, to smooth income, households take steps to protect themselves from adverse income shocks before they occur [47]. To achieve this, households can pool together labour supplies, allocating them across different local employers over time. However, as most farming households in SSA earn wages through agriculture (e.g., from working on neighbouring farms or plantations, and rendering services to local businesses that deal with agricultural supplies) pooling labour supplies across different divisions of the climate-sensitive agriculture industry will not solve their income problems in the event of climatic extremes. Diversifying into non-agricultural activities or more profitable alternatives is difficult for many rural households [64]. The barriers to entry include working capital and vocational skills and or education requirements. Examples from Tanzania and Ethiopia cited in Dercon's study support the view that the poor typically enter into activities with low entry costs such as those linked to subsistence farming or casual agricultural wage employment. Since diversifying income sources is costly for poor rural households, Village Savings and Loans Associations (VSLAs)[6] are sometimes used as a collective means to smooth income. Fumagalli and Martin [65] share findings from a cluster randomised control trial (RCT) carried out between 2009 and 2012 in the Nampula Province of Mozambique, which shows the usefulness of pooling income. Based on the study, VSLA money has been used by households to buffer shortfalls in income due to unforeseen shocks. It is unclear, however, to what extent VSLAs would be effective in responding to covariate risk. If all households in a community are affected by a catastrophic event, informal risk-sharing activities are unlikely to be sufficient. Nonetheless, access to financial markets presents a greater opportunity for income smoothing and less vulnerability to weather shocks [62].

In all, there is an overlap between different types of shocks and behavioural responses to shocks. As the discussion above attests, high-frequency low losses are usually managed at the farm level and mitigated in part through access to household investments [63]. In an ideal world, residual risk (low frequency, medium loss) that cannot be retained by the farmer is better of transferred to third parties, usually insurance companies [45], which is not always an option for smallholders in SSA. Where insurance is an option, smallholders often deem it too costly for their limited income. Nonetheless, transferring a portion of income risk to a third party enables the farmer to have enough money to invest in higher-risk/higher-yield production technologies, such as improved seeds and inputs [20]. When weather-related shocks strike, households that receive indemnity payments have more response options, which notionally should reduce their reliance on detrimental coping strategies [66]. Although smallholder farmers in SSA have developed numerous adaptation mechanisms to cope with weather fluctuations over time, evidence has repeatedly shown that their methods are not adequate to deal with climate change [36]. If climate

[6] VSLAs are typically composed of 15 to 20 self-selecting households, who meet regularly to pool income into a common fund, which can be lent out to group members at group agreed interest rates [65].

change adaptation investments are not made (e.g. by governments, multinational corporations and donor communities), the adaptation mechanisms used by smallholder farmers in SSA will not keep up with climate change impacts [22]. The Paris Agreement underlined the global importance of adaptation and contains provisions related to adaptation finance that follow guidelines from the Cancun Adaptation Framework [67]. Paragraph 28 of the Cancun Adaptation Framework stressed the need to explore options for risk-sharing and risk insurance, including options for micro-finance to reduce the devastating impacts of disasters among vulnerable populations [68].

4. Weather index insurance

Risk-sharing or risk transfer is a risk management strategy that involves the contractual shifting of risk from one party to another [51]. Risk transfer is most often achieved through an insurance policy, where the insurance carrier assumes the defined risks for the policyholder in exchange for a fee, or insurance premium [69]. Agricultural insurance is one risk transfer tool that farmers can use to manage risks that cannot be mitigated at the farm level [30]. It offers a promising means of cushioning in times of climate change-induced loss and damage for smallholder farmers [35]. Globally, however, less than 20% of smallholder farmers have any form of agricultural insurance [22]. Although the estimated global agricultural insurance premium volume almost doubled in the period 2004–2007, it remained low in African countries where it roughly reached an average of 0.13% of the 2007 agricultural GDP [70]. As a result, some scholars claim that only about 1.3% of the smallholder farmers in SSA have agricultural insurance [71]. Raithatha and Priebe [22] set the figure at 3%, while a more recent study suggests that the figure is around 3.5% which at any rate is far below the rates in Asia (46.2%) and Latin America (15.8%) [72]. Despite the low uptake of agricultural insurance by smallholder farmers in SSA, agriculture insurance is firmly believed can reduce the economic impact of severe weather events and help stimulate economic development through supporting agricultural growth, poverty alleviation, and the development of rural finance [14]. Based on the functional objective of agriculture insurance, it is an income smoothing *ex ante* strategy, actioned before the occurrence of a shock event [16].

There are various types of agriculture insurance, the main ones being, indemnity-based crop insurance (e.g., named peril crop insurance and multiple peril crop insurance) and index-based insurance (e.g., index-based livestock insurance, area yield index insurance and weather index insurance). This chapter looks specifically at weather index insurance (WII). Weather index insurance has been presented as an important risk transfer mechanism that can assist smallholder farmers to deal better with climate risk [22, 35, 73]. The underlying risk for a WII product is the behaviour of the specific weather variable that contributes to production losses [14]. WII focuses on weather-related shocks because rainfall and temperature patterns for instance pose a serious threat for farmers [20]. The pervasive nature of catastrophic weather events is especially well-suited for index products, which explicitly insure against covariate shocks (ibid). Unlike traditional insurance, index-based insurance compensates policyholders according to a pre-determined index value [69] that serves as a proxy for losses rather than upon the assessed losses for individual policyholders [51]. Thus, some of the advantages of WII are that it has low operational costs, fast claim settlement speed and low risk of moral hazard and adverse selection [35].

Low operational costs give WII a critical advantage over traditional insurance, yet the hedging effectiveness of weather index-based insurance tends to be diminished by the often imperfect correlation between the index and realised losses. This is caused for instance, by the non-insurable difference between the weather events happening at the farm site and those occurring at the reference weather station, which is referred to as geographical basis risk [74]. In light of this, some of the drawbacks of WII include high basis risk, high actuarial difficulty, and high set-up costs [75].

The earliest applications of WII in emerging economies in the Americas and Asia are said to have taken place respectively in Mexico in 2002, followed by India in 2003 [47]. In SSA, the first application of weather index is said to have taken place in Malawi in 2005 [76] followed by Ethiopia in 2006 [77]. Almost 2 decades later, however, index insurance markets are still very thin in most African countries. To lessen the limitations of WII, insurance providers have initiated changes to their products being guided by scholarly recommendations and emerging best practices. Some of the key recommendations submitted by the scholarly community include interlinking reliable weather data with location-specific crop and agronomic conditions using flexible geospatial crop modelling tools (see [78]), interlinking WII with subsidies (see [79]) and interlinking WII with microfinance (see [16]). The mixed results of many WII pilot projects to date, for example, as presented by the lack of widespread implementation of even those projects considered successful, followed by the consistently low adoption rate by smallholder farmers, warrant an investigation into the changes needed for the products to become more scalable and sustainable.

5. Bundling weather index insurance with microfinance: expectations vs. reality

Smallholder farmers often do not qualify for credit provided by mainstream banks due to the lack of usable collateral (e.g. savings, reliable earnings, effective land titles and other tangible and intangible assets) to guarantee loan repayments [49, 80]. In addition, the large fluctuations in farm revenue generally make it less commercially attractive to lenders, thus hampering credit provision to the agriculture sector [16]. Credit constraints discourage farmers from investing in higher-risk/higher-yield production technologies, such as improved seeds and inputs [20], which would otherwise boost their capacity to withstand the negative impacts of extreme weather events. In some instances, however, if no collateral is present, lenders may require crop insurance to securitize the repayment of the loan [16]. Thus, crop insurance can facilitate credit. Microfinance Institutions (MFIs) specialise in the supply of credit to segments of the population that is typically unattended by mainstream banks. The promise of microfinance is centred on the awarding of microloans to the poorest of the poor without requiring collateral [81]. What makes microfinance different from traditional forms of credit is its focus on small loans and other low-cost financial services which the poor can use to generate income and become self-reliant [82, 83]. However, while insurance may in some instances unlock credit, bundling microfinance with insurance is far from being the panacea for the credit constraint problem [21]. This is why more insight into the impact of linking insurance and credit is needed, particularly since the adoption rate of WII in SSA has remained low even in cases where microfinance has been made available.

Studies have indicated an uptake of less than a fourth of the smallholder population [80], which shows clearly that demand for WII is low. Actual demand according to the preceding scholars varies from 2 to 40% or 50% maximum. In general, low demand is ascribed to several factors which include farmer budgetary constraints, lack of trust in financial institutions, poor understanding of the contract, and the often imperfect correlation between the index and realised losses (basis risk) [84]. Marr et al. [80] have gone on to group the reasons for low demand into 3 categories namely, (1) neoclassical (i.e., risk aversion, risk mitigation, basis risk and price), (2) behavioural (i.e., understanding, trust and education), and (3) pecuniary determinants capturing credit and liquidity constraints (i.e., wealth, liquidity, credit and income). To weigh in briefly on the effect of the given determinants of low demand, firstly, it has been noted already in this chapter that smallholders are generally risk averse, which causes them to depend more on traditional risk mitigation strategies. Secondly, because, their risk mitigation strategies are limited, they are among the most vulnerable populations to climate change. Thirdly, when presented with risk mitigation strategies such as insurance, smallholders are not always willing to pay for indemnity. Aside from being risk averse, they are poor and often credit and liquidity constrained. Inevitably, price is a crucial factor that the smallholders consider before signing up for an insurance policy. There are thus tensions between what must be charged to insure low-probability high-consequence events and the willingness of households to pay for insurance products designed to protect against losses caused by these events [33].

Fourthly, basis risk interacts with other factors such as price and is an important factor known to drive price beyond the reach of smallholders. To increase demand for WII, suppliers need to focus on minimising basis risk. Even as basis risk is an inherent problem for index insurance, it can be reduced through product design and application [47]. To increase demand for WII, suppliers need to additionally educate smallholders about the benefits of insurance, which should be followed up by cultivating relationships of trust [85]. There is a further need for suppliers to come up with innovative ways to make insurance more attractive to smallholders. This involves adapting financial services and products to match the risk profile of the market demographic [33], for example through bundling WII with microfinance.

5.1 Expectations

Bundling index-insurance with credit is a practice that is widely debated in literature but mainly at a theoretical level [80]. There are several benefits that come with combining microcredit with insurance, some of which have already been discussed in this chapter. Since both insurance and credit are recognised as important tools for smoothening and enhancing income [16], it is believed that when bundled together, they can enhance on-farm efforts (e.g., through increased input, improved seed varieties and investments in and specialised and diversified farming) to mitigate climate risks. Meyer et al. [21] are of the view that neither credit nor insurance markets can exist independently in low-collateral environments. This makes perfect sense considering that insurance can ensure the success of credit by promoting lending to smallholders in credit constrained environments where farmers have weak collateral to offer, and systemic risks are the main cause of loan defaults. While credit on the other hand can ensure the success of insurance by enhancing household income and protecting farmers against the financial risk of crop failure. Linking the two contracts thus seems beneficial for farmer productivity, food systems resilience and incidentally, the growth of rural financial markets. A potential downside of this practice, however, which cannot be overlooked by this chapter is that, if a loss occurs which is not covered by the insurance because the index was not correlated to the realised loss and an indemnity payment was not triggered, the farmer may not be able to repay their loan. On its own, index insurance can harm farmers by extracting insurance payments while providing little or no actual risk coverage [20]. When combined with credit, the farmer may be worse off than if their loan were not insured because they have to pay the insurance premium as well as repay the loan [21]. This shows that while insurance could unlock credit and produce desired results such as higher investments, it could also produce undesired results such as higher default rates (ibid).

5.2 Reality

A few empirical studies have been carried out to understand the credit insurance linkage in different parts of SSA, and the results have been conflicted. Among these, a study by Giné and Yang [19] sought to test whether reducing risk through WII induces greater demand for credit among smallholder farmers in Malawi. Half the farmers were randomly selected to be offered credit to purchase high-yielding hybrid maize and groundnut seeds for planting. The other half were offered a similar credit package but were also required to purchase (at actuarially fair rates) a weather insurance policy that partially or fully forgave the loan in the event of poor rainfall. The uptake of credit was 33% for farmers offered a loan without insurance and 17.6% for farmers offered a loan bundled with weather insurance. The findings suggest that smallholders do not always value insurance as the demand for credit fell when bundled with insurance. An explanation for the behavioural response given by the authors is that farmers understood that they were implicitly insured by the limited liability inherent in the loan contract so that going for a loan bundled with insurance (for which an insurance premium was charged) would effectively increase the interest rate on the loan. On the other hand, the overall poor uptake rate could be taken to mean that smallholders generally do not trust financial institutions [86].

In a study carried out by Karlan et al. [87]. A randomised control trial was conducted to investigate whether price risk affected the demand for credit by smallholders in Eastern Ghana. Farmers were offered loans with an indemnity component that forgave 50% of the loan if crop prices dropped below a threshold price. A control group was offered a standard loan product at the same interest rate. Loan uptake was high among all farmers. The indemnity component had little impact on the uptake or other outcomes of interest. The indemnity product had incorporated insurance into the loan rather than as an add on, to avoid potential choice overload problems that arise sometimes when too many choices cause stagnation in decision making. Yet, findings showed a high take-up rate of credit despite indemnity, which made it difficult for the authors to assess heterogeneity in behavioural response. What is apparent from the findings is that insurance made no difference to the demand for credit. This again implying that smallholders do not always value insurance. To explain the outcome, the authors suggested among other reasons that, the farmers perhaps did not understand the contract.

In a different study carried out by Mishra et al. [88] in Northern Ghana, results also found no evidence that insurance has a significant impact on increasing the uptake of credit. The study investigated whether coupling agricultural loans with micro-level and meso-level drought index insurance can stimulate the demand and supply of credit and increase technology adoption. Based on empirical findings, if at all, bundling loans with insurance increased the likelihood of loan applications for female farmers. Gallenstein et al. [84] published a paper on the same population in

Northern Ghana. The authors investigated the willingness to pay for drought index insurance backed loans and found out that insurance lowered overall demand for loans. In fact, adding an insurance policy to an agricultural loan reduced the demand for credit as 75.3% of the population were willing to pay the market interest rate for the uninsured loan. What is also apparent from the findings of this study is that smallholders do not always value insurance. In this case, insurance had a bearing on demand for credit, albeit in a negative way.

Different results were observed, however, in a study carried out in Machakos County, Kenya by Ndegwa et al. [89]. The authors sought to investigate the causal effect of bundling WII with credit on uptake of agricultural technology among smallholders. 1170 sample households were randomly assigned to one of three research groups, namely, control, risk contingent credit and traditional credit. Based on the findings the average credit uptake rate was 33% with the uptake of bundled credit being significantly higher than that of traditional credit. In this case, insurance was seen to influence the uptake of credit. By and large, the study observed that risk rationing was among the key reasons responsible for the negative credit uptake among smallholders.

In another study, Pelka et al. [74] analysed the influence of weather variations on the repayment performance of credit among smallholder farmers in Madagascar. The farmers studied primarily grow rice in monoculture. The weather risk for rice cultivation in the central highlands of Madagascar is the excessive amount of rain in the harvest period (between the end of February to April), which reduces rice yields and, thus, leads to revenue losses for farmers. Findings demonstrated a high correlation between precipitation and credit risk, where credit risk is defined as whether or not a borrower can pay back all loan instalments by the due date. Thus, findings revealed in particular that, the credit risk of loans granted to smallholders increased in the harvesting period due to the excessive amount of precipitation. Based on the analysis given by the authors, credit risk would reduce significantly if the farmers had weather index insurance policies. This assumption is based on the hypothesis that, "the effect of weather events on the repayment performance of loans equals the effect of the returns of weather index-based insurance on the repayment performance of loans" Pelka et al. [74]. As such, the authors surmise that weather index-based insurance might have the potential to mitigate a portion of the risk in agricultural lending. In this study, the authors do not seem to argue for the bundling of credit and WII, but instead, propose that WII would be instrumental in mitigating credit risk in cases where lending is involved which would work only where the weather index is perfectly correlated to the realised loss. To avoid issues of credit risk, the weather index insurance programs in Malawi often bundle credit with mandatory weather index insurance [78]. However, while making insurance mandatory is good in that it assures worried lenders, the downside is that it may discourage farmers from seeking loans [21] as seen in experiments carried out in Malawi and Ghana earlier cited in this section.

6. Discussion and conclusion

A review of the literature showed mostly mixed results regarding the impact of bundling WII with microfinance among smallholders in SSA. The literature confirmed the premise that, even where microfinance has been made available, the demand for WII has remained consistently low across the sub-continent. Thus, a wide gap still exists between the expectations of what WII can achieve for smallholder farmers in dealing with climate change risk, and the reality that is on the ground, which is that current demand varies from 2 to 40% (50% at the most). While WII may not provide complete protection against losses, it can improve the financial protection coverage needed for smallholders to effectively deal with the financial consequences of high-magnitude climatic loss events. In this way, WII can play an instrumental role in creating an enabling environment for rural financial services including banking and microfinance. For WII to work, it must complement existing risk management strategies, to ensure all round cover against climate change risks.

The chapter focused mainly on demand side dynamics paying considerable attention to the risk behavioural responses of the smallholders. It is crucial to understand how farmers respond to solutions designed to mitigate against risk as this will help to establish the effectiveness and compatibility of the measures apropos the target market. Based on the reviewed studies, the determinants of low demand for WII are many, ranging from risk aversion, liquidity and credit constraints, lack of trust in financial institutions, poor understanding of the indemnity contract to risk rationing. To improve demand for WII, suppliers need to design products to match the needs of target markets. A needs-based approach or deficit model recognises all needs, including underlying needs as valid claims. And so, insurance providers must be fully cognizant of community needs in their entirety for them to package WII more attractively. This would entail tackling more than just weather risk. Some insurance providers are already doing this. For example, research has shown that the uptake of WII is higher in Ethiopia when insurance is channelled through group-based informal insurance schemes *iddir* (a funeral society) or when bundled with input schemes [78]. Bundling insurance with microfinance is another way of catering to a community's secondary needs through targeting liquidity and constraints. However, evidence has shown that, this does not always work in communities with lower risk-taking behaviour. This is why a needs-based approach should be carried out alongside a people-centered market research of the target population.

Demographical information and behavioural economics make generalisations about populations which can help insurance providers to know what the customers are looking for and how their product meets customer needs [90]. Since WII takes on an anti-poverty approach, insurance providers should go beyond tactical strategies, and understand and view things from the perspectives of smallholder farmers. Thus, customer empathy is a requirement for the design of WII packages that meet the underlying needs of customers, while factoring in customer feelings about the products being offered. A typical market research seeks to understand the obvious characteristics of population (e.g., age, sex, income, employment, level of education, farm size, cropping activities). While a person-centered market research would seek to understand further information such as, how cultural beliefs and attitudes/religious views/willingness to adopt change/willingness to pay for change/ value placed on change (in monetary terms) influence technological preferences. Other information that could be sought by insurance providers include, household structure/headship and gender practices, to ascertain who does what? who has what? and who decides what? at the household level. SSA is home to more than 500 million women who account for about half of the continent's population [91][7]. Based on data

[7] According to Menashe-Oren & Stecklov [92], SSA is characterised by balanced sex ratios at birth, so the primary factors creating divergence in rural/urban age structures are sex differences in mortality and migration.

from 45 countries in SSA for the periods 1980–2015, until the ages of 15–19, there are more boys than girls in the rural sector and fewer boys than girls in the urban sector, which changes dramatically between the ages 20–24 [92]. This suggests that in a lot of countries in SSA, there are more women than men who live and work in rural areas from the age of 20 onwards. This is consistent with reports which state that, in SSA, women are responsible for much of the food production in rural areas [93]. According to WorldBank [91], the share of labour varies across countries, ranging from 24% in Niger to 56% in Uganda, but remains consistently well below the commonly cited 60–80%. Despite their contribution to agriculture, women in male headed households have very little say in decision-making compared to women who head their own homes (female headed households) [94]. The point is, if women are a major demographic in rural areas, gender differences and practices are important factors that should be incorporated into the design and application of WII in SSA. In a study on Northern Ghana carried out by Gallenstein et al. [84], bundling loans with micro-insurance was seen to increase the likelihood of loan applications for female farmers more than men. An analysis into such behavioural patterns could help WII providers to package their products in a gender sensitive manner so as to appeal to the needs of both male and female smallholders, which will potentially increase demand.

The more information is understood about the characteristics and preferences of the target population, and the more inclusive the insurance product or package is, the more likely it is to influence demand in a positive way. For as long as WII suppliers do not genuinely put the people first, combining WII with other innovations will not increase demand. Bundling WII with key farm inputs such agricultural inputs (i.e., fertilisers, seeds, loans, etc.), key agricultural institutions (e.g., Agri-banks, input suppliers, farmers' organisations, etc.) has not boosted demand for WII in Malawi [27]. From the lessons learned in this chapter, a 'One Size Fit All' WII design does not work well in SSA – what worked in Machakos County, Kenya did not work in Eastern and Northern Ghana.

Acknowledgements

This publication was made possible (in part) by a grant from Carnegie Corporation of New York. The statements made and views expressed are solely the responsibility of the author.

Conflict of interest

The author declares no conflict of interest.

Notes/thanks/other declarations

I would like to acknowledge my academic supervisor Professor Mark New whose comments enabled me to improve this chapter.

Author details

Dorcas Stella Shumba
African Climate and Development Initiative (ACDI), University of Cape Town, Cape Town, South Africa

*Address all correspondence to: stella.shumba@uct.ac.za

References

[1] Niang I, Ruppel OC, Abdrabo MA, Essel A, Lennard C, Padgham J, et al. Africa. In: Barros VR, Field CB, Dokken DJ, Mastrandrea MD, Mach KJ, Bilir TE, et al editors. Climate Change 2014: Impacts, Adaptation, and Vulnerability. Part B: Regional Aspects. Contribution of Working Group II to the Fifth Assessment Report of the Intergovernmental Panel on Climate Change. Cambridge, MA: Cambridge University Press; 2014

[2] AFDB. Feed Africa: Strategy for Agricultural Transformation in Africa 2016-2025. Abidjan: African Development Bank Group (AFDB); 2016

[3] Diop M. Foresight Africa 2016: Banking on agriculture for Africa's Future. Washington, DC: Brookings Institute; 2016

[4] OBG. Agriculture in Africa. Oxford, UK: Oxford Business Group; 2021

[5] OECD/FAO. OECD-FAO Agricultural Outlook 2016-2025. Special Focus: Sub-Saharan Africa. Paris: OECD Publishing; 2016

[6] Shimeles A, Verdier-Chouchane A, Boly A. Introduction: Understanding the challenges of the agricultural sector in Sub-Saharan Africa. In: Shimeles A, Verdier-Chouchane A, Boly A, editors. Building a Resilient and Sustainable Agriculture in Sub-Saharan Africa. Cham: Palgrave Macmillan; 2018

[7] Giller KE. The food security conundrum of sub-Saharan Africa. Global Food Security. 2020;**26**:100431. DOI: 10.1016/j.gfs.2020.100431

[8] Goedde L, Ooko-Ombaka A, Pais G. Winning in Africa's Agricultural Market. 2019. Available from: https://www.mckinsey.com/industries/agriculture/our-insights/winning-in-africas-agricultural-market

[9] Abraham M, Pingali P. Transforming smallholder agriculture to achieve the SDGs. In: Paloma SG y, Riesgo L, Louhichi K, editors. The Role of Smallholder Farms in Food and Nutrition Security. Cham: Springer International Publishing; 2020. pp. 173-209. DOI: 10.1007/978-3-030-42148-9_9

[10] Gollin D. Smallholder agriculture in Africa: An overview and implications for policy. In: Working Paper October 2014. London: IIED; 2014

[11] Gollin D, Morris M, Byerlee D. Technology adoption in intensive post-green revolution systems. American Journal of Agricultural Economics. 2005;**87**(5):1310-1316

[12] Demeke M, Kiermeier M, Sow M, Antonaci L. Agriculture and Food Insecurity Risk Management in Africa: Concepts, Lessons Learned and Review Guidelines. Rome: FAO; 2016

[13] ASFG. Supporting Smallholder Farmers in Africa: A Framework for an Enabling Environment. Africa: African Smallholder Farmers Group (ASFG); 2013

[14] Collier B, Skees JR, Barnett B. Weather index insurance and climate change: Opportunities and challenges in lower income countries. The Geneva Papers. 2009;**34**:401-424

[15] Akotey JO, Adjasi CKD. Microinsurance and consumption smoothing among low-income households in Ghana. The Journal of

Developing Areas. 2018;**52**(4):151-165. DOI: 10.1353/jda.2018.0057

[16] Asseldonk MV, Burger K, d'Hotel EM, Muller B, Cotty T, Meijerink G. Linking Crop Insurance and Rural Credit. Paris: AGRINATURA-EEIG; 2012

[17] Farrin K, Miranda MJ. A heterogeneous agent model of credit-linked index insurance and farm technology adoption. Journal of Development Economics. 2015;**116**:199-211. DOI: 10.1016/j.jdeveco.2015.05.001

[18] Gallenstein R, Flatnes JE, Dougherty JP, Sam AG, Mishra K. The impact of index-insured loans on credit market participation and risk-taking. Agricultural Economics. 2021;**52**(1): 141-156. DOI: 10.1111/agec.12611

[19] Giné X, Yang D. Insurance, credit, and technology adoption: Field experimental evidence from Malawi. Journal of Development Economics. 2009;**89**(1):1-11

[20] Jensen ND, Barrett CB. Agricultural index insurance for development. Applied Economic Perspectives and Policy. 2016;**39**(2):199-219

[21] Meyer R, Hazell P, Varangis P. Unlocking Smallholder Credit: Does Credit-Linked Agricultural Insurance Work? Washington D.C: World Bank; 2017

[22] Raithatha R, Priebe J. Agricultural Insurance for Smallholder Farmers: Digital Innovations for Scale. London: GSMA; 2020

[23] Berhanu M, Oljira Wolde A. Review on climate change impacts and its adaptation strategies on food security in sub-Saharan Africa. Agricultural Social Economic Journal. 2019;**19**(3):145-154. DOI: 10.21776/ub.agrise.2019.019.3.3

[24] Blanc É. The Impact of Climate Change on Crop Production in Sub-Saharan Africa. New Zealand: University of Otago; 2011

[25] Brown OLI, Hammill A, McLeman R. Climate change as the 'new' security threat: implications for Africa. International Affairs (London). 2007;**83**(6):1141-1154. DOI: 10.1111/j. 1468-2346.2007.00678.x

[26] Gizaw MS, Gan TY. Impact of climate change and El Niño episodes on droughts in sub-Saharan Africa. Climate Dynamics. 2017;**49**(1-2):665-682. DOI: 10.1007/s00382-016-3366-2

[27] Makaudze EM. Weather Index Insurance for Smallholder Farmers in Africa: Lessons Learnt and Goals for the Future. Stellenbosch: African SUN Media; 2012

[28] UNDRR. Human Cost of Disasters 2000-2019. Geneva, Switzerland: UN Office for Disaster Risk Reduction (UNDRR); 2020

[29] Mano R, Nhemachena C. Assessment of the economic impacts of climate change on agriculture in Zimbabwe: A ricardian approach. Policy Research Working Paper 4292. Washington DC: World Bank; 2007

[30] WorldBank. Zimbabwe: Agriculture Sector Disaster Risk Assessment. Washington DC: World Bank; 2019

[31] Coulibably BS. Foresight Africa: Top Priorities for the Continent 2020-2030. Washington, DC: The Brookings; 2020

[32] Carter MR, Little PD, Mogues T, Negatu W. The long-term impacts of short-term shocks: poverty traps and environmental disasters in ethiopia and honduras. In: ASIS Collaborative Research Support Program (CRSP) Brief

Number 28. Madison, WI: Department of Agricultural and Applied Economics, University of Wisconsin; 2005

[33] Skees JR. Challenges for use of index-based weather insurance in lower income countries. In: 101st EAAE Seminar. Berlin, Germany: Management of Climate Risks in Agriculture; 2007

[34] Bjornlund V, Bjornlund H, Van Rooyen AF. Why agricultural production in sub-saharan africa remains low compared to the rest of the world – A historical perspective. International Journal of Water Resources Development. 2020;**36**(1):S20-S53. DOI: 10.1080/07900627.2020.1739512

[35] Weber EJ. Weather Index Insurance in Sub-Saharan Africa. 2019. Available from: https://ssrn.com/abstract=3396489

[36] Boko M, Niang I, Nyong A, Vogel C, Githeko A, Mcdany M, et al. Africa. In: Parry ML, Canziani OF, Palutikof JP, Linden PJVD, Hanson CE, editors. Climate Change Impacts, Adaptation and Vulnerability. Contribution of Working Group II to the Fourth Assessment Report of the Intergovernmental Panel on Climate Change. Cambridge, UK: Cambridge University Press; 2007

[37] Miller KA, Mcunu N, Anhäuser A, Farrow A, Santillo D, Johnston P. Weathering the Storm: Extreme Weather Events and Climate Change in Africa. Amsterdam, Netherlands: Greenpeace; 2020

[38] Gommes R, Petrassi F. Rainfall Variability and Drought in Sub-Saharan Africa. Rome, Italy: Food and Agriculture Organisation (FAO); 1996

[39] Hulme M, Doherty R, Ngara T, New M, Lister D. African climate change: 1900-2100. Climate Research. 2001;**17**(2):145-168

[40] WMO. State of the Climate in Africa 2019. Geneva: World Meteorological Organization (WMO); 2020

[41] Engelbrecht F, Adegoke J, Bopape M-J, Naidoo M, Garland R. Projections of rapidly rising surface temperatures over Africa under low mitigation. Environmental Research Letters. 2015;**10**(8):085004

[42] Woetzel J, Pinner D, Samandari H, Engel H, Krishnan M, McCullough R, et al. How will African farmers adjust to changing patterns of precipitation? In: Climate Risk and Response. Case Study: Agriculture in Africa. McKinsey Global Institute; 2020. Available from: https://www.mckinsey.com/~/media/mckinsey/business%20functions/sustainability/our%20insights/how%20will%20african%20farmers%20adjust%20to%20changing%20patterns%20of%20precipitation/mgi-how-will-african-farmers-adjust-to-changing-patterns-of-precipitation.pdf

[43] Williams CJR, Kniveton DR. Introduction. In: Williams CJR, Kniveton DR, editors. African Climate and Climate Change: Physical, Social and Political Perspectives. Cham: Springer; 2011

[44] AFDB. Climate change in Africa. In: African Development Bank at COP25. Available at. Abidjan: African Development Bank Group (AFDB); 2019

[45] Tedesco, I. A holistic approach to agricultural risk management for improving resilience. In Proceesings of 2nd International Workshop on Modelling of Physical, Economic and Social Systems for Resilience Assessment. Luxembourg; European Commission Joint Research Centre; 2017

[46] Zhang L. Assessing the Demand for Weather Index Insurance in Shandong

Province, China University of Kentucky]. 2008. Available from: https://uknowledge.uky.edu/gradschool_theses/559

[47] GlobalAgRisk. Designing Agricultural Index Insurance in Developing Countries: A GlobalAgRisk Market Development Model Handbook for Policy and Decision Makers. Lexington, KY: GlobalAgRisk; 2009

[48] Morduch J. Income smoothing and consumption smoothing. Journal of Economic Perspectives. 1995;**9**(3):103-114. DOI: 10.1257/jep.9.3.103

[49] Skees JR, Murphy A, Collier B, McCord MJ, Roth J. Scaling Up Index Insurance: What is needed for the next big step forward? Berlin: Kreditanstalt für Wiederaufbau (German Financial Cooperation); 2007

[50] Camerer CF, Kunreuther H. Decision processes for low probability events: Policy implications. Journal of Policy Analysis and Management. 1989;**8**(4):565-592. DOI: 10.2307/3325045

[51] WorldBank. Weather Index Insurance: Guidance for Development Practitioners. In Agriculture and Rural Development Discussion Paper 50. Washington DC: World Bank; 2011

[52] Lekprichakul T. Ex Ante and Ex Post Risk Coping Strategies: How Do Subsistence Farmers in Southern and Eastern Province of Zambia Cope? Japan Research Institute for Humanity and Nature: Kyoto; 2009

[53] Abid M, Ali A, Rahut DB, Raza M, Mehdi M. Ex-ante and ex-post coping strategies for climatic shocks and adaptation determinants in rural Malawi. Climate Risk Management. 2020;**27**:100200. DOI: 10.1016/j.crm.2019.100200

[54] Frankenberger T, Swallow K, Mueller M, Spangler T, Downen J, Alexander S. Feed the Future Learning Agenda Literature Review: Improving Resilience of Vulnerable Populations. Rockville, MD: Westat; 2013

[55] Barnett BJ, Barrett CB, Skees JR. Poverty traps and index based risk transfer products. World Development. 2008;**36**(2008):1766-1785

[56] Reyes CM, Agbon AD, Mina CD, Gloria RAB. Agricultural insurance program: Lessons from different country experiences. In: PIDS Discussion Paper Series, No. 2017-02. Quezon City: Philippine Institute for Development Studies (PIDS); 2017

[57] Carter MR, Lybbert TJ. Consumption versus asset smoothing: Testing the implications of poverty trap theory in Burkina Faso. Journal of Development Economics. 2012;**99**(2012):255-264

[58] Shumba D. Understanding the Gender Dimensions of Environmental Change: An Exploration of the Experiences and Perceptions of Zimbabwean Rural Men and Women. New Zealand: Massey University, 2017

[59] Dercon S. Risk, insurance, and poverty: A review. In: Dercon S, editor. Insurance Against Poverty. Oxford: Oxford University Press; 2004

[60] Swift J. Why are rural pople vulnerable to famine. IDS Bulletin. 2006;**37**(4):41-49

[61] Janzen SA, Carter MR. The impact of microinsurance on consumption smoothing and asset protection: Evidence from a drought in Kenya. In: Paper prepared for Presentation at the Agricultural & Applied Economics Association's 2013 AAEA & CAES Joint

Annual Meeting. Washington, DC; 4-6 August 2013

[62] Sugiyanto C, Kusumastuti SY, Donna DR. Managing Risks: How do Poor Households Smooth Their Income and Consumption? (An Examination of Poor Households in Yogyakarta, Indonesia). Institute for Money Technology and Financial Inclusion (IMTFI); 2012. Available from: https://www.imtfi.uci.edu/files/blog_working_papers/2012-3_sugiyanto.pdf

[63] WorldBank. Agriculture for Development. Washington D.C: World Bank; 2008

[64] Dercon S. Income risk, coping strategies, and safety nets. The World Bank Research Observer. 2002;**17**(2): 141-166. DOI: 10.1093/wbro/17.2.141

[65] Fumagalli L, Martin T. Income smoothing, child labor and schooling: A randomized field experiment in the Nampula Province of Mozambique. Milan, Italy: AlpPop The Alpine Population Conference, Dondena Centre for Research on Social Dynamics; 25-28 January 2015

[66] Jensen ND, Barrett CB, Mude AG. Index insurance and cash transfers: a comparative analysis from Northern Kenya. Journal of Development Economics. 2017;**129**(November): 14-28

[67] UNFCCC. (2015). Adoption of the Paris Agreement, 21st Conference of the Parties. New York: United Nations Framework Convention on Climate Change.

[68] UNFCCC. The Cancun Adaptation Framework: Reopor of the Conference of the Parties on its Sixteenth Session held in Cancun from 29 Novermber to 10 December 2010. New York: United Nations Framework Convention on Climate Change; 2010

[69] Skees JR, Collier B. The Potential of Weather Index Insurance for Spurring a Green Revolution in Africa. Nairobi, Kenya: AGRA Policy Workshop; 2008

[70] Di Marcantonio F, Kayitakire F. Review of pilot projects on index-based insurance in Africa: Insights and lessons learned. In: Tiepolo M, Pezzoli A, Tarchiani V, editors. Renewing Local Planning to Face Climate Change in the Tropics. Cham: Springer International Publishing; 2017. pp. 323-341. DOI: 10.1007/978-3-319-59096-7_16

[71] Hess U, Hazell P. Innovations and Emerging Trends in Agricultural Insurance: How Can We Transfer Natural Risks Out of Rural Livelihooods to Empower and Protect People? Bonn, Germany: Deutsche Gesellschaft für Internationale Zusammenarbeit (GIZ) GmbH; 2016

[72] Nshakira-Rukundo E, Kamau JW, Baumüller H. Determinants of uptake and strategies to improve agricultural insurance in Africa: A review. Environment and Development Economics. 2021;**26**(5-6):605-631. DOI: 10.1017/S1355770X21000085

[73] Binswanger-Mkhize HP. Is there too much hype about index-based agricultural insurance? Journal of Development Studies. 2012;**48**(2): 187-200

[74] Pelka N, Musshoff O, Weber R. Does weather matter? How rainfall affects credit risk in agricultural microfinance. Agricultural Finance Review. 2015;**75**(2):194-212. DOI: 10.1108/AFR-10-2014-0030

[75] Kemeze FH. The impact of agricultural insurance on the demand for supplemental irrigation: A randomized controlled trial experimental evidence in Northern Ghana. In: Shimeles A, Verdier-Chouchane A, Boly A, editors. Building a Resilient and Sustainable Agriculture in Sub-Saharan Africa. London: Palgrave Macmillan; 2018

[76] Mapfumo S. Weather Index Crop Insurance: Implementation, Product Design, Challenges and Successes – Lessons Learned in the Field. MicroEnsure; 2008. Available from: https://www.findevgateway.org/sites/default/files/publications/files/mfg-en-paper-weather-index-crop-insurance-implementation-product-design-challenges-and-successes-lessons-learned-in-the-field-nov-2008.pdf

[77] Vhurumuku E. Use of weather-based index as a tool to reduce food insecurity and vulnerability: A case of Ethiopia. In: Makaudze EM, editor. Weather Index Insurance for Smallholder Farmers in Africa: Lessons Learnt and Goals for the Future. Africa: African SUN Media; 2012

[78] Tadesse MA, Shiferaw BA, Erenstein O. Weather index insurance for managing drought risk in smallholder agriculture: Lessons and policy implications for sub-Saharan Africa. Agricultural and Food Economics. 2015;**3**(26):1-21

[79] Carter MR, Janvry Ad, Sadoulet E, Sarris A. Index-based weather insurance for developing countries: A review of evidence and a set of propositions for up-scaling. In: Development Policies. France: Foundation for Studies and Research on International Development (FERDI); 2014

[80] Marr A, Winkel A, van Asseldonk M, Lensink R, Bulte E. Adoption and impact of index-insurance and credit for smallholder farmers in developing countries. Agricultural Finance Review. 2016;**76**(1):94-118. DOI: 10.1108/AFR-11-2015-0050

[81] Ruben M. The Promise of Microfinance for Poverty Relief in the Developing World. Proquest CSA Discovery Guides; 2007. Available from: https://www.findevgateway.org/sites/default/files/publications/files/mfg-en-paper-the-promise-of-microfinance-for-poverty-relief-in-the-developing-world-may-2007.pdf

[82] Goldberg M, Palladini E, Bank W. Managing Risk And Creating Value With Microfinance. Washington, DC: World Bank; 2010

[83] Pomeranz D. The Promise of Microfinance and Women's Empowerment: What Does the Evidence Say? London: Ernest & Young; 2014

[84] Gallenstein R, Mishra K, Sam A, Miranda M. Willingness to pay for insured loans in Northern Ghana. Journal of Agricultural Economics. 2019;**70**:640-662. DOI: 10.1111/1477-9552.12317

[85] Singh P, Agrawal G. Efficacy of weather index insurance for mitigation of weather risks in agriculture: An integrative review. International Journal of Ethics and Systems. 2019;**35**(4):584-616. DOI: 10.1108/IJOES-09-2018-0132

[86] Langyintuo A. Smallholder farmers' access to inputs and finance in Africa. In: Paloma SG y, Riesgo L, Louhichi K, editors. The Role of Smallholder Farms in Food and Nutrition Security. Cham: Springer International Publishing; 2020. pp. 133-152. DOI: 10.1007/978-3-030-42148-9_7

[87] Karlan D, Kutsoati E, McMillan M, Udry C. Crop price indemnified loans for farmers: A pilot experiment in

rural Ghana. The Journal of Risk and Insurance. 2011;**78**(1):37-55. DOI: 10.1111/j.1539-6975.2010.01406.x

[88] Mishra K, Gallenstein R, Sam AG, Miranda MJ, Toledo P, Mulangu F. You are Approved! Insured Loans Improve Credit Access and Technology Adoption of Ghanaian Farmers. 2017. Available at: https://thedocs.worldbank.org/en/doc/570041495654735804-0010022017/original/D2Mishraetal.ABCA20170518.pdf

[89] Ndegwa MK, Shee A, Turvey CG, You L. Uptake of insurance-embedded credit in presence of credit rationing: evidence from a randomized controlled trial in Kenya. Agricultural Finance Review. 2020;**80**(5):745-766. DOI: 10.1108/AFR-10-2019-0116

[90] Bahlinger D. Innovate to Win: Why Market Research is Key to Insurance Industry Success. Washington, DC: Milliman; 2020

[91] WorldBank. Inequalities in Women's and Girls' Health Opportunities and Outcomes: A Report from sub-Saharan Africa. Washington D.C: World Bank; 2016

[92] Menashe-Oren A, Stecklov G. Rural/urban population age and sex composition in sub-Saharan Africa 1980-2015. Population and Development Review. 2018;**44**(1):7-35. DOI: 10.1111/padr.12122

[93] FAO. Women, Agriculture and Rural Development: A Synthesis Report of the Africa Region. Rome: FAO; 1995

[94] Lowe-Morna C, Dube S, Makamure L, Robinson KV. SADC Gender Protocol Report. Johannesburg: Gender Links; 2014

Chapter 4

Toward Safe Food Systems: Analyses of Mycotoxin Contaminants in Food and Preventive Strategies Thereof for Their Formation and Toxicity

Dikabo Mogopodi, Mesha Mbisana, Samuel Raditloko, Inonge Chibua and Banyaladzi Paphane

Abstract

Mycotoxin contaminants in food pose a threat to human and animal health. These lead to food wastage and threaten food security that is already a serious problem in Africa. In addition, these affect trading and especially affect incomes of rural farmers. The broad impacts of these contaminants require integrated solutions and strategies. It is thus critical to not only develop strategies for analysis of these toxins but also develop removal and preventive strategies of these contaminants to ensure consumer safety and compliance with regulatory standards. Further within the aim of promoting food safety, there is need for operational policy framework and strategy on the management of these contaminants to promote their mitigation. This chapter discusses integrated strategies for monitoring and control of mycotoxin contamination in food matrices to promote their mitigation and build resilient food systems in Africa and thus reinforce efforts to reach sustainable food security.

Keywords: food safety, mycotoxins, nanotechnology, analytical strategies, food security

1. Introduction

Food safety indirectly affects a wide range of social, economic, and environmental processes including food production and hence environmental impacts of agriculture, food trade, and energy use [1]. Foodborne illness, in particular, places an undue burden on health and socioeconomics of society, and this burden is the highest in developing countries especially in marginalized communities. Thus, the integration of food safety considerations is critical in achieving a wide range of sustainable development goals (SDGs) including SDG2 (*End hunger, achieve food security and improved nutrition, and promote sustainable agriculture*) [2]. It is important to make food safety a development priority and to ensure that food security policies and initiatives give attention to food safety.

In order for African Governments to make food safety a public health priority, there is need for rigorous analysis of food contaminants that would give evidence on the burdens of food safety and thus lead to establishing and implementing effective and resilient food safety systems [3]. Of concern is the presence of chemical contamination that poses an enormous threat to food safety and security, and these influence the development of African agri-food system. Chemical contamination imposes a huge economic burden across the health and other sectors [4]. Chemical contamination also leads to food loss, which could otherwise have served millions of people and assisted in achieving food security [5]. Food loss not only threatens food security but also represents the lost labor, capital, water, energy, land, and other resources that went into producing the food and thereby threatening sustainability [2]. Chemical contamination includes many substances such as agrochemicals, pesticides, heavy metals [6], persistent organic pollutants, and natural toxins [7]. Among chemical contaminants that are troublesome are naturally occurring toxins and these include mycotoxins, marine biotoxins, cyanogenic glycosides, and toxins occurring in poisonous mushrooms [8]. It is of particular interest to focus on mycotoxins due to their severity in Africa and their impact on agro-economies [9–13].

Mycotoxins are secondary metabolites of a range of filamentous fungi and saphrophytic molds [14]. Among all the toxic filamentous fungi species, *Aspergillus, Fusarium, and Penicillium* are important genera, producing regularly widely studied toxins including aflatoxins, patulin, ochratoxin A (OTA), deoxynivalenol (DON), trichothenes: T-2 toxin, fumonisin, tremorgenic toxins, ergot alkaloids, and zearalenone (ZON) [15]. Mycotoxins can contaminate food or food crops throughout the food chain, in the field or after harvest and during storage [16]. In addition to food- and feed-born intoxication, humans can also be affected through exposures *via* surface water contamination. Pathogenic fungi, including *Fusarium* species, have been demonstrated to be capable of continuing to produce their secondary metabolites in water [17], and this process has been indicated to be a potential route of human exposure to mycotoxins [18].

1.1 Impact of mycotoxins on public health

The consumption of mycotoxins-contaminated food/feed products has had an adverse impact on public health for many centuries [19]. Mycotoxins can be found in many food products including cereals, nuts, spices, dried fruits, apples, and coffee beans [20]. Exposure to mycotoxins can produce both acute and chronic toxicities ranging from death to deleterious effects on the central nervous, cardiovascular, pulmonary, and digestive systems of most farm animals and humans. Mycotoxins may also be carcinogenic, mutagenic, teratogenic, and immunosuppressive [12, 19].

Aflatoxins are among the most potent carcinogens of all mycotoxins. Studies have revealed that aflatoxins occur at extremely high levels in many African countries such as Ghana, Benin, Togo, Egypt, Guinea, and Gambia [20]. Repetitive incidents of aflatoxicosis, which, in severe cases, lead to death, have been reported. The greatest recorded fatal mycotoxin-poisoning outbreak occurred in Africa in 2004 where a 125 people in Kenya died due to consumption of contaminated maize [9]. A similar outbreak occurred in Eastern Kenya in 2005 where 75 cases were admitted in Hospital resulting in 25 deaths. Maize samples collected from these areas had high aflatoxin B1 (AFB1) levels with 55% contaminated above the Kenyan legal limit of 20 μg/kg [10].

AFB1 levels have been extensively linked to human liver cancer in which they act synergistically with HBV hepatitis B virus infection [10, 21]. There is up to 30 times greater risk of acquiring liver cancer from chronic infection with hepatitis B virus and dietary exposure to aflatoxin as compared with exposure to either of the two factors alone [21]. Both aflatoxin exposure and chronic hepatitis B infection predominate in rural Africa, which explains why the highest incidence of liver cancer occurs in Africa. In Tanzania, there was about 1480 per 100,000 persons cases of aflatoxin-induced liver cancer in 2016 [12]. Further AFB1 could also lead to increased susceptibility to infectious diseases such as malaria and HIV-AIDS [10].

Consumption of fumonisins has been associated with elevated human esophageal cancer incidence in various parts of Africa [10, 22]. Fumonisins have also been implicated in the high incidence of neural tube defects in rural populations of Eastern Cape province, the former Transkei region of South Africa [11, 22]. Fumonisins may also cause stunted growth in children. A study carried out to investigate the relationship between infant and young child growth and fumonisin exposure revealed that children with fumonisins intake of greater than the maximum tolerable daily intake (PMTDI) were significantly shorter (1.3 cm) and lighter (328 g) compared with children whose fumonisin intake is less than the PMTDI [20]. Recently, children in Tanzania showed impaired growth, which is associated with exposure to fumonisns from maize [23]. Another study done in sorghum grown in different parts of Northern Uganda showed that 80% of all samples contained aflatoxins, 93% fumonisins, and 67% OTA. The presence of mycotoxins in staple such as sorghum has been linked to the development of edema and kwashiorkor in undernourished children in this region [24].

Aflatoxin exposure in young children in West Africa has also been associated with Reye's syndrome, child neurological impairment, Kwashiorkor, and stunted growth [25]. The chronic incidence of aflatoxin in diets is evident from the presence of aflatoxin M1 (AFM1) in human breast milk in Ghana, Nigeria, Sierra Leone, and Sudan as well as in umbilical cord blood samples in Ghana, Kenya, Nigeria, and Sierra Leone [9]. Another study on aflatoxin exposure in the Gambia revealed that aflatoxins can be transported from the mother to the infant. This shows a significant association between maternal exposure to aflatoxin and impaired infant growth [26].

1.2 Economic impact of mycotoxins

The economic impacts of mycotoxins to human society can be thought of in terms of the direct market costs associated with lost trade or reduced revenues due to contaminated food or feed, and the human health losses from the adverse effects associated with mycotoxin consumption covered in Section 1.1. Mycotoxins are known to affect almost one quarter (25%) of global feed and food output [27]. This leads to huge agricultural and industrial losses in billions of dollars [20]. About 10% of the 2010 Kenyan maize harvest was withdrawn from the food supply in a responsible move taken by the Kenyan government to protect public health, which translates to economic losses [16]. These toxins account for economic losses in the magnitude of millions of dollars due to reduced agricultural production. In Africa, factors such as poverty and climate change further complicate the mycotoxin situation; thus, the economic impact due to mycotoxins is alarming [19]. This impact includes high cost of research and regulatory activities aimed at reducing health risks because of the existence of causal relationships between mycotoxins and their impact on health.

In domestic markets, economic losses occur at various levels, from the commodity producers to the brokers, the processors, and the animal producers. Several countries, particularly some industrialized ones, have set specific regulations defining maximum admissible levels for major mycotoxins in numerous commodities. Limits for AFB1 in foodstuffs range from 0 to 30 μg/kg, while those for total aflatoxins range from 0 to 50 μg/kg [28]. As of 2003, only 15 African countries, accounting for approximately 59 percent of the continent's population, are known to have specific mycotoxin regulations [29], and this is still the current status to date. In countries like Ethopia, only a few food commodities have mycotoxin legislation largely because they are exported to European and American markets [28]. While these regulations limit their presence in food and feed, these also adversely affects access to attractive export market for many developing countries due to the difficulty in meeting required standards [1]. For example, Africa could earn up to US$1 billion per year from groundnut exports by regaining the 77% share of the global groundnut export market it enjoyed in the 1960s instead of the current share of 4%, which is valued at just US$64 million [1].

1.3 Mycotoxin contamination: what is it to Africa?

Mycotoxin research has attracted huge interest among scientists, farmers, and policy makers and regulatory bodies alike. Despite mycotoxins being a much more pronounced problem in the developing world than in the developed world, much of the work in this area is concentrated in the developed world, while Africa, especially Sub-Saharan Africa, is lagging behind. Only few and fragmented studies have been conducted on mycotoxins in Africa (examples are shown in **Table 1**). This is of concern given that most of African countries rely on staple food such as sorghum and maize and other oil seeds such as groundnuts that are subject to contamination by a range of fungi, both in the field and after harvest. This predisposes a high number of populations in Africa to consumption of mycotoxin contaminated food products and thus increases the chance of chronic and detrimental exposure to mycotoxins [34]. Further, Africans rely on preservation of grains through traditional storage, where the grains stored for more than a few days are susceptible to fungal attack.

Increased climate variability and harsh climate conditions in Africa such as high relative humidity and high temperatures conducive for mycotoxigenic fungal colonization and mycotoxin production pre- and/or post-harvest [46] may aggravate the situation. The stress of hot dry conditions, especially in places such as Botswana and Namibia, may result in significant mycotoxigenic fungal infections during the preharvest phase and hence mycotoxin production. Climate change can also increase host susceptibility to hull cracking [46]. As a result, this can lead to decreased phytoalexin production, which increases susceptibility of peanuts to mycotoxin and may compromise maize kernel integrity leading to increased mycotoxin contamination.

All these factors require a rigorous mycotoxin management system, especially the continued monitoring of mycotoxins in Africa. Thus, Africa is challenged with driving mycotoxin research to (a) provide scientific evidence for consumers from health and economic perspective; (b) to provide regulatory bodies with data for relevant risk of exposure and risk assessment to enable them to set regulatory legislations for mycotoxins in food commodities, as well as (c) to ensure that international regulatory levels are met. It is within this context that it is necessary to come up with cost-effective strategies in determining the identity and level of mycotoxins in food commodities as well as to come up with sustainable preventive strategies. Without an

Country	Year	Mycotoxin(s)/fungal contamination	Matrix	References
Angola	2017	*Aspergillus and penicillium*	Arabica coffee and Robusta coffee	[5]
Botswana	2013	Aflatoxins and fumonisins	Peanuts, peanut butter, and sorghum	[30]
	2011	ZEA and fumonisins	Maize and sorghum grains and meals	[31]
Ghana	2021	Aflatoxins	Maize	[32]
	2019	Aflatoxins	cereals and cereal based foods	[33]
	2018	aflatoxins, fumonisins, DON, T-2 toxin, ZEA and ochratoxin	maize, maize silage, other cereals	[34]
Kenya	2021	Aflatoxin, citrinin, fumonisin, OTA, diacetoxyscirpenol, T2 HT2	Rice	[35]
	2020	Aflatoxins and fumonisins	Maize	[36]
Namibia	2019	Patulin, aflatoxins, and fumonisins	Sorghum malts	[37]
Namibia, Kenya, and Nigeria	2018	Aflatoxins, fumonisins, DONl, T-2 toxin, ZON, and ochratoxin	Maize, maize silage, other cereals	[34]
Nigeria	2020	DON, fumonisins, moniliformin, aflatoxins, and citrinin	Cheese balls, garri (cassava-based), granola, and popcorn	[38]
Rwanda	2019	Aflatoxins and fumonisins	Maize	[39]
	2018	Aflatoxins	Soybean (*Glycine max L.)*	[40]
South Africa	2018	Aflatoxins, fumonisins, ochratoxins, HT-2 toxin, T-2 toxin, ZON, DON, and 15-acetyl-DON	Maize	[41]
	2018	Aflatoxins, fumonisins, OTA, sterigmatocystin, 3-acetyl DON, roquefortine C	Food spices	[42]
Togo	2019	Aflatoxins, fumonisins, and trichothecenes	Maize and sorghum	[43]
	2020	Aflatoxins	Maize	[44]
Zambia	2017	Aflatoxins	Groundnut and maize	[45]
Zimbabwe	2013	Aflatoxins and fumonisins	Peanuts, peanut butter, and sorghum	[30]

Table 1.
Examples of mycotoxins studies in Africa.

aggressive research program to prevent, treat, and contain outbreaks of mycotoxins in grain, grain producers will suffer the consequences of reduced marketability of their products. In this regard, nanotechnology-based solutions present themselves as attractive solutions and the use of affordable detections such as point-of-care (POC) diagnosis and electrochemistry are areas that present a lot of potential.

2. Analytical strategies toward mycotoxin adsorption and detection

The accurate and rapid qualitative and quantitative analysis for mycotoxins has been topic of interest by many researchers [47, 48]. A mycotoxin analysis method should be simple, rapid, reproducible, robust, accurate, sensitive, and selective to enable simultaneous determination. Analytical methods for the determination of mycotoxins commonly have the following steps: sampling, homogenization, extraction, and cleanup, which might include sample concentration and then detection [49].

2.1 Cost-effective strategies for adsorption of mycotoxins (either for extraction or for decontamination)

Several strategies on pre-harvest and post-harvest prevention of mycotoxin contamination have been reported including the use of resistant varieties, the use of biological and chemical agents, crop rotation, improved drying methods, good storage conditions, and irradiation. However, these methods do not solve the problem as mycotoxins still get detected in food ready for consumption [50]. Therefore, greater attention should be paid to mycotoxin adsorption or removal strategies as they have greater potential in complete elimination of mycotoxins from food commodities. These adsorption strategies are also very useful for extraction of mycotoxin in contaminated samples prior to instrumental analysis, needed especially for trace analysis. An efficient method for adsorption of mycotoxin should be inexpensive, able to adsorb or remove/inactivate the mycotoxins without producing toxic residues and affecting the technological properties, nutritive value, and palatability of products [51]. Several adsorption materials are discussed herein.

2.1.1 Zeolites

Zeolites are micro-porous crystalline-hydrated aluminosilicates structurally based on three-dimensional anionic network of SiO_4 and AlO_4 tetrahedra linked to each other by sharing all of the oxygen atoms [52]. The potential for using zeolites as mycotoxin adsorbents is based on their adsorption capacity, cation-exchange, dehydration-rehydration, and catalysis features. Zeolites can also be modified specifically to enhance selectivity of specific mycotoxins. Mycotoxins are structurally diverse; thus, they have varying chemical and physical properties. Some are polar, others are non-polar, and there are several that fall in between. This diversity can be resolved by such a material that can change its properties under various physicochemical conditions [52].

Surfactant-modified zeolites have proven to be effective adsorbents of mycotoxin and potential food additives due to their "non-toxic" traits. The clinoptilolite type that has been approved by European Food Safety Authority (EFSA) Panel on Food Contact Materials, Enzymes, Flavorings and Processing Aids (CEF) is one of the safe substances for feed and food additives [53]. The *in vitro* mycotoxins adsorption by natural clinoptilolite-heulandite rich tuff-modified with octadecyldimethyl benzyl ammonium chloride (Do) and dioctadecyldimethyl ammonium chloride (Pr) (organo-zeolites) has been investigated [54]. Results from the mycotoxin-binding studies showed that the organo-zeolites effectively adsorbed AFB1, ZON, OTA, and the ergopeptine alkaloids.

ZON adsorption by organozeolites prepared *via* treatment of the natural zeolites—organoclinoptilolites (ZCPs) and organophillipsites (PCPs) with cetylpyridinium chloride (CP), has also been studied [55]. Results showed that adsorption of ZON increases with increasing amounts of CP at the zeolitic surfaces for both ZCPs and PCPs even though the adsorption mechanism was different. The increased adsorption of ZON with increasing amount of organic cation at the zeolitic surface confirmed that CP at both zeolitic surfaces is responsible for ZON adsorption. Although there has not been much work done on multi-mycotoxin adsorption by zeolites, studies show that there is potential in that area.

Due to their adsorption efficiency, zeolites have also developed for the analytical determination of mycotoxins, especially aflatoxins and ZON. Aflatoxins in milk have successfully been determined with an ionic liquid-modified magnetic zeolitic imidazolate framework-8 (M/ZIF-8) [56] and the application potential of M/ZIF-8 was extended successfully for the trace liposoluble pollutants analysis in foodstuffs. Natural zeolite treated with benzalkonium chloride has also showed great potential as an OTA and ZON adsorbent [55].

2.1.2 Molecularly imprinted polymers (MIPs)

MIPs are synthetic polymers with a predetermined selectivity for a certain analyte or several analytes that are structurally similar, making them ideal for separation and adsorption purposes. MIPs have been widely investigated as suitable adsorbents for mycotoxin analysis and determination [57–59] and only have been applied to food commodities to solve the challenge associated with detecting trace quantity of mycotoxins in food. AFB1-specific molecularly imprinted solid phase extraction sorbent has been developed for the selective pre-concentration of toxic AFB1 in child-weaning food, tsabana. The MIPs successfully achieved a pre-concentration factor of 5 and therefore significantly increased AFB1 signal intensity for easier detection [59].

MIPs have also been applied to extract AFM1 from milk spiked with 0.5–50 ng/mL AFM1. The MIPs removed 87.3–96.2% of the AFM1 without any notable effects on the milk composition [60]. MIPs that constituted of (i) Fe_3O_4, to make the MIP magnetic, (ii) chitosan (CS), and SiO_2 to improve the biocompatibility, stability and dispersibility of the MIP, were developed for removal of patulin from apple juice. This Fe_3O_4@SiO_2@CS-GO@MIP demonstrated to be a promising adsorbent with the adsorption capacity of 7.11 mg/g maximally and ability to remove over 90% of the total patulin in apple juice [61].

2.1.3 Carbon nanomaterials

The application of nanotechnology in adsorbents is especially attractive due to increased adsorption capacities of nanomaterials. Nanotechnology is a field of science, which deals with production, manipulation, and use of materials ranging in nanometers [62] with unique and improved properties of commercial and scientific relevance such as large surface-to-volume ratio and improved physiochemical properties such as color, solubility, strength, diffusivity, toxicity, magnetic, optical, thermodynamic properties [63]. In particular, the large surface area-to-volume ratios of nanomaterials can greatly enhance the adsorption capacities of sorbent materials.

Carbon nanoforms have large surface area per weight, colloidal stability upon various pH [64], strength, elasticity, and great conductivity and thus have great potential as mycotoxin adsorbents [65]. Fullerene, an allotrope of carbon has been found to adsorb aflatoxins. Another form, nanodiamonds, has the same advantages as carbon nanomaterials and is considered inexpensive [65]. Furthermore, their chemical structure allows surface modifications including carboxylation, hydrogenation, and hydroxylation which could enable effective adsorption of mycotoxins. The binding and mechanism of mycotoxins and nanodiamonds have been studied. Nanodiamond aggregates (~40 nm) have been shown to adsorb AFB1 and OTA *via* electrostatic interactions with functional groups on their surfaces [66] and demonstrated adsorption capacities greater that clay mineral, which are conventional adsorbents for mycotoxins.

Single/multiwalled carbon nanotubes (CNT) have been utilized in solid phase extraction of various mycotoxins due to their good adsorption capacity. A multi-walled CNT-based magnetic solid-phase extraction sorbent for the determination of ZON and its derivatives were developed and applied in maize samples [67]. The main parameters affecting the cleanup efficiency were investigated using ultra-high-performance liquid chromatography–tandem mass spectrometry (LC–MS), and high purification efficiencies for all analytes were obtained. The method proved to be a powerful tool for monitoring ZON and its derivatives in maize. The good adsorption capacity of CNT has also been utilized in extraction of tricothecenes [68, 69] and aflatoxins [70].

2.2 Cost-effective methods for the detection and analysis of mycotoxins

There are numerous analytical methods having different technical details for accuracy, which have been developed for analysis of mycotoxins [71]. Commonly used methods to analyze mycotoxins are thin-layer chromatography, high-performance liquid chromatography with UV or fluorescence detection (FD), LC–MS [71], gas chromatography–mass spectroscopy, and immunoanalytical techniques with enzyme-linked immunosorbent assay (ELISA) being the most prevailing method [72]. Whereas these methods are offering good detection limits and exceptional specificities and sensitivities, they are still drawbacks associated with these methods. These methods are time-consuming, and they use expensive analytical instruments, and require a lot of technical knowledge and operational expertise. They are therefore unsuitable for point-of-care diagnosis and will certainly not be accessible to farmers and many developing country laboratories. Therefore, the development of rapid, simple, relatively easy to use, and possibly non-instrumental cost-effective and convenient sampling and accurate detection methods for mycotoxin analysis are extremely essential and desirable. Methods with such properties are especially attractive for routine laboratory and on-site screening by untrained personnel and could also be affordable to farmers and to African Laboratories.

2.2.1 Lateral flow immunoassays

The lateral flow immunoassay (LFIA) has gained increasing interest and exhibits promise as a tool to overcome the complexities associated with traditional methods of mycotoxin analysis [73]. With LFIA, expensive equipment is not required, less skill is involved in administering LFIAs, and there is easy interpretation of results. The user-friendly operation and easy storage of the LFIA platform allow them to be used at the

POC or industry setting as well as for in-home diagnoses/farm diagnosis especially with remote settings, administered with little training and with little chance of error [73, 74]. The POC diagnosis would also enable the decentralization of laboratory testing to POC sites. LFIA also offers advantages of prolonged shelf-life, small volumes required, rapid screening, and sometimes sensitive detection. Rapid detection of mycotoxin levels in food is of key importance in both mycotoxin monitoring and exposure assessment [71].

Recently, LFIA has been studied to detect mycotoxins such as AFB1, ZON, OTA and T-2 toxin DON, and fumonisin B1 [73, 74]. A one-step lateral flow test has been developed for the quantitative determination of total type B fumonisins in maize with a test range up to 4000 μg/kg and a limit of detection of 199 μg/kg [75]. A multiplex LFIA with luminescent quantum dots as label was developed with cutoff limits of 1000, 80, and 80 μg/kg for DON, ZON, and T2/HT2-toxin, respectively. The LFIA gave within 15 minutes with a low false-negative rate of less than 5% [73]. Further, LFIA has been used for the determination of AFB1, ZON, DON where analysis of naturally contaminated maize samples showed high sensitivity of LFIA proven by a good agreement between the multiplex LFIA and LC–MS/MS (100% for DONs and AFs, and 81% for ZONs) [74].

While traditionally built commercial LFIAs have many advantages, issues including poorer sensitivity and lower specificity than laboratory tests such as LC–MS and HPLC affect their efficacy and availability to the full market potential. Decreasing these disadvantages and complexity of these tests may increase the availability of diagnostic testing and quality of food commodities to farmers unable to make it to expensive testing facilities. To overcome this, several strategies are currently being developed such as reducing the components utilized in the manufacturing of these tests, which will consequently reduce cost and increase the manufacturability, improving adsorption capabilities and improving detection capabilities [76].

2.2.1.1 Improvement of LFIAs using electrospun nanofibers

With LFIAs, bio-reagents are immobilized in defined areas of the strip, normally referred to as the membrane, where the formation of colored bands due to the accumulation of suitably labeled species yields a yes/no information [77]. In particular, the analytical response is observed in the test line (T-line), while a second control line (C-line) allows to verify that the test has been correctly performed and therefore that results are reliable. There is potential for use of electrospinning to develop adsorbent pad and the support membrane for use in lateral flow device to improve adsorption flow rate and hence decrease incubation time [78, 79]. In conventional LFIA, nitrocellulose is used as a solid phase support. These are affordable, simple to produce, and easy to use in remote settings. These same materials can be used in conjunction with electrospinning technology to develop novel platforms for the detection of mycotoxins.

Electrospinning is a technique that utilizes electrostatic force to process a variety of native and synthetic polymers into highly porous materials composed of nanoscale to micron-scale diameter fibers. By nature, electrospun materials exhibit an extensive surface area and highly interconnected pore spaces and thus offer the advantages of high surface area-to-volume ratio for active reaction sites, tunable porosity and morphology, and high mechanical strength. For the ability to directly regulate the physical properties of an electrospun material through the manipulation of the fundamental variables such as electrospinning solvent and the air gap distance, accelerating voltage affords considerable control over the process. Further electrospun nanofibers can be functionalized very easily and materials can easily be combined together to make fibers and thus manipulate nanofiber composition to get the desired properties and function. Electrospun fibers can also be deposited unto other surfaces such as microfibrious mats. Electrospinning has shown great potential including water and air filtration as well as a gateway to the development and fabrication of physiologically relevant tissue engineering scaffolds, hemostatic agents, wound care products, and solid phase drug and peptide delivery platforms. Despite the growing research in this area, electrospinning techniques have not been widely employed for the development of LFIAs. Although the potential application of combining electrospun nanofiber membranes and biosensing has been recognized, limited studies have been done in this area of LFIAs. To date, electrospinning has not penetrated to any great extent into product lines designed for diagnostic and research applications.

Electrospun materials, by nature, exhibit an extensive surface area-to-volume ratios and therefore increase chances of interaction with target analytes such as mycotoxins [63]. Increasing the surface area of the detector substrate offers the advantage of increasing the number of sensing sites available without increasing the amount of overall sample required. A small volume electrospun mat can provide a very large surface for sensing and easy access for mycotoxins to the sensing sites [63]. The sequential deposition of the discreet, individual fibers that are formed in this process also results in a unique and complex interconnected network of pores. Thus, exploiting these characteristic to fabricate LFIA platforms designed for mycotoxins detection is desirable. The electrospun membrane can then be manipulated with gold nanoparticles (NPs) and antibodies to achieve functionality required for the mycotoxin detection. Gold nanoparticles are the most preferred candidate materials and have been widely used for the fabrication of aflatoxin-sensing devices. Gold nanoparticles offer excellent compatibility with antibodies, and their functionality remains unaffected even after immobilization. A fiber-based immunoassay system could also be incorporated in multiple configurations, which may not necessitate individual housing and packaging of tests.

Developing a fiber-based immunoassay system, by incorporating immunoassay technology that is currently used for diagnostic tests into a fiber-based system, presents a great potential. This could increase the sensitivity, decrease the number of components in manufacturing, reduce cost, and facilitate simpler and more comfortable sample collection to simplify the procedure. Electrospun membranes have been tested as immunoassay substrates. Polycaprolactone on nitrocellulose has been successfully electrospun membrane to form a hydrophobic coating to reduce the flow rate and increase the interaction rate between the targets and gold NPs-detecting probes conjugates [79]. This resulted in the binding of more complexes to the capture probes. With this approach, the sensitivity of the PCL electrospin-coated test strip was increased by approximately 10-fold as compared with the unmodified test strip. The approach holds great potential for sensitive detection of targets at point-of-care testing.

2.2.1.2 Improvement of detection in LFIAs

As there is an increasing need for high-performing LIFA in the clinical, environmental, self-diagnosis, agriculture, and food safety areas, conventional LFIA having readout errors to the naked eye is up against some major problems such as poor quantitative discrimination and low analytical sensitivity. To make the most out of LFIA's advantages such as rapid point-of-care diagnosis, LFIA readers measuring the optical densities of the LFIA detection area have been developed for point-of-care applications [80] provided for quantitative or semi-quantitative analysis.

Further to provide the basis for a global monitoring of mycotoxins, highly sensitive, low-cost diagnostic tests developed can also be linked to smart phones applications as shown in **Figure 1**. The resulting digital information can be transmitted to a database of mycotoxin occurrence developed country by country and thus improved communication channels within the food chain. This could lead to comprehensive information systems that can support farm management decisions and thus help producers of many crops to produce higher quality and/or avoid losses, and also increase consumer confidence in agro-food products. A simple, rapid, and accurate one-dot LFIA detection method for AFB1 has been developed for point-of-care diagnosis [80] using competition between colloidal gold-AFB1-BSA conjugates for antibody-binding sites in the test zone. This was coupled with smartphone application for quantitative or semi-quantitative analysis.

2.3 Electrochemical detection of mycotoxins

Electrochemistry provides powerful analytical techniques that are sensitive, reliable, portable, and low-cost procedures that are associated with food safety [81, 82]. Electrochemistry deals with relationship between electrical energy and chemical energy and inter-conversion of one form to another. To transform the toxin interaction to analytical signal, a variety of electrochemical techniques have been used.

Amperometry is an important electrochemical analysis method in food analysis. In amperometry, the potential of the working electrode is constant and the resulting current from Faradaic processes occurring at the electrode is monitored with the function of time. It has a working response over a wide range of mycotoxin concentrations that gives an improved signal to ratio since the current is integrated over relatively longer time intervals [83].

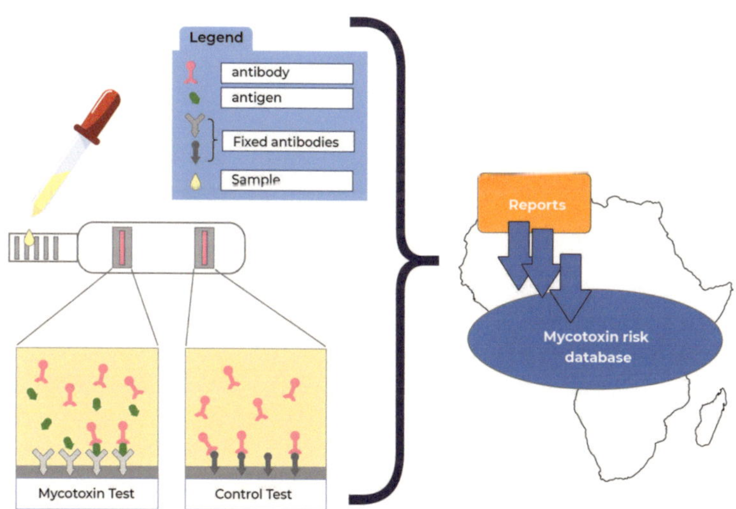

Figure 1.
Low-cost rapid mycotoxin test system combined with ICT solutions.

Voltammetry is another method in the analysis of mycotoxins. The current in the cell is measured with respect to the variation of the potential in the cell. Constant or varied potential is applied at the electrode surface, and the resulting current is measured with a three-electrode system (work, auxiliary, and reference electrode). Chemically modified electrodes are employed for highly sensitive electrochemical determination of mycotoxins. Hernandez-Hernandez et al. 2021 studied ZON using cyclic voltammetry (CV), differential pulse voltammetry (DPV), and electrochemical impedance spectroscopy (EIS). The method for the determination ZON was developed and applied for the quantitative analysis with low detection limits and multiplex analysis [84].

2.3.1 Electrochemical sensors

A biosensor is an analytical device that incorporate a bio-component or bio-receptor such as isolated enzymes, whole cell, tissues, aptamers with a suitable transducing system to detect chemical compound [85]. The numerous examples in the literature illustrate the high potential of the electrochemical biosensors in mycotoxin analysis, contributing to their sensitive determination in a variety of food and commodities. Measurement of the signal is generally electrochemical for biological, and this bio-electrochemical serves as transduction component in electrochemical biosensors. The biological reaction generates change in signal for conductance or impedance, measurable current, or change accumulation, which can be measured by conductometric, potentiometric, or amperometric techniques. The interaction between the target molecule and the electrical signal of bio-component produced can be measured [86].

Immunosensors are devices based on the detection of analyte-antibody interaction. Three main groups have been developed, which are luminescent or colorimetric sensors, surface plasmon resonance, and electrochemical sensors. An electrochemical immunosensor for the simultaneous detection of fumonisin B1 and DON has been designed and fabricated, which attained very low detection limits [87]. Furthermore, a third-generation enzymatic biosensor for quantification of sterigmatocystin (STEH), which was based on modified glassy carbon electrode, has been developed. The biosensor was also used to determine STEH in corn samples inoculated with *Aspergillus flavus*, which is an aflatoxins fungus producer [88].

2.3.1.1 Nanosensors

In many situations, it is necessary to detect multiple analytes or pathogens simultaneously, especially in mycotoxins detection where various mycotoxins can contaminate one single product. This would not be possible with conventional sensors. Sensors in nanoscale are especially attractive for such purposes. Nanosensors are characterized by one of the following attributes: Either the size of the sensor or its sensitivity is on the nanoscale or the spatial interaction distance between the sensors and the object is given in nanometers. These have advantages of improved sensitivity, specificity, and limits of detection, and reduced assay complexity and cost. Relatively small amount of analyte is required to register a response due to the small area of the sensing surface. Recently, a CeO_2 NPs-based sensor to detect OTA was developed [89]. The biosensor was assembled by functionalizing CeO_2 particles with OTA-specific ssDNA aptamers resulting in higher dispersibility and activity. Changes in the redox properties at the CeO_2 surface upon binding of the ssDNA and its target, measured using TMB, enabled rapid visual detection of OTA. In the presence of OTA, the ssDNA aptamer changed its structure from loose random coils to a compact tertiary form following target binding. As a result, a decreased catalytic effect against TMB oxidation was observed. The system was able to detect as low as 0.15 nM OTA.

During fungal growth, carbon dioxide is secreted due to the metabolic activity of microorganisms. In particular, gas nanosensors can be applied to detect the presence of CO_2 [89]. The detection of CO_2 is critical for environmental monitoring, chemical safety control, and many industrial applications; hence, nanosensors have been developed to assess changes in CO_2 concentration [90]. Electrochemical CO_2 nanosensors have been developed based on the principle that when CO_2 comes in contact with a semiconductor nanomaterial layer, a surface interaction may occur through oxidation/reduction, electron charge transfer, adsorption, or chemical reaction. The chemical interaction of the adsorbate (CO_2) with adsorbent semiconducting nanomaterial causes a charge depletion layer with upward bending energy bands that lead to change in electrical properties [91]. Although literature is scarce on CO_2 nanosensors associated with mycotoxin monitoring, there is a great potential in the area.

3. Preventive strategies

3.1 Food packaging

It is important to maintain the integrity of the food during storage and transportation through the supply chain before reaching the end consumer. Food packaging is one of the most critical steps in the food industry to protecting and preserving food commodities from any unacceptable alteration in quality and safety [92]. Traditional packaging systems such as use of polyethylene, polypropylene, and polyethylene terephthalate have several limitations related to extending shelf-life and maintaining the safety of food products. Thus, food packaging continues to evolve along with the innovations in material science and technology critical for food commodity preservation and effective distribution. Moreover, the increased desire of both food producers and consumers for quality food is encouraging researchers to seek novel, innovative, and resourceful food packaging systems with committed food safety, quality, and traceability and also to find ways to improve food quality while least compromising nutrition product value [93]. Innovative packaging systems facilitate communication at the consumer levels. These interventions and developments in food packaging must be commercially feasible and effectively acceptable, which must meet regulatory guidelines along with a justified outcome that outweighs the associated expenses of added novel technology [93].

Nanotechnology, in particular, has brought advances in the domain of food packaging. It offers a variety of options in the improvement of food packaging based on functionality nanomaterials, which can significantly address the food quality, safety, and stability concerns and thus reduce food waste and economic losses associated with mycotoxin contamination.

Advanced technologies based on applications of nanomaterials for food packaging, including active and intelligent packaging systems, have been developed in response to increased concerns for food safety and stringent regulatory requirements, and market globalization [94].

3.1.1 Active packaging

An active packaging is a designed packaging system that incorporates components that would release or absorb material into or from the packaged food or the food environment [94] thereby stimulating actions, which extends the shelf-life, and improves or maintains food quality and safety and/or sensory properties of the food product. Nanotechnology can be used to incorporate the active constituent into a food package material. Active packaging incorporates robust ways to control oxidation, microbial growth, hydrolysis, and other degradation reactions. The most promising active packaging technologies applicable to mycotoxin control include antimicrobial packaging, which significantly improve the micro-biological safety, oxygen scavengers, and moisture regulators/absorbers [94].

3.1.1.1 Antimicrobial active packaging

An antimicrobial packaging in particular antifungal active packaging is attractive in dealing with mycotoxins. This packaging allows its interaction with the food product or the headspace inside to reduce, inhibit, or retard the growth of spoilage or pathogenic microorganisms that may be present on food surfaces [95] and thus extends food shelf-life. Antimicrobial packaging could be achieved either by incorporation of nanomaterial active agent onto or applying a coating layer onto or within the packaging material. The active agent can inhibit the essential metabolic pathways of microorganisms or destroy cell wall/membrane structure. Higher surface area-to-volume ratio of nanomaterials antimicrobial agents in comparison with classical material enables their efficient inhibitory activity against food microbes resulting in an enhanced reactivity as photocatalysts and improved interactions between NPs and microbial membranes.

Nanomaterials such as chitosan NPs, metal NPs (AgNPs, Copper NPs and gold NPs), and metal oxide NPs (TiO_2, ZnO, MgO, and CuO) and CNTs are suitable agents that are well known for their antimicrobial activity and thus show great potential in providing antimicrobial and scavenging activity to food packaging. AgNPs are known to be inhibitory against multiple fungi [62, 96]. The AgNPs have been shown to inhibit fungal growth, when they are deposited over multilayered linear low-density polyethylene (LLDPE), and this resulted in 70% reduction of *Aspergillus niger* [76]. In another study, the application of 45 ppm Ag NPs caused a decrease in mycotoxin production (up to 80%) and changes in the enzymatic profile in *Aspergillus niger* [97]. The biosynthesized AgNPs showed outstanding activities for inhibiting four mycotoxigenic fungal strains (including *Alternaria alternata*, *A. ochraceus*, *Aspergillus flavus*, and *Fusarium solani*) [98]. Chitosan/silver, chitosan/gold, and chitosan/cinnamaldehyde nanocomposite films have also demonstrated antimicrobial activity against *Aspergillus niger* [99]. TiO_2 NPs, used as a food additive and for food contact material, have been applied to food packaging [92]. ZnO NPs have been an extremely promising antifungal agents for inhibiting the growth of mycotoxin-producing fungi [98]. CuNPs with the size range of 3–10 nm have also been found to have a superior antifungal activity toward *Fusarium oxysporum* [100]. NPs are especially attractive when exploiting eco-friendly energy-efficient, cost-effective, and green approaches. The use of extract of *Cymbopogan citratus* (DC) stapf, commonly known as lemon grass [100] and leaf extract of *Cinnamomum camphora* [101] in NPs synthesis, has been reported and has been found to be efficient in terms of reaction time as well as stability of the synthesized NPs. Essential oil-loaded biopolymeric nanocarriers also show promising antimicrobial and antioxidant activity and are suitable material for active food packaging due to inhibition of microbial growth in different food products [102].

3.1.1.2 Incorporation of moisture repellents and moisture absorbers in food packaging

Excess water reduces food shelf-life as it can promotes fungal proliferation inducing undesired changes in food quality. Thus, the moisture absorbers that are active non-migratory packaging and anti-wetting agents can be used in food packaging to reduce food water activity and provide an environment less suitable for mycotoxin-causing fungi [94]. Anti-wetting/moisture repellents can be made up of hydrophobic coatings on the surfaces of packaging materials.

Another strategy could involve the preparation of nano-engineered silicate-based hybrids coated onto both the intercalated and exfoliated silicate-based nano-composites. These materials are known to play an important role as agents that prevent the permeability of gaseous agents (e.g., O_2, CO_2). An attractive feature of using nano-engineered silicate-based hybrids arises from the fact that they are among minerals that are widely found in nature abundantly. Silicate minerals can have the surface easily modified due to the high possibility of ion exchange whereby a hydrophobic silicate can be modified/converted to an organophilic by exchanging a cation on its surface with an organic cation.

3.2 Smart packaging/intelligent packaging systems

In processing facilities, packaged foods are tested randomly during a production run. The downside to this is that there is no assurance that unsampled packages meet quality and safety standards. Recent efforts have thus been directed to the development of intelligent packaging systems that allow for real-time monitoring of food quality and boosting communicating with suppliers or the consumer at any point of the supply chain, or at the time of use [103]. These give ability to continually monitor the content of a package headspace and also provide a means to assess the safety and quality of the contained food long after it has left the production chain [62]. This can assist in ensuring adequate control after delivery to the supermarket, which is often not possible.

Intelligent systems use different innovative communication methods, which include sensors (already discussed under 2.3.1.1), indicators, and data carriers, that can measure changes in the environmental conditions inside packaging. These systems are attractive in mycotoxin research. The inclusion of nanosensors especially in food packaging systems could help in detecting the spoilage-associated changes and mycotoxin-causing fungi and thus can be alerted consumer and producer on food contamination [104]. These selective and sensitive nanosensors have been efficiently incorporated into food packaging, applied as labels or coatings to add an intelligent function to food packaging [105].

4. Conclusion

Analytical detection methods for mycotoxin that are affordable, easy to operate, and including LFIAs and electochemistry have been discussed. LFIA especially offers point-of-care diagnosis, which could be affordable to laboratories and farmers.

The means of improving the LFIAs such as using electrospinning for production of membrane are recommended for increasing the acceptability LFIA. Food packaging is recognized as a means of preventing/controlling formation of mycotoxins. Aggressive research programs and yet affordable are needed to prevent, treat, and contain outbreaks of mycotoxins in grain, and grain producers and thus increase marketability of African products.

Author details

Dikabo Mogopodi[1*], Mesha Mbisana[1], Samuel Raditloko[1], Inonge Chibua[1] and Banyaladzi Paphane[2]

1 University of Botswana, Gaborone, Botswana

2 Botswana University of Agriculture and Natural Resources, Gaborone, Botswana

*Address all correspondence to: dikmog@yahoo.co.uk

References

[1] Kraemer K, et al. The critical role of food safety in ensuring food security. In:Good Nutrition: Perspectives for the 21st Century.Basel, Switzerland: Karger Publishers; 2016. pp. 312-325. DOI: 10.1159/000452395

[2] Vågsholm I, Arzoomand NS, Boqvist S. Food security, safety, and sustainability—Getting the trade-offs right. Frontiers in Sustainable Food Systems. 2020;**4**:16. DOI: 10.3389/FSUFS.2020.00016

[3] Kussaga JB, Jacxsens L, Tiisekwa BP, Luning PA. Food safety management systems performance in African food processing companies: A review of deficiencies and possible improvement strategies. Journal of the Science of Food and Agriculture. 2014;**94**(11): 2154-2169. DOI: 10.1002/JSFA.6575

[4] Cai X, Gao Y, Sun Q, Chen Z, Megharaj M, Naidu R. Removal of co-contaminants Cu (II) and nitrate from aqueous solution using kaolin-Fe/Ni nanoparticles. Chemical Engineering Journal. 2014;**244**:19-26. DOI: 10.1016/J.CEJ.2014.01.040

[5] Thakali A, MacRae JD. A review of chemical and microbial contamination in food: What are the threats to a circular food system? Environmental Research. 2021;**194**:110635. DOI: 10.1016/J.ENVRES.2020.110635

[6] Mogopodi D, Paphane B, Mmolawa TB, Lenamile O. Investigation of disposal processes by manufacturing companies in Gaborone. The International Journal of Agriculture and Environmental Research. 2018;**4**(11): 6-14. DOI: 10.5281/ZENODO.1745078

[7] Rather IA, Koh WY, Paek WK, Lim J. The sources of chemical contaminants in food and their health implications. Frontiers in Pharmacology. 2017;**8**:830. DOI: 10.3389/FPHAR.2017.00830

[8] Fletcher MT, Blaney BJ. Mycotoxins. The Encyclopedia of Food Grains Second Definition. 2016;**2**(4):290-296. DOI: 10.1016/B978-0-12-394437-5.00112-1

[9] Probst C, Njapau H, Cotty PJ. Outbreak of an acute aflatoxicosis in Kenya in 2004: Identification of the causal agent. Applied and Environmental Microbiology. 2007;**73**(8):2762. DOI: 10.1128/AEM.02370-06

[10] Shephard GS. Impact of mycotoxins on human health in developing countries. Food Additives & Contaminants: Part A. 2008;**25**(2):146-151. DOI: 10.1080/02652030701567442

[11] Shephard GS et al. Multiple mycotoxin exposure determined by urinary biomarkers in rural subsistence farmers in the former Transkei, South Africa. Food and Chemical Toxicology. 2013;**62**:217-225. DOI: 10.1016/J.FCT.2013.08.040

[12] Kimanya ME, Routledge MN, Mpolya E, Ezekiel CN, Shirima CP, Gong YY. Estimating the risk of aflatoxin-induced liver cancer in Tanzania based on biomarker data. PLoS One. 2021;**16**(3):e0247281. DOI: 10.1371/JOURNAL.PONE.0247281

[13] Degraeve S et al. Impact of local pre-harvest management practices in maize on the occurrence of fusarium species and associated mycotoxins in two agro-ecosystems in Tanzania. Food Control. 2016;**59**:225-233. DOI: 10.1016/J.FOODCONT.2015.05.028

[14] Pérez-Fuentes N et al. Single and combined effects of regulated and

emerging mycotoxins on viability and mitochondrial function of SH-SY5Y cells. Food and Chemical Toxicology. 2021;**154**:112308. DOI: 10.1016/J.FCT.2021.112308

[15] Martínez-Culebras PV, Gandía M, Boronat A, Marcos JF, Manzanares P. Differential susceptibility of mycotoxin-producing fungi to distinct antifungal proteins (AFPs). Food Microbiology. 2021;**97**:103760. DOI: 10.1016/J.FM.2021.103760

[16] Kebede H, Liu X, Jin J, Xing F. Current status of major mycotoxins contamination in food and feed in Africa. Food Control. 2020;**110**:106975. DOI: 10.1016/J.FOODCONT.2019.106975

[17] Picardo M, Filatova D, Nuñez O, Farré M. Recent advances in the detection of natural toxins in freshwater environments. TrAC Trends in Analytical Chemistry. 2019;**112**:75-86. DOI: 10.1016/J.TRAC.2018.12.017

[18] Russell R, Paterson M. Zearalenone production and growth in drinking water inoculated with fusarium graminearum. Mycological Progress. 2007;**6**(2):109-113. DOI: 10.1007/S11557-007-0529-X

[19] Magnoli AP, Poloni VL, Cavaglieri L. Impact of mycotoxin contamination in the animal feed industry. Current Opinion in Food Science. 2019;**29**:99-108. DOI: 10.1016/J.COFS.2019.08.009

[20] Wu F, Groopman J, Pestka J. Public health impacts of foodborne mycotoxins. Annual Review of Food Science and Technology. 2014;**5**(1):351-372. DOI: 10.1146/ANNUREV-FOOD-030713-092431

[21] Groopman J, Kensler T, Wild C. Protective interventions to prevent aflatoxin-induced carcinogenesis in developing countries. Annual Review of Public Health. 2008;**29**:187-203. DOI: 10.1146/ANNUREV.PUBLHEALTH.29.020907.090859

[22] Marasas WFO et al. Fumonisins disrupt sphingolipid metabolism, folate transport, and neural tube development in embryo culture and In vivo: A potential risk factor for human neural tube defects among populations consuming Fumonisin-contaminated maize. The Journal of Nutrition. 2004;**134**(4):711-716. DOI: 10.1093/JN/134.4.711

[23] Mollay C, Kassim N, Stoltzfus R, Kimanya M. Childhood dietary exposure of aflatoxins and fumonisins in Tanzania: A review. Cogent Food & Agriculture. 2020;**6**(1):1859047. DOI: 10.1080/23311932.2020.1859047

[24] Wokorach G, Landschoot S, Anena J, Audenaert K, Echodu R, Haesaert G. Mycotoxin profile of staple grains in northern Uganda: Understanding the level of human exposure and potential risks. Food Control. 2021;**122**:107813. DOI: 10.1016/J.FOODCONT.2020.107813

[25] Egal S et al. Dietary exposure to aflatoxin from maize and groundnut in young children from Benin and Togo, West Africa. International Journal of Food Microbiology. 2005;**104**(2):215-224. DOI: 10.1016/J.IJFOODMICRO.2005.03.004

[26] Turner P et al. Aflatoxin exposure in utero causes growth faltering in Gambian infants. International Journal of Epidemiology. 2007;**36**(5):1119-1125. DOI: 10.1093/IJE/DYM122

[27] Eskola M, Kos G, Elliott CT, Hajšlová J, Mayar S, Krska R. Worldwide contamination of food-crops with mycotoxins: Validity of the widely cited 'FAO estimate' of 25%. Critical Reviews in Food Science and Nutrition.

2019;**60**(16):2773-2789. DOI: 10.1080/10408398.2019.1658570

[28] Ayelign A, De Saeger S. Mycotoxins in Ethiopia: Current status, implications to food safety and mitigation strategies. Food Control. 2020;**113**:107163. DOI: 10.1016/J.FOODCONT.2020.107163

[29] Food and Agriculture Organization of the United Nations. Mycotoxin regulations in 2003 and current developments. In: Worldwide Regulations for Mycotoxins in Food and Feed 2003. pp. 9-28, 2004. Accessed: Nov. 01 2021. [Online]. Available: ftp://ftp.fao.org/

[30] Mupunga I. A Comparative Study of Natural Contamination with Aflatoxins and Fumonisins in Selected Food Commodities from Botswana and Zimbabwe. Johannesburg: University of South Africa; 2013

[31] Mokgatlhe TM, Siame AB, Taylor JE. Fungi and fusarium mycotoxins associated with maize (Zea mays) and sorghum (Sorghum bicolor) in Botswana. African Journal of Plant Science and Biotechnology. 2011;**5**(1):26-32

[32] Korley Kortei N, Akomeah Agyekum A, Akuamoa F, Baffour VK, Wiisibie Alidu H. Risk assessment and exposure to levels of naturally occurring aflatoxins in some packaged cereals and cereal based foods consumed in Accra, Ghana. Toxicology Reports. 2019;**6**:34-41. DOI: 10.1016/J.TOXREP.2018.11.012

[33] Kortei N et al. The occurrence of aflatoxins and human health risk estimations in randomly obtained maize from some markets in Ghana. Scientific Reports. 2021;**11**(1):1-13. DOI: 10.1038/S41598-021-83751-7

[34] Gruber-Dorninger C, Jenkins T, Schatzmayr G. Multi-mycotoxin screening of feed and feed raw materials from Africa. World Mycotoxin Journal. 2018;**11**(3):369-383. DOI: 10.3920/WMJ2017.2292

[35] Mutiga SK et al. Multiple mycotoxins in Kenyan rice. Toxins. 2021;**13**(3):203. DOI: 10.3390/TOXINS13030203

[36] Birgen JK, Cheruiyot RC and Exodus Akwa T. Exodus Akwa, "Mycotoxin contamination of stored maize in Kenya and the associated Fungi". The Journal of Plant Pathology. 2020;**2**(1):7-13. DOI: 10.36959/394/620

[37] Nafuka S, Misihairabgwi J, Bock R. Variation of fungal metabolites in sorghum malts used to prepare namibian traditional fermented beverages Omalodu and Otombo. Toxins (Basel). 2019;**11**(3):165. DOI: 10.3390/TOXINS11030165

[38] Misihairabgwi JM, Ezekiel CN, Sulyok M, Shephard GS, Krska R. Mycotoxin contamination of foods in Southern Africa: A 10-year review (2007-2016). Critical Reviews in Food Science and Nutrition. 2019;**59**(1):43-58. DOI: 10.1080/10408398.2017.1357003

[39] Niyibituronsa M et al. Assessment of aflatoxin and fumonisin contamination levels in maize and mycotoxins awareness and risk factors in Rwanda. African Journal of Food, Agriculture, Nutrition and Development. 2020;**20**(5):16420-16446. DOI: 10.18697/AJFAND.93.19460

[40] Niyibituronsa M et al. Evaluation of mycotoxin content in soybean (Glycine max L.) grown in Rwanda. African Journal of Food, Agriculture, Nutrition and Development. 2018;**18**(3):13808-13824. DOI: 10.18697/AJFAND.83.17710

[41] Meyer H, Skhosana ZD, Motlanthe M, Louw W, Rohwer E. Long term monitoring (2014-2018)

of multi-mycotoxins in South African commercial maize and wheat with a locally developed and validated LC-MS/MS Method. Toxins (Basel). 2019;**11**(5): 271. DOI: 10.3390/TOXINS11050271

[42] Motloung L et al. Study on mycotoxin contamination in south African food spices. World Mycotoxin Journal. 2018;**11**(3):401-409. DOI: 10.3920/WMJ2017.2191

[43] Hanvi DM, Lawson-Evi P, De Boevre M, Goto CE, De Saeger S, Eklu-Gadegbeku K. Natural occurrence of mycotoxins in maize and sorghum in Togo. Mycotoxin Research. 2019;**35**(4):321-327. DOI: 10.1007/S12550-019-00351-1

[44] Baglo DE, Faye A, and Fall M. "Determination of aflatoxin in maize produced in two regions of Togo". Advances in Food Technology and Nutritional Sciences – Open Journal. Jun 2020;**6**(1):42-46. DOI: 10.17140/AFTNSOJ-6-167

[45] Kachapulula PW, Akello J, Bandyopadhyay R, Cotty PJ. Aflatoxin contamination of groundnut and maize in Zambia: Observed and potential concentrations. Journal of Applied Microbiology. 2017;**122**(6):1471-1482. DOI: 10.1111/JAM.13448

[46] Botana LM, Sainz MJ. Climate Change and Mycotoxins. Berlin, Germany: Walter de Gruyter GmbH & Co KG; 2015

[47] Guo W et al. Development of a QuEChERS-Based UHPLC-MS/MS Method for Simultaneous Determination of Six Alternaria Toxins in Grapes. Toxins (Basel). 2019;**11**(2):87. DOI: 10.3390/TOXINS11020087

[48] Agriopoulou S, Stamatelopoulou E, Varzakas T. Advances in occurrence, importance, and mycotoxin control strategies: Prevention and detoxification in foods. Food. 2020;**9**:518. DOI: 10.3390/foods9020137

[49] Alshannaq A, Yu JH. Occurrence, toxicity, and analysis of major mycotoxins in food. International Journal of Environmental Research and Public Health. 2017;**14**(632):1-20. DOI: 10.3390/ijerph14060632

[50] Salim SA, Sukor R, Ismail MN, Selamat J. Dispersive liquid-liquid microextraction (DLLME) and LC-MS/MS analysis for multi-mycotoxin in Rice bran: Method development, optimization and validation. Toxins (Basel). 2021;**13**(280):1-21. DOI: 10.3390/toxins13040280

[51] Pankaj SK, Shi H, Keener KM. A review of novel physical and chemical decontamination technologies for aflatoxin in food. Trends in Food Science and Technology. 2018;**71**:73-83. DOI: 10.1016/J.TIFS.2017.11.007

[52] Breck D. Zeolite Molecular Sieves Structure, Chemistry and Use, New York. New York: John Wiley & Sons; 1974

[53] EFSA. Food contact materials, enzymes and processing aids|EFSA. EFSA Journal. 2013;**11**:3155 Accessed: Nov. 01, 2021. [Online]. Available: https://www.efsa.europa.eu/en/science/scientific-committee-and-panels/cep

[54] Tomašević-Čanović M, Daković A, Rottinghaus G, Matijašević S, and Duričić M. "Surfactant modified zeolites— New efficient adsorbents for mycotoxins". Microporous and Mesoporous Materials.2003;**61**(1-3): 173-180. DOI: 10.1016/ S1387-1811(03)00365-2

[55] Marković M et al. Ochratoxin A and zearalenone adsorption by the natural

zeolite treated with benzalkonium chloride, Colloids and Surfaces A: Physicochemical and Engineering Aspects. 2017;**529**:7-17. DOI: 10.1016/j.colsurfa.2017.05.054

[56] Gao S et al. Determination of aflatoxins in milk sample with ionic liquid modified magnetic zeolitic imidazolate frameworks. Journal of Chromatography B. 2019;**1128**:121778. DOI: 10.1016/J.JCHROMB.2019.121778

[57] Lucci P et al. Molecularly imprinted polymer as selective sorbent for the extraction of zearalenone in edible vegetable oils. Foods. 2020;**9**(10):1439. DOI: 10.3390/FOODS9101439

[58] Liang Y et al. An amino-functionalized zirconium-based metal-organic framework of type UiO-66-NH 2 covered with a molecularly imprinted polymer as a sorbent for the extraction of aflatoxins AFB1, AFB2, AFG1 and AFG2 from grain. Microchimica Acta. 2019;**187**(1):1-8. DOI: 10.1007/S00604-019-3959-7

[59] Semong O, Batlokwa BS. Development of an aflatoxin B1 specific molecularly imprinted solid phase extraction sorbent for the selective pre-concentration of toxic aflatoxin B1 from child weaning food, Tsabana. Molecular Imprinting. 2017;**5**(1):1-15. DOI: 10.1515/molim-2017-0001

[60] Bodbodak S, Hesari J, Peighambardoust SH, Mahkam M. Selective decontamination of aflatoxin M1 in milk by molecularly imprinted polymer coated on the surface of stainless steel plate. International Journal of Dairy Technology. 2018;**71**(4):868-878. DOI: 10.1111/1471-0307.12551

[61] Sun J et al. Removal of patulin in apple juice based on novel magnetic molecularly imprinted adsorbent Fe_3O_4@SiO_2@CS-GO@MIP. LWT. 2019;**118**(1):108854. DOI: 10.1016/J.LWT.2019.108854

[62] Duncan TV. Applications of nanotechnology in food packaging and food safety: Barrier materials, antimicrobials and sensors. Journal of Colloid and Interface Science. 2011;**363**(1):1-24. DOI: 10.1016/J.JCIS.2011.07.017

[63] Oketola AA, Torto N, Oketola AA, Torto N. Synthesis and characterization of poly(styrene-co-acrylamide) polymers prior to electrospinning. Advances in Nanoparticles. 2013;**2**(2):87-93. DOI: 10.4236/ANP.2013.22015

[64] Gibson N et al. Colloidal stability of modified nanodiamond particles. Diamond and Related Materials. 2009;**18**(4):620-626. DOI: 10.1016/J.DIAMOND.2008.10.049

[65] Horky P, Skalickova S, Baholet D, Skladanka J. Nanoparticles as a solution for eliminating the risk of mycotoxins. Nanomaterials. 2018;**8**(9):727. DOI: 10.3390/NANO8090727

[66] Puzyr A, Purtov K, Shenderova O, Luo M. The adsorption of aflatoxin B1 by detonation-synthesis nanodiamonds. Biochemical and Biophysical Research Communications. 2007;**417**(1):299-301. DOI: 10.1134/S1607672907060026

[67] Han Z et al. Multi-walled carbon nanotubes-based magnetic solid-phase extraction for the determination of zearalenone and its derivatives in maize by ultra-high performance liquid chromatography-tandem mass spectrometry. Food Control. 2017;**79**:177-184. DOI: 10.1016/J.FOODCONT.2017.03.044

[68] Dong M et al. Multi-walled carbon nanotubes as solid-phase extraction

sorbents for simultaneous determination of type a trichothecenes in maize, wheat and rice by ultra-high performance liquid chromatography-tandem mass spectrometry. Journal of Chromatography. A. 2015;**1423**:177-182. DOI: 10.1016/J.CHROMA.2015.10.068

[69] Dong M et al. Determination of type a trichothecenes in coix seed by magnetic solid-phase extraction based on magnetic multi-walled carbon nanotubes coupled with ultra-high performance liquid chromatography-tandem mass spectrometry. Analytical and Bioanalytical Chemistry. 2016;**408**(24):6823-6831. DOI: 10.1007/S00216-016-9809-0

[70] Singh C et al. Carboxylated multiwalled carbon nanotubes based biosensor for aflatoxin detection. Sensors and Actuators B: Chemical. 2013;**185**:258-264. DOI: 10.1016/J.SNB.2013.04.040

[71] Rahmani A, Jinap S, Soleimany F. Qualitative and quantitative analysis of mycotoxins. Comprehensive Reviews in Food Science and Food Safety. 2009;**8**(3):202-251. DOI: 10.1111/J.1541-4337.2009.00079.X

[72] Tittlemier S, Cramer B, Dall'Asta C, Iha M, Lattanzio V. Developments in mycotoxin analysis. World Mycotoxin Journal. 2019;**12**(1):3-29. DOI: 10.3920/WMJ2018.2398

[73] Foubert A et al. Development of a rainbow lateral flow immunoassay for the simultaneous detection of four mycotoxins. Journal of Agricultural and Food Chemistry. 2016;**65**(33):7121-7130. DOI: 10.1021/ACS.JAFC.6B04157

[74] Song S et al. Multiplex lateral flow immunoassay for mycotoxin determination. Analytical Chemistry. 2014;**86**(10):4995-5001. DOI: 10.1021/AC500540Z

[75] Molinelli A, Grossalber K, Krska R. A rapid lateral flow test for the determination of total type B fumonisins in maize. Analytical and Bioanalytical Chemistry. 2009;**395**(5):1309-1316. DOI: 10.1007/S00216-009-3082-4

[76] Sánchez-Valdes S, Ortega-Ortiz H, Valle LFR, Medellín-Rodríguez FJ, Guedea-Miranda R. Mechanical and antimicrobial properties of multilayer films with a polyethylene/silver nanocomposite layer. Journal of Applied Polymer Science. 2009;**111**(2):953-962. DOI: 10.1002/APP.29051

[77] Liu S et al. Nanozyme amplification mediated on-demand multiplex lateral flow immunoassay with dual-readout and broadened detection range. Biosensors & Bioelectronics. 2020;**169**:112610. DOI: 10.1016/J.BIOS.2020.112610

[78] Yew C, Azari P, Choi J. Electrospun polycaprolactone nanofibers as a reaction membrane for lateral flow assay. Polymers (Basel). 2018;**10**(12):1387. DOI: 10.3390/POLYM10121387

[79] Yew CHT, Azari P, Choi JR, Li F, Pingguan-Murphy B. Electrospin coating of nitrocellulose membrane enhances sensitivity in nucleic acid-based lateral flow assay. Analytica Chimica Acta. 2018;**1009**:81-88. DOI: 10.1016/J.ACA.2018.01.016

[80] Lee S, Kim G, Moon J. Performance improvement of the one-dot lateral flow immunoassay for aflatoxin B1 by using a smartphone-based Reading system. Sensors. 2013;**13**(4):5109-5116. DOI: 10.3390/S130405109

[81] Fernández H. Mycotoxins quantification in the food system: Is there any contribution from electrochemical biosensors? Journal of Biosensors and Bioelectronics. 2013;**04**(03):e121. DOI: 10.4172/2155-6210.1000E121

[82] Fernandez H, Electroanalytical Properties of Mycotoxins and their Determinations in the Agroalimentary System. 2012 https://www.researchgate.net/publication/287267796_Electroanalytical_properties_of_mycotoxins_and_their_determinations_in_the_agroalimentary_system (Accessed 01 November 2021)

[83] Raeisossadati MJ et al. Lateral flow based immunobiosensors for detection of food contaminants. Biosensors & Bioelectronics. 2016;**86**:235-246. DOI: 10.1016/J.BIOS.2016.06.061

[84] Hernández-Hernández AA et al. A novel voltammetric approach for the quantification of aflatoxin b1 using a bismuth-modified electrode. The Electrochemical Society. 2021;**168**(2): 026512. DOI: 10.1149/1945-7111/ABE349

[85] Evtugyn G, Porfireva A, Kulikova T, Hianik T. Recent achievements in electrochemical and surface plasmon resonance aptasensors for mycotoxins detection. Chemosensors. 2021;**9**(7): 180. DOI: 10.3390/CHEMOSENSORS9070180

[86] Rovina K, Shaeera SN, Vonnie JM, Yi SX. Recent biosensors technologies for detection of mycotoxin in food products. Mycotoxins and Food Safety. IntechOpen; 2019. pp. 1-17. DOI: 10.5772/INTECHOPEN.89022

[87] Lu L, Gunasekaran S. Dual-channel ITO-microfluidic electrochemical immunosensor for simultaneous detection of two mycotoxins. Talanta. 2019;**194**:709-716. DOI: 10.1016/J.TALANTA.2018.10.091

[88] Nieto DC et al. Development of a third-generation biosensor to determine sterigmatocystin mycotoxin: An early warning system to detect aflatoxin B 1. Talanta. 2019;**194**:253-258. DOI: 10.1016/J.TALANTA.2018.10.032

[89] Biji KB, Ravishankar CN, Mohan CO, Srinivasa Gopal TK. Smart packaging systems for food applications: A review. Journal of Food Science and Technology. 2015;**52**(10):6125-6135. DOI: 10.1007/S13197-015-1766-7

[90] Rezk MY, Sharma J, Gartia MR. Nanomaterial-Based CO_2 Sensors. Nanomater. 2020;**10**(11):2251. DOI: 10.3390/NANO10112251

[91] Shinde PV et al. Room-temperature synthesis and CO_2-gas sensitivity of bismuth oxide nanosensors. RSC Advances. 2020;**10**(29):17217-17227. DOI: 10.1039/D0RA00801J

[92] Sharma C, Dhiman R, Rokana N, and Panwar H. "Nanotechnology: An untapped resource for food packaging". Frontiers in Microbiology. 2017;**0**(SEP): 1735. DOI: 10.3389/ FMICB.2017.01735

[93] Vanderroost M, Ragaert P, Devlieghere F, De Meulenaer B. Intelligent food packaging: The next generation. Trends in Food Science and Technology. 2014;**39**(1):47-62. DOI: 10.1016/J.TIFS.2014.06.009

[94] Drago E, Campardelli R, Pettinato M. Innovations in smart packaging concepts for food: An extensive review. Foods (Basel, Switzerland). 2020;**9**(11):1628. DOI: 10.3390/FOODS9111628

[95] de F Soares FN, Pires ACS, Camilloto GP, Santiago-Silva P, Espitia PJP, Silva WA. Recent patents on active packaging for food application. Recent Patents on Food, Nutrition & Agriculture. 2010; **1**(2):171-178. DOI: 10.2174/1876142910901020171

[96] Bradley EL, Castle L, Chaudhry Q. Applications of nanomaterials in food

packaging with a consideration of opportunities for developing countries. Trends in Food Science and Technology. 2011;**22**(11):604-610. DOI: 10.1016/J. TIFS.2011.01.002

[97] Pietrzak K, Twarużek M, Czyżowska A, Kosicki R, and GB. "Influence of silver nanoparticles on metabolism and toxicity of moulds". Acta Biochimica Polonica. 2015;**62**(4): 851-857. DOI: 10.18388/ ABP.2015_1146

[98] Abdel-Hadi AM, Awad MF, Abo-Dahab NF, and Elkady ME. "Extracellular synthesis of silver nanoparticles by aspergillus terreus: Biosynthesis, characterization and biological activity." Biosciences, Biotechnology Research Asia. Dec 2014;**11**(3):1179-1186. DOI: 10.13005/ BBRA/1503

[99] Youssef AM, Abdel-Aziz MS, El-Sayed SM. Chitosan nanocomposite films based on Ag-NP and Au-NP biosynthesis by bacillus subtilis as packaging materials. International Journal of Biological Macromolecules. 2014;**69**:185-191. DOI: 10.1016/J. IJBIOMAC.2014.05.047

[100] Geetha N, Geetha T, Manonmani P, Thiyagarajan M. Green synthesis of silver nanoparticles using cymbopogan citratus (dc) Stapf. extract and its antibacterial activity. Australian Journal of Basic and Applied Sciences. 2014;**8**(3):324-331

[101] Huang H, Yang X. Synthesis of polysaccharide-stabilized gold and silver nanoparticles: A green method. Carbohydrate Research. 2004;**339**(15): 2627-2631. DOI: 10.1016/J.CARRES. 2004.08.005

[102] Maurya A, Prasad J, Das S, Dwivedy AK. Essential oils and their application in food safety. Frontiers in Sustainable Food Systems. 2021;**5**:133. DOI: 10.3389/FSUFS.2021.653420

[103] Mustafa F, Andreescu S. Chemical and biological sensors for food-quality monitoring and smart packaging. Foods. 2018;**7**(10):168. DOI: 10.3390/FOODS 7100168

[104] Majid I, Ahmad Nayik G, Mohammad Dar S, Nanda V. Novel food packaging technologies: Innovations and future prospective. Journal of the Saudi Society of Agricultural Sciences. 2018;**17**(4):454-462. DOI: 10.1016/J. JSSAS.2016.11.003

[105] Kuswandi B, Wicaksono Y, Abdullah A, Yook Heng L, Ahmad M. Sensing and instrumentation for food quality and safety smart packaging: Sensors for monitoring of food quality and safety. Sensing and Instrumentation for Food Quality. 2011;**5**:137-146. DOI: 10.1007/s11694-011-9120-x

Section 2

Illustrative Case Studies

Chapter 5

Social Resilience in Local Food Systems: A Foundation for Food Security during a Crisis

Tanya Zerbian, Mags Adams and Neil Wilson

Abstract

The Covid-19 pandemic has presented new challenges for food production, distribution, and consumption and has exacerbated existing inequalities in access to food. However, it has also provided new opportunities for local communities to work differently, to increase collaboration, and to improve outcomes for those most in need. This chapter focuses on how various local food initiatives within a specific UK city, Preston in NW England, interact, cooperate and collaborate, and the changes to these interactions during a crisis. The findings derive from a social network analysis (SNA) conducted during summer 2020 examining how relationships changed during the crisis, and online semi-structured interviews. Using resilience as a framework to understand these dynamics, the chapter argues that social preconditions, such as a previously organised local food network in partnership with local authorities, have helped communities to self-organise and respond to difficult circumstances. Moreover, it also highlights the ways in which responses to major disruption (Covid-19) can bring about the collective questioning of current models of emergency food provisioning and create stronger collaborative bonds within already organised networks. We demonstrate that such processes could potentially improve food insecurity outcomes by combining locally grown food and dignified food access options.

Keywords: food resilience, social capital, food security, local food systems, Covid-19, local food initiatives

1. Introduction

The global Covid-19 situation has presented new food production, distribution, and consumption challenges and has potentially exacerbated existing inequalities for those in deprived areas. Significantly, the implications of the Covid-19 pandemic on global food supply chains and food systems' resilience have aggravated food insecurity indicators. As defined by the Food and Agriculture Organisation (FAO), food security is a condition that "exists when all people, at all times, have physical, social and economic access to sufficient, safe and nutritious food that meets their dietary needs and food preferences for an active and healthy life" ([1], p. 49). The FAO estimates that up to 811 million people worldwide faced hunger in 2020 – up to 161 million more than in 2019 – as conflict, climate extremes, and economic slowdowns, aggravated by the Covid-19 pandemic, continued to increase in frequency and intensity [2]. The World Food Program (WFP) calculated that the number of acutely food insecure people in the countries where it operates reached more than 271 million people directly due to the aggravating impact of the Covid-19 pandemic. In the UK, it is estimated that the number of people experiencing food insecurity quadrupled due to lack of food in shops, economic impacts, and isolation brought about by the pandemic [3].

As well as these challenges, the Covid-19 situation presents new opportunities for local food initiatives to work differently, increase collaboration, and improve outcomes for those most in need. Local food initiatives usually refer to social innovations that aim to address environmental and social issues derived from current food system structures, reconfiguring food supply chains and relations within a locality [4]. The collective responses of local food initiatives to the disruption caused by Covid-19 provide the perfect space to increase knowledge about how local food systems – collaborative networks that integrate individual local food initiatives efforts [5] – and could potentially lead to better food security outcomes. Case studies have increasingly documented how networked responses in diverse local communities during the Covid-19 crisis managed to respond to rising food insecurity needs and the opportunities this might provide for food systems change [3, 6]. Our research aimed to expand this body of literature by providing knowledge about how various local food initiatives interact, cooperate, and collaborate, how these changed during the Covid-19 pandemic and what this means for a local food system. To date, there are few studies that have investigated the changing structure of local food systems using a comparative research design before and during a disruption. Lessons learned from this examination might help local responses to future crises such as the climate crisis and other external stresses that affect food systems and society.

We focus on the local food system of the Local Authority Area of Preston in the Lancashire region of the UK. In the first section of the chapter, food security resilience is introduced. By providing an overview of the concepts of resilience and social capital, a theoretical framework is presented that is used to unpack the dynamics of Preston's local food system. The following section outline the methodology used to study Preston's local food system – namely, a social network analysis (SNA) conducted during 2020, examining collaborative relationships before and during the crisis, and online semi-structured interviews with a subset of local food initiatives. Next, the results from the research are presented in order to illuminate the changing characteristics of the local food system and its potential outcomes. The final section returns to the concept of food security resilience, using social capital as a proxy, to highlight important lessons learned from the case study presented, namely the relevance of previous social preconditions to ensure adaptation and response.

2. Social resilience, a key factor in addressing food security needs during a crisis

2.1 Food security resilience; beyond ecology

Resilience is a concept that holds different meanings depending on the various situations in which it is being used [7]. Ecology literature usually frames resilience as a technical concept that refers to the "capacity of a system to withstand shocks and external pressures while maintaining its basic structure, processes, and functions" ([8], p. 601) In this context, resilience was perceived as an isolated 'outcome' rather than connected to specific abilities, as many academics and practitioners now recognise [9]. Resilience thinking has expanded from this initial narrow definition by integrating adaptability and transformability as crucial ingredients [10, 11]. Social theory has contributed to this reconceptualisation adding essential dimensions, such as agency and collective action, to the concept [12]. As such, resilience is defined at the communal rather than individual level, focusing on coordinated efforts and cooperative adaptation [13]. Here, resilience refers to the ability of a given community or group to cope with external shocks and disturbances to its infrastructure and functioning [10]. It involves both the capacity to learn and adapt to ongoing pressures using existing economic, social, and environmental resources while also developing new strategies and capabilities [11].

Both literature and practice have increasingly acknowledged the potential of resilience thinking to contribute to food security. Tendall et al. [14] develop the notion of food security resilience at the system level by breaking it down into four components: robustness (the capacity to withstand the disturbance in the first place before any food security is lost); redundancy (the extent to which elements of the system are replaceable, affecting the capacity to absorb the perturbing effect of the disturbance and avoid as much food insecurity as possible); flexibility and thus rapidity (or the speed with which the food system can recover any lost food security); and finally, resourcefulness and adaptability (how much of the lost food security is recovered). More broadly, it has been argued that food security resilience is "about the capacities of households and communities, to deal with adverse events in a way that does not affect negatively their long-term wellbeing and/or functioning" ([12], p. 806). Although Tendall et al.'s [14] definition offers a strong starting point to understand how particular local food systems have been able to respond to the Covid-19 pandemic, resilience variables such as those proposed are difficult to observe and measure, and there is no current consensus on how to do so [7].

Therefore, to understand how local food systems can contribute to food security and what is needed to address external stresses, this study assessed the changes in *resilience capacities* (the inputs required to achieve resilience) of Preston's local food system. Although these capacities cannot be regarded as a proxy for the *actual* resilience of a system, there is a direct linkage between them and the potential of a system to be resilient [7]. Thus, they are helpful variables for understanding why a particular system might successfully respond to a specific crisis. Building on literature that integrates social theory into resilience thinking, this study concentrated on social resilience capacities of local food systems using social capital as an analytical tool, which other scholars have regarded as a key feature of community and social resilience [10, 12, 15].

Overall, there is not a universal definition of social capital [16]. Adler and Known [17] categorised definitions of social capital depending on whether their focus was on an individual or a collective group, and divided the definitions into three categories. The first refers to social capital as a resource that an individual has as a result of their external linkages with other actors [13]. The second category focuses on the structure of relations of multiple actors that give the collectivity cohesiveness, which facilitate common goals. In this category, social capital is defined as "the features of social organisation, such as trust, norms, and networks, that can improve the efficiency of society by facilitating coordinated actions" ([18], p. 167). It is thus defined by its function to facilitate certain action within a social structure [19]. The third category of social capital refers to both external linkages and internal linkages of a social grouping. The current study adopts the second view of social capital, as it allows the analysing of local food systems' structure and the collective characteristics that facilitate action in times of crisis. In this regard, it moves away from focussing on an individual resource pool to address adversity towards the social resilience capacities of local food systems as a whole.

To aid the analysis of social capital influence upon the response of local food systems to emergencies, two forms of social capital are examined: bonding and bridging social capital. Bonding usually refers to strong and emotional connections, such as friends or family, among individuals that commonly share similar characteristics in class, race, attitudes, and available information and resources [17, 18, 20]. Bridging describes loose relationships that enables information to be exchanged across diverse groups [16]. Bridging social capital, in contrast to bonding social capital, usually appears in more open networks, increasing chances to expand and access new relationships, information, resources, and opportunities [21].

2.2 The changing relationships of local food initiatives pre- and during Covid-19

The methodology used in this study involved a three-phase process. Phase I consisted of an initial internet search to identify a preliminary list of local food initiatives supporting one or more areas that contribute to the sustainability and food security of the Preston, Lancashire area. Local food initiatives in Preston were identified based on their nature as a component of a local food system as characterised by Clément [22]. Clément identifies local food initiatives as those that focus on direct local food marketing, local food procurement, food access programmes, and food education and policy [21]. We added an overarching criteria of having a specific focus on improving food security and sustainability at the local level and follow ethical principles to differentiate them from the conventional food system [23]. We initially identified 44 organisations in Preston that could be considered local food initiatives working within the local food system.

Phase II involved gathering survey data from key personnel working in these organisations to establish which local food initiatives have active relationships and collaborations and which are more marginal within Preston's local food system. The survey identified how these connections have changed since the Covid-19 crisis developed and enabled comparison with pre-Covid-19 relationships. To do this, we asked questions relating to the scale of interactions between organisations before and during the crisis. To answer these questions participants had to indicate which option best described their relationship with other organisations in the local food system. The scale used in the study was derived from the four Cs of interorganisational partnering to respond to a disaster and Himmelman's collaboration continuum [24, 25]. Reflecting increasing degrees of interaction and integration with other organisations, the options provided were 'communicating' (exchange of ideas and information), 'sharing' (communicating and sharing of resources for mutual benefit), and 'collaborating' (communicating, sharing and working together to create something new). Based on the definitions of bonding and bridging social capital, collaborating refers to the former, while communicating and sharing to the latter.

The survey analysis was coupled with SNA to measure the social capital features of the local food system, following a network approach to social capital, which focuses on the patterns and collection of relationships within a group [26]. SNA has been identified as beneficial for demonstrating the relationships among food systems' actors both visually and numerically [27]. Gephi, an open-source platform for visualising and analysing network graph data, was used to analyse network-based questions to assess the overall characteristics of the local food system and identify central actors within it. Of the 44 identified organisations, 21 local food initiatives completed the survey. Although there are various methods available to impute the missing data of non-respondents, doing so can create biased network measures and metrics [28]. Missing data in this context is missing at random and the probability of it being missing is unrelated to the value of the missing connections and observed organisational attributes [29]. Therefore, the analysis was based on the 21 responses from local food initiatives that we received. Phase III included semi-structured interviews with key stakeholders in the local food system and will be discussed further in Section 2.3.

2.2.1 The social network of Preston's local food system

Data about social networks is depicted as sociograms. Sociograms are graphs showing network actors (in our case these are local food initiatives which are represented as 'nodes' in the network) and their relationships (these are the connections between the local food initiatives and are represented as 'edges') [30]. Relationships (edges) can be directed (having a certain quality that can be different in both directions) or undirected (where the type of relationship is not specified). We gathered information about both, as knowing the direction of the edges can provide information about reciprocal relationships. Reciprocal relationships denote the level of trust between organisations because it reflects the cultivation and utilisation of tangible and intangible resources by network members for the common interest [16, 21]. **Figures 1** and **2** illustrate the sociograms of the relationships among organisations before Covid-19 and during Covid-19. For the SNA, we concentrated on measures of connectivity and centrality[1], as they represent some of the fundamental structural properties of importance to any network and have been used to clarify the vulnerability of networks [30].

Table 1 shows the local food system's connectivity network measures, comparing pre-and during Covid-19. Network diameter is the longest distance between any two nodes (i.e., how many edges are between the two most distant nodes). A short network diameter means it is possible to move through the network in a very few steps through a small number of nodes and implies that an idea or resource will spread quickly across the network, signalling integration to the system [31]. The average path length is the mean distance between all possible pairs of nodes in the network; the closer to 1, the more connected the network [32]. In the case of Preston, with a diameter of 2 and an average path length of approx. 1.5 even before Covid-19, the local food system was already 'compact' [33].

Similarly, network density – the number of identified links divided by the maximum possible number of links [32] – remains between 0.44 and 0.45. This measure captures the bonding social capital within the local food system, reflecting sociological ideas like cohesion, solidarity, and membership, by calculating how many edges exist between actors compared to how many edges between actors are possible; the closer to 1, the more connected the network is [34]. In terms of resilience, having a medium network density, low diameter, and average path length means that resources

[1] Connectivity is an aggregate metric that gives information about the cohesiveness of the network as a whole; the interconnectedness of actors. Centrality is a measure relating to individual nodes. It indicates which nodes possesses critical positions in the network [27].

Figure 1.
Sociogram pre-Covid-19 - Preston's local food system.

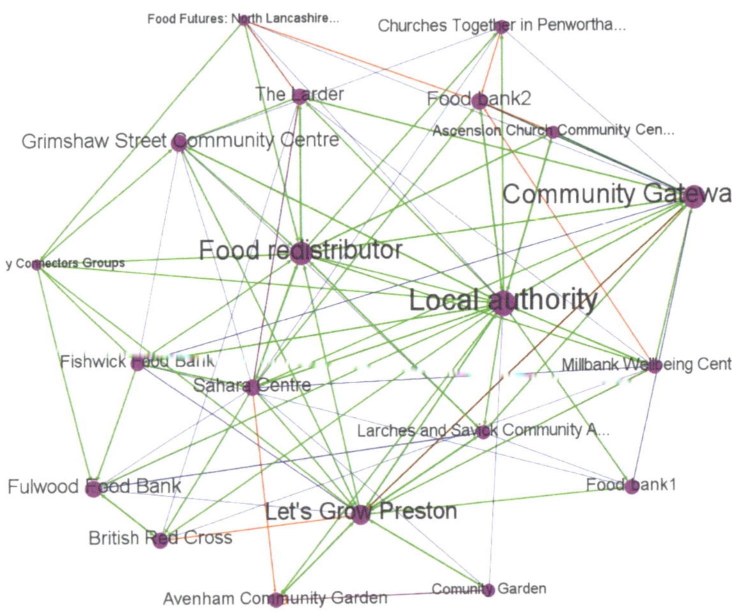

Figure 2.
Sociogram during Covid-19 - Preston's local food system.

Metric	Pre-Covid-19	during Covid-19
Network Diameter	2	2
Network Density	0.442	0.453
Average Path Length	1.568	1.553

Table 1.
Connectivity measures in Preston's local food system.

can spread quickly between organisations. In times of crisis, such connectivity can facilitate rapid social action and setting up new processes and activities without the potential for duplication of activity and attendant waste of resources, making it easier to respond to changing situations such as Covid-19. This could explain the successful response to food insecurity described by participants (see Section 2.3.). Based on these measures, it could be argued that Preston's local food system already possessed a strong level of bonding social capital, as it demonstrates collective cohesiveness. However, as will be seen next, this changes when looking at the *types* of relationships present.

Figure 1 illustrates the overarching interconnectivity between organisations of Preston's local food system before Covid-19. The size of the nodes in the sociograms indicates the importance of an organisation within the network. The edges (connections) are coloured based on the type of relationship: blue: communicating, red: sharing, green: collaborating. The local food system before Covid-19 already shows a high number of edges between the many organisations within it. Approximately half of edges were collaborative relationships, and the other half were communicating and sharing connections (see **Figure 1**). Notably, the sociogram pre-Covid-19 presents a small network of organisations, which share collaborative ties with the same initiatives. In this regard, there was a strong presence of bridging social capital exemplified through weaker ties such as communicating or resource sharing, with a sub-group of organisations with an enhanced bonding social capital reflected through collaborative relationships.

Comparing the sociograms before and during Covid-19, it can be identified that the pandemic has affected the associations between local food systems' members, although the overall features of the local food system remain the same. Significantly, it has increased the quality of interactions. **Figure 2** illustrates a higher number of green coloured, collaborative relationships across the local food system, accounting for 60% of the edges. In this regard, many weaker connections in the form of sharing and communicating pre-Covid-19 were replaced by collaborations during-Covid-19, signalling the creation of bonding social capital from previous connections based on bridging social capital.

Despite the overarching interconnectivity between organisations within Preston's local food system, it can be identified that a small number of organisations have particularly central roles in the network, which has been strengthened during Covid-19. To understand the role of specific organisations within the network, we used centrality measures to identify the most connected actors in the network that hold a significantly higher than average number of links [31]. In-degree centrality is the number of edges pointing towards a node, i.e., how popular or sought-after a given organisation is. Out-degree centrality denotes the outgoing connections of a node with other organisations, which refers to the sociability or outreach of an organisation [31]. This is important to understand the social resilience capacities of a local food system, as it points to particularly influential and prominent actors that could facilitate rapid response, network organisation, or those holding the resources needed to adapt. **Table 2** presents the degree centrality per organisation. The nodes in **Figures 1** and **2** are sized according to their in-degree centrality score, which indicates the number of incoming links a local food initiative possesses. From this, four organisations, the local authority, the food redistributor, CGA (a community housing association), and Let us Grow Preston (LGP - a network of community gardens), can be identified as having high levels of in-degree and out-degree centrality. As such, they hold an advantageous position concerning their roles and leadership within the local food system. This has remained during Covid-19, albeit with the scores increasing for each organisation, indicating an increased number of connections.

Name	In-degree		Out-degree		Betweenness C.		Eigenvector C.	
	Pre-Covid	During Covid	Pre-Covid	During Covid	Pre-Covid	During Covid	Pre-Covid	During Covid
Local authority	13	15	16	16	0.239	0.354	0.942	0.960
CGA	11	13	8	9	0.053	0.094	0.953	0.989
Food redistributor	11	12	8	7	0.053	0.066	1.000	1.000
Let us Grow Preston	9	10	12	13	0.119	0.122	0.720	0.709
Food bank2	7	7	2	2	0.000	0.000	0.584	0.536
Fulwood Food Bank	6	7	0	2	0.000	0.055	0.569	0.519
British Red Cross	6	6	1	1	0.003	0.002	0.571	0.522
Sahara Centre	6	6	15	14	0.086	0.053	0.635	0.572
The Larder	6	6	7	6	0.027	0.111	0.619	0.560
Avenh. C.Garden	5	5	4	3	0.016	0.006	0.436	0.401
Grimshaw St. Community C.	5	7	3	4	0.001	0.007	0.509	0.524
Fishwick Food Bank	4	5	1	8	0.001	0.005	0.451	0.450
Food bank1	4	5	5	2	0.003	0.000	0.465	0.500
Larches and S. Community A.	4	4	9	7	0.010	0.006	0.534	0.506
Millbank Wellbeing C.	4	4	7	8	0.004	0.007	0.487	0.449
Ascension Church	3	3	0	4	0.000	0.001	0.352	0.407
Community C. Groups	3	1	3	6	0.008	0.005	0.187	0.012
Churches Together	2	4	3	3	0.001	0.003	0.287	0.423
Comunity Garden	2	3	3	3	0.000	0.005	0.200	0.234
Food Futures	2	1	6	6	0.003	0.054	0.184	0.077

Table 2.
Centrality measures per node.

Betweenness centrality measures how often a node lies on the shortest path between two other notes. This helps to identify the brokers or gatekeepers, those with links that stretch well beyond their local network neighbours, as these nodes are the critical actors on the path for routes of exchange. Eigenvector centrality measures the influence of a node in a network concerning the importance or connectedness of its neighbours [35]. Both betweenness and eigenvector centrality refers to the effect that an organisation may have within a network. Based on their eigenvector and betweenness scores (see **Table 2**), the local authority and LGP are also the most strategically located overall to create links with other local food initiatives and share information and resources [31, 36]. The position of these organisations has been strengthened during Covid-19, indicating their potential role in structuring an organised response to the crisis, act as a bridge to facilitate information exchange and new information flows (bridging social capital), and increasing trustful connections (bonding social capital).

The following section uses data from semi-structured interviews to build on these findings and provide explanations for why Preston's local food system has remained relatively unchanged in terms of overall characteristics, but more significantly changes in relation to the strength of ties. It explains how the previous structure of the local food system helped a coordinated response to the crisis, and the role of LGP and the local authority in facilitating coordination.

2.3 The importance of previous connections for self-organisation and adaption

In addition to the survey and SNA, we conducted semi-structured, in-depth interviews with a purposively selected subset of survey respondents. Of the 21 respondents to the survey, nine participated in this Phase. Additionally, to gain a deeper insight into Preston's local food system, two local food researchers who had been involved in collaborative work within the local food system before Covid-19 were interviewed. Interviews lasted between 45 and 90 minutes, were conducted online following Covid-19 restrictions, and were recorded with the participant's consent. Interviews were transcribed, and analysis was supported by NVivo software, following Stake's [37] guidelines to qualitative case study analysis, which focuses on pattern recognition across the collected data. The use of case study analysis was intended to gather further explanatory details about the local food system and its changes.

As the SNA has shown, Preston's local food system already had a high degree of connections before Covid-19, including both bonding and bridging social capital. This is mainly because Preston's local authority had created a space in 2019 where local food initiatives within Preston could share their approach to food insecurity, could discuss various models of food aid provision, and foster mutual learning. According to participants, this initiative was taken up very positively by local food initiatives:

> *"My feeling is that they definitely, the meeting I went to, there was an enthusiasm around sharing and working together. There was a collective kind of wanting to do that [...]" (local food expert).*

This demonstrates the potential for developing bonding social capital was present before COVID-19, fostering stronger collective sharing and mutual learning. With the facilitation of the local authority, this embryonic food poverty alliance was working closely with LGP, a community gardens network initiated by the local authority, to grow and collect surplus food from allotments and gardens to use the produce in food insecurity schemes and nutrition education. These events prior to Covid-19 further suggest the centrality of local authorities in fostering coordinated approaches towards food-related issues and increasing social capital within local food systems. In addition, while the local food system was not necessarily demonstrating strong *collaborative* ties pre-Covid-19, as seen in the previous section, it reveals that providing opportunities to share information (bridging) is important in facilitating coherence between organisations and that can lead to increased bonding social capital in local food systems.

Interview findings corroborated the centrality of the local authority and the importance of previous relationships, as found through the SNA, to respond to the Covid-19 food insecurity crisis in the city. Covid-19 acted as a catalyst for the food poverty alliance by strengthening ties that pre-existed the pandemic. Pre-existing relationships that previously simply shared information, extended to collectively working towards a common purpose. In March 2020, the local authority called for a joint meeting of the food poverty alliance and other local food initiatives working on food access and LGP, leading to the creation of a WhatsApp group for coordination. Multiple interviewees reinforced the importance of the council's leadership in ensuring the successful organisation of networked responses:

> *"And that I think, really, it's just having that permanency, 'cause a lot of the organisations involved in the community food hub and the network are charity-based. So, they can't necessarily focus on that side of um, sort of leading on the project, so what [the local authority] have been doing is they've taken that kind of lead to coordinate things, and I think it definitely needs somebody like that to focus on it, 'cause we are all funding dependent, we might not be here tomorrow, but it still needs somebody to carry on and push that forward" (community food hub).*

The importance of the local authority role in coordinating the food poverty alliance is not only because many local food initiatives are reliant on external funding. Participants, including the local authority, perceived that the alliance was moderated and formed in an inclusive and accepting manner, leading to a feeling of building collective realities and a shared mission under a notion of diversity:

> *"And I think that is partly because from the onset I think we've all recognised that each of the groups are unique and offer their own individual services and I think that has been key. We are not, certainly the network isn't trying to mould everybody to deliver one certain service. It's actually recognising that everybody is [...] unique and special in their own rights" (local authority).*

This signals a high level of respect among the participants of the food poverty alliance, acknowledging the uniqueness of each. Significantly, this indicates that bonding social capital and cohesiveness can still be present in non-homogenous groups, leading to a closely connected network, yet open enough to accept new entries. This acknowledgment of diversity within the alliance has led to the development of new connections. Interviewees agreed that Covid-19 prompted new relations between organisations, which might not have been considered previously. Covid-19 prompted a closer collaboration between food banks organised by diverse faith and ethnic groups and community gardens and sustainable food initiatives. This lead to a cross-fertilisation of beliefs, demographics, and purposes. In terms of social resilience capacity, this meant that bridging social capital was invigorated, promoting channels for the food poverty alliance to expand and potentially build stronger links with heterogenous groups. Indeed, the ability to respond quickly to Covid-19 in terms of food access was attributed to the strengthening of the relationships among these diverse groups:

> *"I know from an organisational point of view, how much I became under pressure at end of March to about July and then is continuing and couldn't have done it without my partners and then having those conversations. And as you know, everybody was learning, we went from face-to-face meetings to learning a technology that nobody was au fait with [...]. Even though, there were difficult times, we got to do it all." (community centre).*

This experience emphasises the importance of developing trust and mutual support in collaborative relationships. In Preston's case, Covid-19 acted as a catalyst to reach higher levels of these attributes, helping member organisations to collectively overcome the challenges imposed by COVID-19 due to the increased strength of their connections. This increased coherence and thus new-found bonding capital among local food initiatives also meant a better response to food access concerns that might have been overlooked otherwise. Notably, this was related to the increased information sharing among organisations and the exchange of food and resources. While talking about the benefits of joint coordination, one participant explained how, with the help of various providers, they were able to respond to a gap in food access for students in the city:

> *"It came to light through one of the other organisations... There is about three or four hundred students from South India who are in Preston and... The university were just, just 'go away and leave us alone'. So, between us, between the various food providers we got on to the Vice Chancellor and said, 'What are you doing? You should be helping these people'. And... The university said, 'Oh, well we are shut down and we can't do this, and we can't do that...' And we said, 'Yes you can get a key and open the door to one of your big rooms and between us we will find food and the students can come to this one spot'" (community food market).*

This communication between the food initiatives and the university ultimately led to a process being put in place to support these students. The university was not one of the organisations identified for the SNA as they are not a significant part of the local food system in the city, but this example illustrates how a local food system with strong bridging and bonding capital can swiftly identify and support other organisations outside of already established platforms. Furthermore, the ability to feed back to the food poverty alliance was highlighted as important for making sure that those in vulnerable positions were receiving food according to their needs, culture, and eating habits. Significantly, these examples elicited reflection across the local food initiatives, and led to discussions that questioned the adequacy of some of the models and food currently being used:

> *"So, in a crisis situation sometimes you have to do things because if it's a matter of you know somebody going hungry [...] But I said that this is a plan strategy we need [...] be supporting our local small local businesses who are struggling, who may go out of business, who may be forced into poverty if we don't support them. So, you just perpetuate in that cycle and he, he's, I think he's going to get it now" (food hub).*

> *"I was having a meeting the other day and saying 'yes, we are giving food parcels out, but what else goes with giving a food parcel, how are we making a difference other than putting that food on that table, but what else has that family learned? [...] What else is happening in the house? Is there other issues? Who is actually talking?'" (community centre).*

The above statements illustrate ways in which having spaces for discussion and knowledge exchange helps initiatives to move beyond a model of emergency food aid that mainly uses surplus food. Indeed, the prominent participation of LGP, which during the pandemic decided to grow as much food as possible and collect as much fresh local food from allotments and community gardens for the food poverty alliance, has signalled a possible mechanism for introducing other local and sustainable food to address food insecurity needs. The local authority reflects this sentiment:

> *"And then of course, LGP have been key to this, because LGP work with all the local allotments [...], so LGP have been providing all the food hubs with fresh produce and continue to do so. I know in some of the areas they've been talking about more community allotments, growing spaces, having gardens where they can grow their own produce and that will definitely without a doubt will be on the agenda going forward." (local authority).*

Although 'it is by no means perfect' and 'there is still a lot to do', as participants mentioned, the development of the local food system in Preston suggests the importance of developing both bridging and bonding social capital through strong collaborative links and information exchange across the diversity of organisations in the local food system to be able to respond better to future crises. Notably, the role of local authorities has been identified as key in such a process. More importantly, the Covid-19 pandemic has fostered the creation of spaces of mutual reflection, whereby the purpose and avenues of emergency food aid are reconsidered, and more sustainable and structural strategies are considered.

3. Social resilience capabilities for improving food security outcomes during crises

This analysis of how the relationships between Preston's local food initiatives changed because of the Covid-19 pandemic reveals the importance of how social resilience capacities can help communities better respond to shocks and disturbances. Within this local food system strong communicative, sharing, and collaborative relationships and connections were already present before the pandemic hit, with engagement occurring across an already highly connected network. Collaboration, mutual sharing, and communication between different types of local food initiative indicate the presence of both bonding (strong collaborative connections) and bridging (loose relations through sharing and communicating) social capital before Covid-19. In particular, the prior formation of a food poverty alliance by the local authority provided the opportunity to construct a relatively cohesive response to food insecurity. Findings highlight that the critical component of these ties is the quick mobilisation of resources (e.g., food and information). This provided the capacity during Covid-19 to ensure food access across multiple communities during this major disruption to food systems and society's structures. Reflecting on these features of local food systems in relation to the literature on resilience and social capital, can help us better understand the role of networks of local food initiatives in adaptation, crisis mitigation and collective reflection and what these dynamics could mean for future successful food security responses.

Returning to the two types of social capital used to analyse the food security resilience capacity of Preston's local food system, it can be argued that bonding and bridging social capital worked in complementary but distinct ways before and during the crises [21]. Bonding social capital, due to preparatory work of the food poverty alliance, helped the local food system adapt quickly to new ways of delivering food, whilst bridging capital helped integrate a more diverse set of local food initiatives. As explained by Putnam, bonding social capital fosters mobilising solidarity, allowing communities to 'get by', as in the case of increasing exchange of food and resources in Preston. On the other hand, bridging social capital is essential to 'get ahead', broadening identities and reciprocity across diverse groups [21]. In this regard, despite the presence of a relatively collaborative network before Covid-19, which others have argued can limit possibilities for expansion and inclusion [13], the presence of bridging social capital before Covid-19 might have helped the 'openness' of the alliance to create bridges across local food initiatives in terms of religion, type and beneficiaries. In addition, results show how a particular emergency can increase the level and type of social capital within local food systems, from loose connections based on information sharing to collaborative ties, leading to greater bonding social capital. Increased bonding social capital has been related to trust and a sense of unity within communities [38]. Indeed, interviews highlight new levels of trust and respect among the food poverty alliance and across the local food system, working towards a common aim in a recognition of diversity as a result of newer collaborative relationships.

The literature on local food systems and local food initiatives has increasingly identified the potential benefits of increased collaboration between different types of organisations working on food-related concerns [39–41]. Our findings show that providing the space for local food initiatives to meet helps shape and develop relationships. This has enabled discussions within the local food system about some of the disadvantages of food aid and the potential to develop avenues of support that can bring about better food insecurity solutions. In particular, this has demonstrated the possibility of creating a bridge between organisations working with vulnerable communities and those focusing on local food, spaces which have previously been heavily criticised for being exclusionary and 'elitist' [42]. Moreover, food aid organisations have frequently been presented as supporting short-term strategies that concentrate on emergency patch work and sacrificing long-term solutions, thereby creating dependant and passive recipients of charity whilst also benefiting big corporations along the way [43, 44]. Providing spaces of deliberation for initiatives within the local food system to develop collective responses to food insecurity is shown to increase the possibility of questioning current models of food provisioning and to develop more imaginative structural solutions.

In addition, this study highlights the importance of a neutral organisation, with resources and strategically located in the local food system, to bridge ties between diverse organisations. Preston's case showcases the role of city councils in developing social capital within local food systems [16]. This means that urban food governance – the modes of interaction within local food systems and the operational and decision-making mechanisms that steer changes in it – have the potential to create synergies within local food systems [45]. Notably, given that local food initiatives often have limited capacities to manage collaborative spaces [46, 47], local authorities have the advantaged position to adopt a leading role in forming partnerships and strategies within the local food system and more so in times of crisis. Moreover, the above findings lend support to acknowledging the need for a coordinated response to emergency situations and crisis. However, this does not mean that, after crisis mitigation, no contingency plans should be adopted in these new collaborative spaces. Previous studies have highlighted the lack of consideration of vulnerabilities of food supply structures and crisis management plans in local food strategies and partnerships [48]. In this sense, local authorities should also take advantage of the collectivisation of food security responses to learn from the experience of the Covid-19 pandemic and ensure that structures, in combination with social resilience capacities, are in place to respond effectively to emerging risks.

Although the lessons learnt from Preston's case reveal the importance of social resilience capacities and urban food governance in being able to respond and adapt to sudden emergencies to ensure food security, the long-term impacts of the changes Covid-19 has had on the dynamics of local food systems remain to be seen. Bonding capital could lead to a close network of those already established initiatives, with less opportunity for others to join. Higher levels of trust among the food poverty alliance might also act as a barrier [36]. In particular, there is a risk of stagnation if the considerations resulting from the reflexive discussions and dialogue among local food initiatives does not lead to a broader focus beyond food poverty. Scholars indicate the deficiencies and challenges of a siloed focus of urban food governance spaces, such as diminishing its potential to create more transformative interventions [48, 49].

4. Conclusions

This article has sought to draw attention to the role of social resilience capacities in helping communities to self-organise and respond to difficult circumstances, especially during times of crises and disruption. This study is primarily aimed at revealing the structures needed to ensure that food access is guaranteed across diverse communities in all circumstances. Using SNA and semi-structured interviews with key actors within Preston's local food system, this research has helped shed some light on the relevance of social capital, both bridging and bonding, in developing collective food security responses in times of crises. Although it is essential to ensure physical infrastructures such as food supply chains and storage are in place to support food security, building social infrastructures like cohesion and trust across local food systems should also become a priority in cities to support populations, particularly those most vulnerable, in disaster. A key actor in Preston in developing these processes has been the local authority. As such, the research finds evidence good urban food governance is important for leveraging the collectivisation of food insecurity initiatives. Given that social capital can be fostered or deteriorated [16], a key focus in the future of local food systems, and urban food governance, should be on harnessing the new found bonding social capital to increase cohesiveness, but also seek to build up connections across diverse communities and local food initiatives.

While we acknowledge that our case may not be representative of all local food systems, it provides a place to begin unpacking the relevance of local food initiatives' relations in addressing food security challenges. The inclusion of diversity within already established networks and alliances within local food systems can lead to collective reflexive processes and questioning of current approaches to food system deficiencies. Future research should examine how the increased collaborative ties developed by the Covid-19 pandemic are affecting local food systems' dynamics in the long-term and if these help move those systems beyond charity-based approaches to food insecurity. A particular focus should be if the increased connectedness of communities and local food initiatives due to solidarity remains even when external shocks are no longer a threat, working towards a collective effort to ensure food for all. With increased research in these areas and others, we will begin to better understand the nuanced nature of social capital and local food initiatives relations for food security resilience and creation of long-term solutions to food insecurity within local food systems.

Author details

Tanya Zerbian*, Mags Adams and Neil Wilson
University of Central Lancashire, Preston, UK

*Address all correspondence to: tzerbian1@uclan.ac.uk

References

[1] FAO. The State of Food Insecurity in the World 2001. Rome: FAO; 2002

[2] FAO. The State of Food Security and Nutrition in the World [Internet]. The State of the World. Rome: FAO; 2021 Available from: http://www.fao.org/3/cb4474en/cb4474en.pdf

[3] Loopstra R. Vulnerability to Food Insecurity since the COVID-19 Lockdown [Internet]. Preliminary Report. London: The Food Foundation; 2020 Available from: https://foodfoundation.org.uk/sites/default/files/2021-10/Report_COVID19FoodInsecurity-final.pdf

[4] Levkoe CZ. Towards a transformative food politics. Local Environment. 2011;**16**(7):687-705. DOI: 10.1080/13549839.2011.592182

[5] González De Molina M, Lopez-Garcia D. Principles for designing agroecology-based local (territorial) agri-food Systems: A critical revision. Agroecology and Sustainable Food Systems. 2021;**45**(7):1050-1082. DOI: 10.1080/21683565.2021.1913690

[6] Bellamy AS, Furness E, Nicol P, Pitt H, Taherzadeh A. Shaping more resilient and just food systems: Lessons from the COVID-19 pandemic. Ambio. 2021;**50**(4):782-793. DOI: 10.1007/s13280-021-01532-y

[7] Béné C. Resilience of local food systems and links to food security – A review of some important concepts in the context of COVID-19 and other shocks. Food Security. 2020;**12**(4):805-822

[8] Schipanski ME, MacDonald GK, Rosenzweig S, Chappell MJ, Bennett EM, Kerr RB, et al. Realizing resilient food systems. Bioscience. 2016;**66**(7):600-610

[9] Béné C, Wood RG, Newsham A, Davies M. Resilience: New utopia or new tyranny? Reflection about the potentials and limits of the concept of resilience in relation to vulnerability reduction programmes. IDS Working Papers. 2012;**2012**:1-61

[10] Adger WN. Social and ecological resilience: Are they related? Progress in Human Geography. 2000;**24**(3):347-364. DOI: 10.1191/030913200701540465

[11] Wilson GA. Community resilience: Path dependency, lock-in effects and transitional ruptures. Journal of Environmental Planning and Management. 2014;**57**(1):1-26

[12] Armitage D, Béné C, Charles AT, Johnson D, Allison H. The interplay of well-being and resilience in applying a social-ecological perspective. Ecology and Society. 2012;**17**(4):15. DOI: 10.5751/ES-04940-170415

[13] Aldrich DP. Building Resilience: Social Capital in Post-Disaster Recovery. Chicago: University of Chicago Press; 2012

[14] Tendall DM, Joerin J, Kopainsky B, Edwards P, Shreck A, Le QB, et al. Food system resilience: Defining the concept. Global Food Security. 2015;**6**:17-23

[15] Putnam R, Leonardi R, Nanetti RY. Making Democracy Work. Civil Traditions in Modern Italy. New Jersey: Princeton University Press; 1993

[16] Aldrich DP, Meyer MA. Social capital and community resilience. The American Behavioral Scientist. 2015;**59**(2):254-269

[17] Adler PS, Kwon SW. Social capital: Prospects for a new concept. The

Academy of Management Review. 2002;**27**(1):17-40

[18] Mouw T. Estimating the causal effect of social capital: A review of recent research. Annual Review Sociology. 2006;**32**(1):79-102. DOI: 10.1146/annurev.soc.32.061604.123150

[19] Coleman JS. Foundations of Social Theory. Cambridge, MA: Harvard University Press; 1990

[20] McPherson M, Smith-Lovin L, Cook JM. Birds of a feather: Homophily in social networks. Annual Review of Sociology. 2015;**2001**(27):415-444

[21] Putnam RD. Bowling Alone: The Collapse and Revival of American Community. New York: Simon & Schuster; 2000

[22] Clément C. The New Governance of Sustainable Food Systems: Shared Insights from Four Rural Communities in Canada and the EU [PhD Dissertation]. Ottawa, Ontario: Carleton University; 2016

[23] Jarosz L. The city in the country: Growing alternative food networks in Metropolitan areas. Journal of Rural Studies. 2008;**24**(3):231-244

[24] Martin E, Nolte I, Vitolo E. The Four Cs of disaster partnering: Communication, cooperation, coordination and collaboration. Disasters. 2016;**40**(4):621-643

[25] Himmelmman AT. Collaboration for a Change [Internet]. Minneapolis: HIMMELMAN Consulting; 2002 Available from: http://tennessee.edu/wp-content/uploads/2019/07/Himmelman-Collaboration-for-a-Change.pdf

[26] Woolcock M, Narayan D. Social capital: Implications for development theory, research, and policy. World Bank Research Observer. 2000;**15**(2):225-249

[27] Christensen L, O'Sullivan R. Using social networking analysis to measure changes in regional food systems collaboration: A methodological framework. Journal of Agriculture, Food Systems, and Community Development. 2015;**5**(3):113-129

[28] Huisman M. Imputation of missing network data: Some simple procedures. In: Alhajj R, Rokne J, editors. Encyclopedia of Social Network Analysis and Mining. New York, NY: Springer; 2014

[29] Huisman M, Steglich C. Treatment of non-response in longitudinal network studies. Social Networks. 2008;**30**(4):297-308

[30] Janssen MA, Bodin Ö, Anderies JM, Elmqvist T, Ernstson H, Mcallister RRJ, et al. Toward a network perspective of the study of resilience in social-ecological systems. Ecology and Society. 2006;**11**(1):15

[31] Borgatti SP, Everett MG, Johnson JC. Analyzing Social Networks. London: SAGE Publications Ltd; 2013

[32] Wasserman S, Faust K. Social Network Analysis: Methods and Applications. Cambridge: Cambridge University Press; 1994

[33] Scardoni G, Laudanna L. Centralities based analysis of complex networks. In: Zhang Y, editor. New Frontiers in Graph Theory. London: IntechOpen; 2012. DOI: 10.5772/35846. Available from: https://www.intechopen.com/chapters/29865

[34] Hansen D, Shneiderma B, Smith M, Himelboim I. Analyzing Social Media Networks with NodeXL: Insights from a Connected World. 2nd ed. Cambridge, MA: Elsevier Inc; 2020

[35] Golbeck J. Analyzing the Social Web. Boston: Elsevier Inc.; 2013. DOI: 10.1016/B978-0-12-405531-5.00001-8

[36] Bauermeister MR. Social capital and collective identity in the local food movement. International Journal of Agricultural Sustainability. 2016;**14**(2):123-141. DOI: 10.1080/14735903.2015.1042189

[37] Stake RE. The Art of Case Study Research. Thousand Oaks, CA: Sage Publications, Inc; 1995

[38] Cheshire L, Esparcia J, Shucksmith M. Resiliencia comunitaria, capital social y gobernanza territorial. Ager. 2015;**18**:7-38. DOI: 10.11144/Javeriana.cdr13-77.nrad

[39] Holt-Giménez E, Shattuck A. Food crises, food regimes and food movements: Rumblings of reform or tides of transformation? The Journal of Peasant Studies. 2011;**38**(1):109-144. DOI: 10.1080/03066150.2010.538578

[40] Guthman J. Neoliberalism and the making of food politics in California. Geoforum. 2008;**39**(3):1171-1183. DOI: 10.1016/j.geoforum.2006.09.002

[41] Werkheiser I, Noll S. From food justice to a tool of the status quo: Three sub-movements within local food. Journal of Agricultural and Environmental Ethics. 2014;**27**(2):201-210. DOI: 10.1007/s10806-013-9459-6

[42] Alkon AH, Mares TM. Food sovereignty in US food movements: Radical visions and neoliberal constraints. Agriculture and Human Values. 2012;**29**(3):347-359. DOI: 10.1007/s10460-012-9356-z

[43] McEntee J, Naumova E. Building capacity between the private emergency food system and the local food movement: Working toward food justice and sovereignty in the global north. Journal of Agriculture, Food Systems, and Community Development. 2012;**3**(1):235-253. DOI: 10.5304/jafscd.2012.031.012

[44] Poppendieck J. Sweet Charity?: Emergency Food and the End of Entitlement. New York: Penguin Group; 1999

[45] Wiskerke JSC. On places lost and places regained: Reflections on the alternative food geography and sustainable regional development. International Planning Studies. 2009;**14**(4):369-387. DOI: 10.1080/13563471003642803

[46] Baldy J, Kruse S. Food democracy from the top down? State-driven participation processes for local food system transformations towards sustainability. Politics and Governance. 2019;**7**(4):68-80. DOI: 10.17645/pag.v7i4.2089

[47] Van de Griend J, Duncan J, Wiskerke JSC. How civil servants frame participation: Balancing municipal responsibility with citizen initiative in Ede's food policy. Politics and Governance. 2019;**7**(4):59-67. DOI: 10.17645/pag.v7i4.2078

[48] Zerbian T, de Luis RE. The role of cities in good governance for food security: lessons from Madrid's urban food strategy. Territory, Politics, Governance. 2021;**0**:1-19. DOI: 10.1080/21622671.2021.1873174

[49] Andrée P, Clark JK, Levkoe CZ, Lowitt K. Civil Society and Social Movements in Food System Governance. Oxon: Routledge; 2019

Chapter 6

Self-Sustained Communities: Food Security in Times of Crisis

Kriengsak Chareonwongsak

Abstract

The COVID-19 pandemic has caused an increase in the number of poor people around the world and led to the risk of food insecurity on a global scale. Even in Thailand, a country where food production exceeds domestic demand, the COVID-19 pandemic affects food security. The increased unemployment and the consequent loss of income resulting from the pandemics undermine food accessibility and affordability for many people. This chapter addresses the problem of food insecurity in Thailand during and after the COVID-19 crisis. It provides an analysis of the current status of food insecurity and food system resilience in Thailand and suggests solutions. It also proposes the adoption of a "Food Self-Sustained Community (FSSC)" model, which refers to the concept of building food security in a community. By planning and designing in advance, a community can switch its normal form of production seamlessly to a self-sufficiency model that prepares it for future crises, so that the community can produce enough food for all members without relying on sources outside the community.

Keywords: Food self-sustained communities, food security, food system resilience, crisis, COVID-19

1. Introduction

The spread of COVID-19 has severely affected the well-being of many people. It is not only the health effects but also the containment measures related to the pandemic that affects the economy. FAO estimated that 720–811 million people suffered from famine worldwide in 2020, a 9.9% increase from the previous year [1]. Even in Thailand, which can produce more food than its domestic demand, and by 2020 was the 13th largest food exporter in the world [2], in the face of the COVID-19 pandemic, it was reported that people consume less food or face starvation [3] disclosing a concern about access that surpasses availability.

In every crisis, food security awareness is raised and suggestions are made on how to solve the problems and develop food systems to ensure survival for countries' populations. Many different proposals for food security have been advocated, ranging from global, country, community, household, to individual levels [4–8]. There are seemingly opposite methods, such as market dependence or self-sufficiency [9], protection of domestic markets, and the liberalization of food trade [10, 11]. Players in the food system may be centralized or decentralized, and large or small entities [12, 13]. Food production knowledge and technology may be modern or indigenous [14, 15].

The objective of this chapter is to review and analyze the impact of the COVID-19 pandemic on food security in Thailand and review and analyze food system resilience and the challenges of building such resilience in a Thai context. Then, the Food Self-Sustained Community (FSSC) model will be discussed as an innovative approach to create community food system resilience and make communities competitive in normal times and self-reliant in food in times of crisis.

2. Analytical framework

The conceptual framework developed for considering the impact of the COVID-19 crisis on food security in Thailand will be based on the relationship between food systems and food security. Food systems have the following elements and activities throughout the food supply chain:

- factors of food production (the supply of agrochemicals, such as fertilizers and pesticides, as well as animal feeds, water, and agricultural credit)

- food production (the methods by which agricultural products are produced, namely arable farming, horticulture, animal husbandry, fishery, and forestry),

- food processing (the conversion of agricultural products into consumable food, such as food manufacturing, food preparation, and food preservation),

- food stock, food markets, and trade (such as food distribution channels, food marketing and sales, food exports and imports, and food aid),

- and food consumption (including consumption behavior, demand, and purchasing power).

These elements and activities are linked by food transportation, logistics, and finance [6, 16–18]. The four pillars of food security are food availability, food access, food utilization, and food stability [19].

Based on literature reviews [19–22], this conceptual framework assumes that the elements and activities of food systems and food security are related as follows (**Table 1**)—factors of food production, food production, food processing, and food stock are related to food availability and stability, as they are related to the supply of food products. Food consumption is related to food utilization. Food stocks, markets, trade, logistics, and finance are correlated with food availability, access, and stability because they are activities that relate to food distribution. In addition, the four pillars of food security are also interrelated, for example, food production and food stock affect food availability and food price stability, which affects food accessibility.

For the analysis of the impact of COVID-19 on the Thailand food system, the shocks on the food system are divided into four components—health crisis (the situation due to the outbreak), containment measures (pandemic control measures such as lockdown and the closing of borders), economic crisis (economic depression due to the effects of the outbreak and the containment measures), and the international situation and the response of foreign countries (**Figure 1**).

Food System	Food Security			
	Availability	Access	Utilization	Stability
Factors of production	X			X
Production and Process	X			X
Stock	X	X		X
Market and Trade	X	X		X
Consumption			X	
Logistics and Finance	X	X		X

Note: Definitions of the four pillars of food security are based on FAO's definition in "An Introduction to the Basic Concepts of Food Security," 2008. Availability refers to the availability of a sufficient supply of food. Access refers to the ability of individuals to acquire sufficient food. Utilization refers to the ability of individuals to utilize food to achieve a state of nutritional well-being. Stability refers to the stability of the other three dimensions of food security over time.

Table 1.
Relationship between the food system and food security.

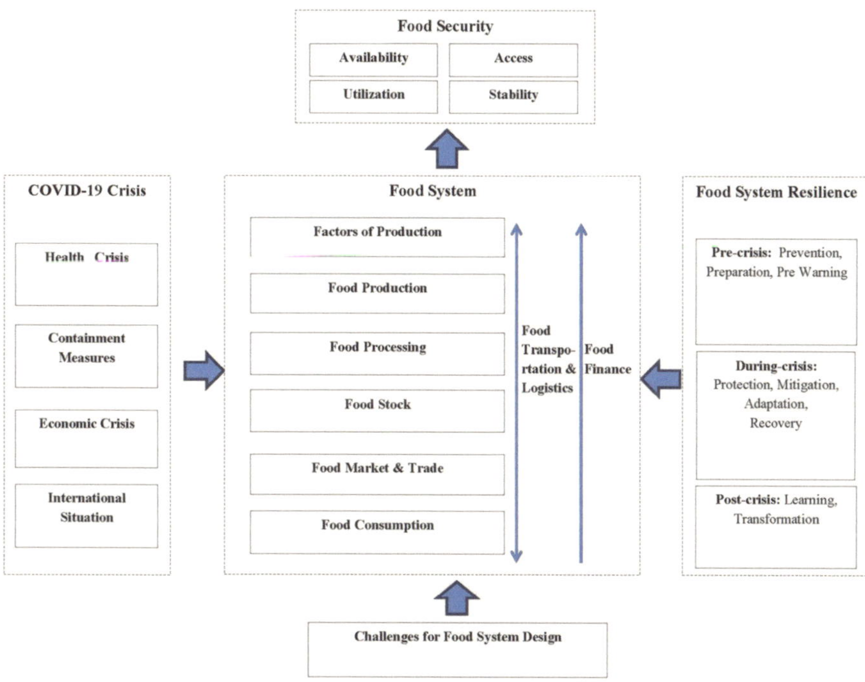

Figure 1.
Framework for analysis—The impact of COVID-19 on food security.

An analysis of food system resilience will also follow the elements and activities of food systems, classified into three periods—pre-crisis, during the crisis, and post-crisis. The term "crisis" means situations where the food system malfunctions and poses a risk of food insecurity due to COVID-19 outbreaks and the responses from governments and other sectors. The pre-crisis food system resilience consists of the ability to prevent crises (prevention), preparedness to deal with the crises (preparation), and the pre-warning system. Food system resilience during a crisis consists of protection from the impact of the crisis (protection), mitigating the effects of the crisis (mitigation), adaptation to cope with the crisis (adaptation), and recovery.

Post-crisis resilience analysis is unrealized. Therefore, the analysis is based on what has been learned (learning) by the authors to provide suggestions for improvement (transformation) of food system resilience in Thailand [23–25]. Other challenges affecting food system design are then analyzed, in particular the trade-off between the system goals and future risks for food security.

3. Impact of COVID-19 on the food system in Thailand

The COVID-19 outbreak in Thailand commenced in January 2020 and the government announced a nationwide lockdown and closed borders for the first time in late March 2020 (these measures were relaxed 3–4 months later). In the first wave of the outbreak, 4237 people were reported as infected. A second wave of the pandemic occurred from late 2020 to March 2021, affecting some areas of the country. As a result, lockdowns were announced for five provinces that had experienced outbreaks, with a total of 24,626 people reported to be infected. Later, a third wave occurred, in April 2021, resulting in the infection of more than 2 million people, as of December 2021 [26], and prompting the government to close down establishments, department stores, restaurants and announce the imposition of a curfew until the end of August 2021. The medical care and state quarantine systems were unable to cope with the situation, therefore, it was necessary to switch to home isolation by allowing those without severe symptoms to be treated at home [27]. The Omicron variant has caused a 4th wave of the Covid-19 outbreak in Thailand, with more infections after the new year 2022. However, the number of infections in the 4th wave was not as high as expected and the symptoms of those infected are less severe, and therefore, the government relaxed closures and containment measures. **Figure 2** shows the level of measures taken by the Thai government to control COVID-19 in line with the

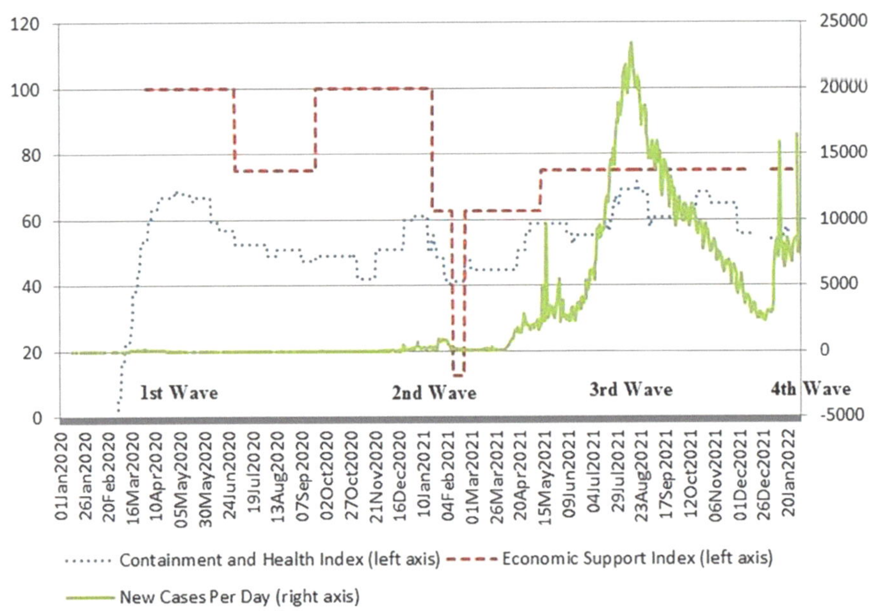

Figure 2.
The Thai government's responses to COVID-19 and daily new cases.

severity of the outbreak [28, 29]. The pandemic and the government control measures have resulted in a generalized economic recession. These factors and situations have affected the food system and caused food insecurity in Thailand.

Note: The Containment and Health Index is a composite index that is calculated from 14 component indicators include eight indicators related to closures and containment measures (namely school closures, workplace closures, cancelation of public events, restrictions on gatherings, reductions in public transport, stay at home requirements, restrictions on internal movement, and International travel controls) and six indicators related to health measures (namely public information campaigns, testing policy, contact tracing, facial coverings, vaccination policy, and the protection of elderly people). The Economic Support Index is a composite index that is calculated from two component indicators related to economic measures namely, Income support and Debt/contract relief for households.

Data source: Hale, Thomas, Sam Webster, Anna Petherick, Toby Phillips, and Beatriz Kira (2020). Oxford COVID-19 Government Response Tracker, Blavatnik School of Government. Data use policy: Creative Commons Attribution CC BY standard.

3.1 Impact on factors of production

The COVID-19 outbreak has caused an increase in the prices of imported production factors because of the imposition of restrictions to contain outbreaks of the virus. This has been especially the case in chemical fertilizers, which have seen large price increases since the middle of 2020, due to the reduced production of raw materials for fertilizer production and the increase in shipping costs due to container shortages for international shipping [30]. For example, the Urea price increased (in USD per metric ton) from $216 in May 2020 to $418 in September 2021.

Thailand is heavily dependent on imports of chemical fertilizers, which comprise almost all of the country's total use [31]. This means that the country's food system will be unable to avoid the impact of COVID-19.

Thailand's agricultural sector faces a problem of labor shortage because most of the country's farms are small and labor-intensive. They also employ a large number of foreign workers, often seasonal migrant labor [32]. The closure of the borders to contain COVID-19 caused foreign workers to panic and many left the country and were then unable to return to Thailand [33]. In the first 6 months of 2020, there was a reduction of around 545,000 foreign workers in Thailand or 18.2% of the total usual number of migrant workers in Thailand [34].

The agricultural sector is also at risk of a shortage of funding for the production of the next cultivation due to losses and lower household income. The increased cost of inputs, with a decrease in revenue due to reduced demand for food (because the lockdown measures have caused the economic recession and have limited the travel of foreign tourists), will cause food producers to suffer losses [35]. In addition, 76% of Thai agricultural households rely on nonagricultural income and 75% of the households have members working outside the agricultural sector [36]. Owing to the recession, nonagricultural workers now have lower incomes and there is increased unemployment. This will cause the total income of agricultural households to decrease as well.

3.2 Impact on food production and processing

The first wave of the COVID-19 outbreak caused the GDP of Thailand's agricultural sector in 2020 to contract by 3.3% compared to the previous year [37]. Factors that contributed to the decline in agricultural GDP were border closure and lockdown measures [38]. However, effective control measures implemented in response to the first wave of outbreak increased the export of some food products, because Thai food products were trusted to be disease-free, while other food-producing countries had more severe outbreaks [39].

However, the second wave of the pandemic, which occurred at the end of 2020, centered on the fishing industry workforce cluster and the country's large seafood wholesale market, severely affected seafood production and caused some countries to ban the import of seafood from Thailand [40]. Similarly, during the third wave of the pandemic outbreaks occurred in factories, including a large food-processing factory. As a result, the factories were shut down to disinfect and control the outbreak among workers, resulting in some food products being in shortage of supply for a period of time [41].

3.3 Impact on food stocks, market, and trade

In the macro view (national scale), food production in Thailand is sufficient to meet the needs of the country's people. But in the micro view (household and individual scales), some people face the problem of not having access to food. The risk of spreading disease in restaurants, wholesale and retail markets of agricultural products caused the government to announce the closure of these places from time to time to limit the spread of the pandemic, resulting in the blockage of the usual food distribution channels [42]. Although the government allowed restaurants and food shops to offer take-home and home delivery meals, home dining behavior resulted in lower consumption than eating at restaurants and food shops. In addition, at certain times COVID-19 also affected food price stability in Thailand. For example, the lockdown during the first wave of the outbreak resulted in soaring rice prices [43] and public anxiety led to food hoarding, resulting in short-term food shortages [42].

3.4 Impact on food consumption

The border closure and lockdown measures greatly reduced food demand due to the disappearance of about 40 million foreign tourists and exports. The economic recession caused by the pandemic control measures resulted in many workers suffering a reduced income and unemployment. It is estimated that up to 6 million workers experienced a reduced income or unemployment [44], especially workers in the tourism sector. Affected people, especially the poor, unemployed workers, and vulnerable groups, have a reduced ability to buy food. A survey conducted by the International Health Policy Program found that as many as 85.4% of low-income residents in urban slums experienced food insecurity due to declining incomes, higher food prices, and difficulty in purchasing food [45]. Similarly, rural smallholder farmers engaged in monocultural agriculture were affected by the lack of channels to sell their produce. Reverse immigration of household members from the city to rural areas increased the pressure on rural households, due to increased household food needs [46]. These people experiencing economic hardships had to adjust their dietary habits by reducing their food consumption and switching to cheaper and less nutritious foods [45].

3.5 Impact on food logistics and finance

The COVID-19 crisis has affected the distribution of food by reducing the flow of food products and finance in the food system. Concerns about the spread of pathogens through food transport have increased costs in food safety control processes. The closure of food retail and wholesale markets has resulted in higher food transportation and distribution costs due to a lack of distribution centers [47]. Higher food logistics costs hinder access to food for people with lower incomes and lower their purchasing power.

The lockdown has also prevented some groups of people from accessing adequate and quality food because alternative food distribution channels have not been developed to replace the old channels that have been closed. For example, patients or people who are quarantined under the home isolation system have difficulty going out to buy food because the authorities require that they must be detained at home. However, no alternative food supply system was provided for this group of people [48]. Closing schools and replacing them with online learning means that schoolchildren in poor families are not able to enjoy quality school lunches. People suffering from malnutrition have been unable to receive nutrients from medical services in hospitals because doctors and nurses have heavy workloads from caring for COVID-19 patients and also due to the cutting of the public health budget allocated for other diseases [3].

4. Food system resilience in Thailand

The COVID-19 crisis has prompted a response from various sectors to intervene in the food system to address food insecurity and improve the adaptation of players and elements in the system. This section comprises a review and analysis of the status of food system resilience in Thailand, both before and during the crisis. Lessons obtained are then used to suggest changes to Thailand's food system during the post-crisis period.

4.1 Factors of production resilience

4.1.1 Pre-Crisis

Thailand's food system is at risk of uncertainty. The agricultural sector has the highest number of poor people compared to other sectors. In addition, in this sector, the elderly account for 46% of the total workers and this percentage is likely to increase [49]. Half of the country's farmers do not own their land and 56% of farmers owning land possess less than 10 rai (4 acres) of land [50]. Land use for energy crops and nonagricultural activities is also increasing, and only 22% of agricultural land is irrigated [51]. Moreover, most agricultural activities are dependent on inputs from foreign producers and large domestic companies, such as producers of chemical fertilizers, pesticides, plant breeding, animal breeding, and animal feed [52].

In the past, the government has continuously issued various policies and measures to solve these problems, for example, taxation of land and buildings to reduce the problem of landholding without use; provision of the Sor Por Kor 4-01 agricultural land title deeds to the poor; re-zoning of agricultural land use and zoning of food crops and energy crops; and development of water management systems and expansion of irrigated areas [53, 54]. However, the solutions to the problems are still difficult to implement. As a result, alternative economy groups have offered food sovereignty as a solution as part of a campaign to enable small farmers to own food inputs independently of the monopoly of big business [55].

4.1.2 During the Crisis

To cope with the COVID crisis, the government has taken measures to alleviate short-term shortages of production factors, such as a project to support subsidies for farmers, a moratorium on debt, a reduction of debt burdens, and extending the loan repayment period for Bank for Agriculture and Agricultural Cooperatives customers [56]. The border closure measure was relaxed temporarily to allow the importation of workers to work in the agricultural sector [34].

4.1.3 Post-crisis

The lesson is that Thailand is at risk of facing food insecurity due to its high dependence on imports of food production factors from abroad, especially chemical fertilizers. At the national level, the development of the production capacity of agricultural inputs is therefore an answer to prevent shocks to the food system, such as the development of the domestic fertilizer industry or promoting organic agriculture to reduce the use of agrochemicals. At the base level, it is difficult for small-scale farmers to be self-reliant on all inputs. But if farmers cannot control or rely on themselves in terms of all the factors of production, there is a risk that food production will be disrupted in times of crisis.

4.2 Food-production and food-processing resilience

4.2.1 Pre-Crisis

Although Thailand can produce more food than the demand, the risk is that the agricultural sector has the lowest productivity compared to other sectors. The agriculture sector accounts for 30% of the workforce, but only 10% of GDP [57]. Most farmers are smallholders, resulting in low productivity because they cannot use high-priced machinery and have to rely on foreign unskilled workers. Most agriculture production is monoculture, resulting in low food diversity. Agricultural products in Thailand are concentrated on just 5 or 6 crops, some of which are non-food crops or those which are low in nutritional value. Vegetable farming occupies 0.9% of the total agricultural land use and concentrates on only eight types of vegetables [58]. In response, the government has promoted large farms to improve productivity and the use of agricultural technology. The Young Smart Farmer project was established to promote the new generation of farmers in the adoption of precision agriculture. On the other hand, some NGOs are trying to promote agroecological sustainable intensification [59].

4.2.2 During the Crisis

Rural areas with diverse food production or a food security system that had been set up in advance were less affected by the crisis. Meanwhile, urban slums offer less food security than rural communities and rural smallholders who cultivate monocultures, and consequently, are affected to a greater extent. Some communities (such as the Karen community, Ban Pa Tung Ngam, Chiang Mai Province) were not seriously affected by the outbreak and lockdown measures because they had a self-sufficient production system and there was a system in place for those affected to receive assistance. For example, highland hill tribe communities consist of largely self-sufficient villages and have a culture of sharing food with the poor. These communities, in addition to producing enough food to consume in the community, can also share food with the people of other communities [60].

The outbreak also led to more qualitative improvements in food production, in particular a focus on the development of food safety standards [61]. Food production for export was also forced to develop safety and sanitation standards, especially fruit exports to China. In addition, the government requires large industrial plants to use "Bubble and Seal" measures to control the spread of the disease in factories [62]. This allows better control and limits the spread of the outbreak, but creates higher costs for entrepreneurs as well.

4.2.3 Post-crisis

The lesson is that the economy of scale is important to the competitiveness of food production, but the economy of scope is essential to food availability and utilization. A community that can produce its own food will be less affected by unexpected shocks than communities that are unable to produce food at all. And communities that are prepared in advance are better able to cope with crises than communities that are not ready. Development of the resilience of the food system must be done before the crisis.

4.3 Food stock, market, and trade resilience

4.3.1 Pre-Crisis

Under normal circumstances, the market mechanism plays a role in ensuring food availability, stability, physical access to food through the reserve, distribution, and trade of food. Food access channels for consumers in Thailand are diverse, ranging from modern trade, e-commerce, community markets, and hawker stalls to mobile grocery stores. However, the channels through which farmers can sell their food products directly to customers and retailers are still limited. The controversy about the market system of agricultural products in Thailand concerns oligopoly or exploitation by middlemen or large businesses. Big agribusinesses will purchase food products only on a contract farming basis with the condition that the farmers must purchase all their inputs from those businesses. On the other hand, the big agribusinesses argue that the mechanism is like a service and a marketing guarantee to farmers, most of whom lack marketing capabilities [63, 64].

4.3.2 During the Crisis

The COVID crisis has led to community adaptation. Community markets have been established on a local level by members of local communities for farmers to bring their products to sell locally, while some farmers have adapted to selling food products directly to consumers through networks of relatives and friends in cities and online systems or online marketplaces [65]. Meanwhile, some communities (such as Ban Pa Pae, Mae Hong Son Province) had already prepared food reserve systems to ensure that community members do not have shortages of the food products they need in times of crisis. For example, community food banks or rice banks, where people in the community stored rice in a collective barn for members to borrow for consumption, on the condition that it must be returned in kind, or as money, with interest in the following year [66].

4.3.3 Post-crisis

According to economic theory, fully competitive markets make food allocation and distribution more efficient. However, the agricultural markets in Thailand are not truly competitive [67]. Moreover, crises tend to affect food markets, to a greater or lesser extent. Therefore, having a food reserve system is essential for maintaining food security at all levels. In addition, the development of marketability, alternative channels, and reserve channels in selling the products of farmers and food producers are important steps, to create continuity in food production for smallholders and reduce food waste caused by unsold products.

4.4 Food consumption resilience

4.4.1 Pre-Crisis

The food access situation in Thailand is determined by economic factors rather than social factors. Thailand has reduced the number and proportion of the poor continuously. The number of people living below the poverty line has continued to decline from 34 million, or 65.17% of the country's total population in 1988, to 4.3 million, or 6.24% in 2019, but there are still 5.4 million near-poor people or 7.79% of the country's population. The Thai government has provided income benefits that are quite inclusive for nearly all groups, from child support subsidies up to the age of 6, school lunch subsidies, a pension for the elderly and the disabled, to a living allowance for the 14.5 million people who hold state welfare cards. Still, these programs provide a relatively limited amount of funding. Moreover, the identification of the poor is not entirely accurate, with inclusion and exclusion errors [68].

4.4.2 During the Crisis

The response to the impact of COVID-19 on food security in Thailand has emphasized the role of the government sector and demand-side interventions. For affected workers who are in the formal economy, unemployment compensation and cash transfer from the Social Security Fund will be provided. But Thailand also has a large number of informal workers, comprising around 54% of the labor force [69]. The government therefore issued economic remedial measures to address the impact of the pandemic and lockdown measures, including cash transfers, conditional cash transfers, reductions in public utility costs, a debt moratorium, and expansion of soft loans for businesses to maintain employment and maintain people's ability to access food.

However, the government aid measures are not enough. Most of them are short-term measures, lasting only 2–3 months during the lockdown. But the economic recession has caused a large number of people to be unemployed and revenues have declined for a longer duration than just during the lockdown period. During the first wave of the pandemic, 30.5 million people, or 40% of the country's population, received cash transfers. However, even though the government's cash transfer measures have covered a large number of people, as many as 3 million people are still missing out on the state aid measures. These include marginalized people, bedridden patients, and those who cannot register for assistance [70].

4.4.3 Post-crisis

The lesson is that tackling poverty and inequality including income insurance (unemployment insurance) is an important factor in reducing the impact of the crisis and maintaining people's ability to access food. But a large number of informal workers creates asymmetric information problems, which prevents governments from helping people affected by food shortages. It also forces governments to take universal measures, which is ineffective in budgeting. The question is, for a developing country like Thailand with a large informal economy, how can the lack of information and income insurance for the poor, marginalized, and other vulnerable groups be solved?

4.5 Food logistics resilience

4.5.1 Pre-Crisis

Thailand lacks planning or preparation of systems for dealing with different types of crises, in particular, a system for allocation of aid and distribution of food and necessities to those affected by crises sufficiently and thoroughly. In several past crises, government measures to address food insecurity have been often ad hoc and failed to provide food for all of these vulnerable groups. Businesses and civil societies, therefore, had to come in and fill the gaps in food systems. However, it was often scattered, redundant, lacking in continuity and organization [71].

4.5.2 During the Crisis

The cooperation of government, business, and civil society has a role to play in closing the gaps in state measures that are inaccessible to some vulnerable groups. Civil society organizations that were taking care of vulnerable groups before the crisis play an important role in providing food through community kitchens and food banks to groups that often do not have access to government aid measures [72]. Networks of civil society organizations also play a role in matching food supply and demand, by purchasing food from smallholder farmers who are unable to sell their products for sale or distribution to people who need food [73]. Likewise, the armed services, including the air force and army, help facilitate food exchanges between far-flung communities, for example, using planes to transport rice products from hill tribe communities in the north in exchange for dried fish, which is a food product of maritime communities in the south [74].

Business organizations' Corporate Social Responsibility activities include the distribution of supplementary food to different groups of people, as well as encouraging people to participate in food donation campaigns. One form of food donation that was very popular in the first wave of the outbreak was "Happiness-sharing Pantries", placing cupboards in public places for people to donate or pick up food to consume [75]. However, the assistance was done by various groups of people in an *ad hoc* way, and there was no central cooperation and organization of assistance systems so that they were comprehensive, adequate, and continuous. One problem with the Happiness-sharing Pantries projects is that some people took all the food from cupboards until there was nothing left to share with others. This problem caused donors to become discouraged and eventually ended the project [76].

4.5.3 Post-crisis

The lesson is that cooperation between government, business, and people sectors is essential to building food security, especially the provision and delivery of food to vulnerable groups. A civil society organization that works closely with a particular community on an ongoing basis will access information on vulnerable groups and will serve as a mechanism that allows food to be delivered to those people who are in real need. But in the macro view, information systems about vulnerable groups and food aid delivery system design are required to make assistance available to everyone. Moreover, ensuring people's food security should not be merely seen as a relief, but should also develop food self-reliance.

5. Challenges of building food system resilience in Thailand

Building food system resilience for food security in Thailand also faces challenges due to a trade-off, or conflict, between several issues, described in the following section.

5.1 Market vs. self-sufficiency

Controversies about food systems inevitably emerge during every crisis, when difficulties are created and many people are exposed to food insecurity risks. Proposals on the food system in Thailand vary between the two extremes of a continuum, self-sufficiency and free trade. The main controversy focuses on whether the Thai agricultural system should be one of market agriculture, which focuses on production for sale in response to market demand, or self-sufficiency agriculture, which focuses on production for one's own consumption. If there is any leftover produce, then this can be sold [4].

The supporting rationale for the market-based production system is to create wealth through specialized production, which enables efficient use of economic resources. Market-based production provides food security because food production increases and prices are lower while consumers still have access to a variety of quality food through market mechanisms [77]. The potential negative aspect of this is that farmers who do not improve productivity could suffer lower incomes, putting them at risk of food insecurity.

However, it is argued that, under normal circumstances, the system of global food trade is not fully free and competition is not fair due to the implementation of measures to protect domestic agricultural markets and subsidize farmers within developed countries. In times of crisis, market mechanisms may fail, to the extent that farmers cannot rely on outside markets. Market-based production also makes the structure of food production homogenous. This makes it more dependent on food imports from foreign countries or from outside the area, which then increases the risk of food insecurity [78].

On the other hand, self-sufficiency production focuses on producing more diverse foods, which reduces the risk of food insecurity [79, 80]. The self-sufficiency production system also focuses on mixed farming and animal husbandry by imitating nature, resulting in high quality and safe food production. It also creates food sovereignty by reducing dependency on imports and inputs from large companies and maintaining the fertility of the soil, as well as water and ecosystems. However, the efficiency, competitiveness [81], and producer motivation of self-sufficiency production have been questioned, because it is seen as requiring farmers to adopt a plain lifestyle without many amenities.

5.2 Macro versus Micro

There is a question about what level the unit of analysis on food security should be: individual, household, community, national or global. In the past, the food security concept emphasized a unit of analysis at the macro level, considering global or national food security. This can be observed from definitions, debates, policies recommendations, and the design of food security indicators, which generally focus on the national or international context, for example, the debates about whether to liberalize food trade or not and the development of international comparative food security indicators. Subsequently, there has been an increase in interest in food security at the micro level, that is at the community, household, and individual scales [14, 82].

Macro-level food security will ensure everyone in the world or an individual country has the opportunity for food security, but that does not mean it will always lead to micro-level food security, especially in times of crisis where food transport is limited or market systems have failed. Emphasis on achieving food self-sufficiency at the national level may distract governments from addressing food security at the household level [83]. Ensuring macro-level food security is often the role of the state, but, in practice, governments are often unable to ensure food security for all citizens because too large a unit creates asymmetric information problems. On the other hand, micro-level food security practices will help fill gaps that the government has failed to cover and alleviate the burden on the government [84]. There is still an argument that it is not possible, even at a national level, to be self-sufficient in all types of food [85]. The question is what is the optimal size of the analytical unit? Is it small enough to ensure that everyone is cared for and large enough to provide adequate food in terms of quality and quantity? In fact, food security at the household and individual levels cannot be guaranteed without national food security. Therefore, building food security may need to be undertaken at all levels but the question is how each level of food security should be organized.

5.3 Efficiency versus stability

A common phenomenon in Thailand is that the countryside serves as a social cushion in times of crisis. Under normal circumstances, many rural people migrate to cities in search of the better economic opportunities that they offer in comparison to rural areas. But every time there is a severe crisis, to survive, people migrate back to their rural homelands [86, 87]. This can be seen in the COVID-19 crisis, where, in the first wave of the outbreak in February–April 2020, it is estimated that 2 million people migrated back to the countryside, and, in the second half of 2020, a monthly average of 200,000 migrated back to the countryside [46]. However, this does not mean that everyone in the city has a country house to migrate back to. Consequently, many people in crisis-affected cities are still at high risk of food insecurity.

At present, the idea of urban farming is gaining more and more attention. But there is a question regarding whether it is necessary for households or urban communities to produce their own food. The price of land in the city is high, therefore, urban food production has a very high opportunity cost compared to rural food production.

However, urban food production has advantages in terms of transportation and logistics costs. Would using urban land to produce food be more cost-effective than buying food from the countryside? On the contrary, if there is no preparation for hedging at all, urban communities will also suffer a lot of damage when a severe crisis occurs.

An interesting question is what should be the cost of hedging for food insecurity risks? The risk management principle states that the cost of hedging is equal to the likelihood of a crisis multiplied by the impact of the crisis. In history, severe crises are likely to occur only occasionally, or infrequently, but if they happen, the impact is so severe that there are many deaths. However, the changes in today's world may be a catalyst for more frequent crises and increase the need for hedging.

Chareonwongsak [88] states that the world has entered the "Pandemic New Normal" era, where pandemics will become more frequent so that it becomes a new normal. The world is more connected and more people live in cities, making pandemics easier to occur and spread faster. This is consistent with the "IPBES Workshop Report on Biodiversity and Pandemics," which indicates that future pandemics will occur more frequently, spread faster, and inflict more damage [89]. There is the possibility of a black swan or an unprecedented crisis because there are new predisposing factors, such as severe climate change and cyber-attacks on countries' financial systems or food chains [90].

6. Suggestions on building food system resilience in Thailand: the FSSC model

The fact that Thailand is a food producer and net exporter makes food security issues seem less of a concern. But the spread and impact of COVID-19 have helped to reveal the fact that the food system in Thailand is still vulnerable to food insecurity for many people. It also reveals the country's under-preparedness to deal with crises. The weakness in the Thai food system is that the Thai government lacks information about people at risk of food inaccessibility due to the large proportion of informal workers while most of the workers in developed countries are formal workers. The government mainly uses macro-level measures, namely cash transfer, to address food inaccessibility. But there is a lack of an alternative system to distribute food to people who have not received help. In a world where crises are more frequent, food system resilience needs to be built to face crises of all forms and levels of severity as well as maintain food security for everyone, therefore, an innovative food system model is required. The food system must be developed at both the macro and micro levels and have the ability to maintain food security in both normal and critical times without exorbitant cost.

The FSSC model presented in this chapter is a proposal for developing food system resilience to protect food security in Thailand. This concept developed from a stream of several concepts—the Mid-stream economy [91], Self-sustained communities [92], and the Linked self-sustained communities [92], applying these concepts in the context of building food security.

This concept stream consists of four main components. First, strength-based production and liberalization of food trade to create wealth during normal times. Second, self-sufficiency in food in times of crisis and at all levels. Third, preparation of a switching mechanism/policy design for readiness in changing the mode, between liberalization in normal situations and self-sufficiency in times of crisis. And fourth, the interconnection of food systems between communities and between all levels to ensure food security at both micro and macro levels.

The development of the FSSC aims to make area-based communities self-sufficient in food in times of crisis for a number of reasons.

First of all, future crises could limit domestic and international food trade and transport. For example, a hyper-inflation crisis or a cyber-attack on the financial system of the country or the world could make it impossible to use the money to buy food. Future pandemic crises could also force governments to use lockdown measures and close borders.

Secondly, the food system at the household level is usually too small to be self-sufficient in food. Meanwhile, countries are too large to be aware of all information and to allocate timely assistance to all people during crises. Therefore, a community that is not so small that it cannot be self-sufficient, or so large that members are not related to each other, is the right unit to maintain food security in times of crisis.

Thirdly, building food security in communities in times of severe crises (which lead to food system failures through wars, disasters, hyperinflation, and similar events) must temporarily integrate all food system activities in the community, to shorten the food supply chain and to build the ability to supply enough food to the people in the community for a given period of time.

Fourth, communities should be self-sufficient in food only in times of crisis in order not to lose the opportunity to create wealth from carrying out economic activities according to the strength of the community during normal times.

The creation of the FSSC has the following strategic proposals:

6.1 Promoting integration into FSSC

FSSCs may be built on the base of existing area-based communities or create new ones by bringing together groups of people who are related and share the common intent to create an FSSC. FFSCs may develop on the concept of Work-Life Integration [93], by creating communities that facilitate people working and living in the same area, as well as the benefit of preventing the effects of epidemics that may occur in the future.

6.2 Designing food systems in the community

Ensuring that communities have enough food in times of crisis must come from setting goals. How many members does the community have? How much food, and how many different types are needed? How long should a community supply food to its members during a crisis? Communities must design and plan in advance where, in times of crisis, they will get their food from, what to produce, how to produce, how much, how to stock input and food products, and how to allocate food products to community members. However, the design of a community food system requires consideration of the conditions, constraints, and context of each community.

6.3 Joint production planning in the community

FSSC may be the solution to the problems in the Thai agricultural sector with many small farmers and elderly workers. FSSC promotes the integration of agricultural farms for joint production planning, procuring, and sharing inputs and resources, including the use of technology and agricultural machinery together which will create an economy of scale. At the same time, farmers in the FSSC may plan to produce a variety of yields to distribute products together and share revenues together. This will allow the community to produce a variety of food products. It also creates an economy of scope and diversification of risks.

6.4 Developing the FSSC system and infrastructure

Developing FSSCs to be able to switch to self-sufficiency, community systems, and infrastructures needs to be done in advance, such as community water storage, community seed banks, community gardens, community alternative energy generation systems, community food banks, community markets and food allocation systems, community data management and information systems (such as projections for production, stock, and community food needs), and community savings promotion and welfare systems.

6.5 Promoting education and R&D on FSSC

FSSC's food production may be unique and differ according to the context and limitations of each community. In times of crisis, where communities cannot rely on sources or agents outside the community, the FSSC food production system tends to be a closed-loop food system, where the outputs and waste from one activity are inputs to other activities until it becomes a cycle or ecosystem. Food production in urban communities with limited space, technology, and methods needs to be developed to optimize the use of space. Also, training for members of the FSSC and the promotion of food system-related R&D in the FSSC needs to be supported.

6.6 Community development based on the strength of the community

In normal times, each FSSC should have a development and production approach that matches the strengths of the community. Each FSSC development should not have the same pattern or produce the same goods and services over and over. But each community should be developed according to its strength, ideology, wisdom, identity, value, image, and uniqueness. Thus, each FSSC will have a unique selling point that will enable it to create more added value for its products and services. Then, a strong economy in a community can also be a better shield against the impact of a crisis.

6.7 Design and preparation of switching mechanisms

The FSSC food system should be developed to be as competitive as possible under normal conditions to enable the FSSC to be able to produce and sell food continuously, without much subsidization or intervention. However, during normal times, it is not necessary for every FSSC to produce all its own food requirements. But a switching mechanism must be designed and prepared to be able to supply food to the entire community in the event of a crisis, such as preparation of a community food reserve system, transformation of vacant spaces in communities and individual households into food production areas, changing the type of food produced to be more versatile, faster yielding, changing cultivation methods for higher yields (despite the fact that the product characteristics may not be as beautiful as before, such as smaller fruits, thinner vegetables), etc. The switching mechanism encompasses the development of leadership, management, morals, and community systems such as structure, processes, rules, and culture that encourage community members to be willing to switch to a self-sufficiency mode.

6.8 Connecting FSSC networks

In fact, it is unlikely that each community will be able to produce food for its own consumption forever without having to rely on the world outside the community at all. Therefore, FSSCs should establish a network to link with other FSSCs and to enable the trading, exchange, and sharing of knowledge, resources, products, and risks. For example, food production planning between communities, the development of food supply chains between communities, the development of food logistics, information and finance between communities, the organization of knowledge sharing and resources among the communities, and the development of food exchange and sharing systems among communities in times of crisis. The link between FSSCs will help support the development of communities in normal times and increase the ability to self-sufficiency and restoration of the community's food system in times of crisis.

6.9 Developing FSSC promotion policy

Governments should develop national policies to promote FSSC, including academic and financial support for FSSC transformation, developing prototypes and learning centers for FSSC in both urban and rural areas, designing urban development and building a community that integrates both workplaces and living facilities in the same area, land use planning and zoning of food production, developing information systems for food system management at the national level, developing early warning systems, developing public-private cooperation systems for food production and distribution in a systematic, thorough and continuous manner, developing international food security cooperation, and the development of food diplomacy.

7. Conclusion

The COVID-19 crisis has affected food security and revealed the shortcomings of the food system in Thailand. The FSSC is an innovative idea resulting from the synthesis of the good points of various food economy systems, with the aim of ensuring food security in both normal and critical times. The development of FSSCs also emphasizes preparation to prevent the impact of crises on food insecurity in communities without creating excessive expenses or opportunity costs. In normal times, FSSCs can also connect to the global market to produce goods and services according to their strengths to create wealth. But communities are designed to be ready to adapt to self-reliance in times of crisis.

However, the FSSC model is still just a concept and it has never been implemented in practice. In addition, the concept development took place from the consideration of Thailand's context, which is a country capable of producing enough food to meet overall domestic demand. Therefore, in applying this concept to other countries with different contexts, it is necessary to adapt it appropriately to the local context. Developing FSSCs involves not just the design of food systems, but the design of communities, which is more complicated because it has to take into account the economic, societal, and political dimensions in each community and also the motivational dimensions, relationships, and other dimensions of human beings. Finally, the FSSC model also needs studies, research, and experimental development of the prototype to improve the model for practical application.

The FSSC model and its associated thoughts have overlays and differentiated parts from City Region Food Systems (CRFS) supported by RUAF [94]. Both concepts have the same goals, namely food security, sustainable development, economic development, and social inclusion and equity. FSSC has a focus on improving area-based community food security and extending communities' connectivity. CRFS focuses on improving the food security of the city-center food system that is linked to the surrounding area. By successfully pushing the FSSC model, it is possible to learn from the CRFS, for example, building cooperation and inclusive participation, formulating an academic-based development strategy and taking into account the context of the food system in each area, developing the capacity of individuals and organizations involved, and building effective systems to drive the development.

Acknowledgements

The author acknowledges the support of the Nation-Building Institute and Institute of Future Studies for Development.

Author details

Kriengsak Chareonwongsak
Nation-Building Institute, Bangkok, Thailand

*Address all correspondence to: kriengsak@kriengsak.com

References

[1] FAO, IFAD, UNICEF, WFP and WHO. In brief to the state of food security and nutrition in the World 2021. In: Transforming Food Systems for Food Security, Improved Nutrition and Affordable Healthy Diets for all. Rome: FAO; 2021. p. 38. DOI: 10.4060/cb5409en

[2] Bangkok Post. Food Exports Poised for 7.1% Growth. 2021. Available from: https://www.bangkokpost.com/business/2070783/food-exports-poised-for-7-1-growth. [Accessed: September 25, 2021]

[3] Mo-suwan L, Balagamwala M. Food and Nutrition. In: Oxford Policy Management and United Nations. Social Impact Assessment of COVID-19 in Thailand. London: Oxford Policy Management; 2020. pp. 107-121. Available from: https://www.unicef.org/thailand/media/5071/file/Social%20Impact%20Assessment%20of%20COVID-19%20in%20Thailand.pdf. [Accessed: September 15, 2021]

[4] FAO. FAO-led global COVID-19 Food Coalition Gains Momentum. 2020. Available from: http://www.fao.org/news/story/en/item/1300989/icode/. [Accessed: September 9, 2021]

[5] Inter-American Institute for Cooperation on Agriculture. International Cooperation is Key to Strengthening Food Security amidst the Pandemic says the Minister of Agriculture of Trinidad and Tobago. 2021. Available from: https://www.iica.int/en/press/news/international-cooperation-key-strengthening-food-security-amidst-pandemic-says-minister. [Accessed: September 10 2021]

[6] Béné C. Resilience of local Food systems and links to Food security – A review of some important concepts in the context of COVID-19 and other shocks. Food Security. 2020;**12**:805-822. DOI: 10.1007/s12571-020-01076-1

[7] Fennell S. Local Food Solutions during the Coronavirus Crisis Could Have Lasting Benefits. 2020. Available from: https://www.cam.ac.uk/stories/globaltolocal. [Accessed: September 10, 2021]

[8] Hunger Project. COVID-19 Resilient Communities: Addressing Food Security. 2020. Available from: https://thp.org/news/covid-19-resilient-communities-addressing-food-security/. [Accessed: September 10 2021]

[9] Johansson A. COVID-19: A catalyst for greater food self-sufficiency? Mycorena. Machinery. 2021;**8**:24. Available from: https://mycorena.com/covid-19-a-catalyst-for-greater-food-self-sufficiency. [Accessed: August 9, 2021]

[10] Clapp J. Food Self-Sufficiency and International Trade: a False Dichotomy?. Background paper prepared for The State of Agricultural Commodity Markets 2015-16. Rome: FAO; 2015. Available from: http://www.fao.org/3/i5222e/i5222e.pdf. [Accessed: August 9, 2021]

[11] Azkhodjaeva R. The role of WTO in food safety during COVID-19 pandemic. Asian Pacific Journal of Environment and Cancer. 2020;**3**(1):41-42. DOI: 10.31557/APJEC.2020.3.1.41-42

[12] Haijun Z, Cook S. Build Resilience of the Food System through Decentralisation, Digitalisation and Diversification: Lessons from China's response to COVID-19. Nutrition Connect. 2020. Available from:

https://nutritionconnect.org/resource-center/blog-38-build-resilience-food-system-through-decentralisation-digitalisation-and. [Accessed: August 9, 2021]

[13] Jansen K. The debate on Food sovereignty theory: Agrarian capitalism, dispossession and agroecology. The Journal of Peasant Studies. 2015;**42**(1): 213-232. DOI: 10.1080/03066150.2014.945166

[14] Sibindi N. Nexus Between Food Security and Trade in the Run-up to the World Food Systems Summit. SAIIA. South Africa 2020. Available from: https://www.jstor.org/stable/resrep27021. [Accessed: August 9, 2021]

[15] Espino A, Itliong K, Ruba CD, Thy O, Barbon WJ, Monville-Oro E, Gummadi S, Gonsalves J. COVID-19 Impact on Local Agri-food system in Cambodia, Myanmar, and the Philippines: Findings from a Rapid Assessment. CCAFS Working Paper no. 357. 2021. Available from: https://cgspace.cgiar.org/bitstream/handle/10568/113843/CCAFS%20WP%20357_Covid%2019_food%20systems.pdf [Accessed: August 10, 2021]

[16] Farrell P, Thow AM, Wate JT, et al. COVID-19 and Pacific Food system resilience: Opportunities to build a robust response. Food Security. 2020;**12**:783-791. DOI: 10.1007/s12571-020-01087-y

[17] Haddad L, Fanzo J, Godfrey S, Hawkes C, Morris S, Neufeld L. The COVID-19 Crisis and Food Systems: Probable Impacts and Potential Mitigation and Adaptation Responses. 2020. Available from: https://www.gainhealth.org/media/news/covid-19-crisis-and-food-systems-addressing-threats-creating-opportunities. [Accessed: December 14, 2021]

[18] HLPE. Nutrition and food systems. A Report by the High Level Panel of Experts on Food Security and Nutrition of the Committee on World Food Security. Rome: FAO; 2017. 152 p. Available from: https://www.fao.org/3/i7846e/i7846e.pdf. [Accessed: December 14, 2021]

[19] FAO. An Introduction to the Basic Concepts of Food Security [Intrnet]. Rome: FAO; 2008. Available from: http://www.fao.org/3/a-al936e.pdf. [Accessed: August 10, 2021]

[20] Pieters H, Guariso A, Vandeplas A. Conceptual Framework for the Analysis of the Determinants of Food and Nutrition Security. FOODSECURE Working paper no. 13. 2013. Available from: https://www.wecr.wur.nl/WECRGeneral/FoodSecure Publications/13_Pieters_Guariso_Vandeplas_ConceptualFramework.pdf. [Accessed: December 10, 2021]

[21] FAO. Trade Reforms and Food Security: Conceptualizing the Linkages. Rome: FAO; 2003. p. 313 p. Available from: https://www.fao.org/3/y4671e/y4671e.pdf. [Accessed: December 14, 2021]

[22] Rivera W M, Qamar M K. Agricultural Extension, Rural Development and the Food Security Challenge. Rome: FAO; 2003. Available from: https://www.fao.org/3/Y5061E/y5061e00.htm#Contents. [Accessed: December 11, 2021]

[23] Sun L, Pang PC, Si YW. Roles of information propagation of Chinese microblogging users in epidemics: A crisis management perspective. Internet Research. 2020;**31**(2):e408. DOI: 10.1108/INTR-11-2019-0490

[24] Saeidabadi M, Farahani SB, Abbasian E, Mirrazi SH. Information

model in crisis management from the perspective of media experts. Journal of Critical Reviews. 2020;7(1):1032-1036. DOI: 10.31838/jcr.07.01.171

[25] Queensland Fire and Emergency Services. Queensland Prevention, Preparedness, Response and Recovery Disaster Management Guidelines. Brisbane: Queensland Government; 2018. p. 2. Available from: https://www.disaster.qld.gov.au/dmg/Documents/QLD-Disaster-Management- Guideline.pdf. [Accessed: December 11, 2021]

[26] Prachachat Business Online. The Number of Coronavirus Cases in April Jumped Three Times Higher than the First Wave. 2021. Available from: https://www.prachachat.net/general/news-651030. [Accessed: August 11, 2021] (in Thai)

[27] Bangkok Post. 100K in Home Isolation. 2021. Available from: https://www.bangkokpost.com/thailand/general/2160663/100k-in-home-isolation. [Accessed: August 10, 2021]

[28] Hale T et al. A global panel database of Pandemic policies (Oxford COVID-19 government response tracker). Nature Human Behaviour. 2021;**5**:529-538. DOI: 10.1038/s41562-021-01079-8

[29] WHO. Daily Cases and Deaths by Date Reported to WHO. WHO Coronavirus (COVID-19) Dashboard. 2021. Available from: https://covid19.who.int/WHO-COVID-19-global-data.csv. [Accessed: August 15, 2021]

[30] Baffes J, Koh W C. Fertilizer Prices Expected to Stay High over the Remainder of 2021. World Bank Blog. 2021. Available from: https://blogs.worldbank.org/opendata/fertilizer-prices-expected-stay-high-over-remainder-2021. [Accessed: August 15, 2021]

[31] TMB Analytics. Expect the Chemical Fertilizer Market in Year 2021 to Grow More than 2.5%. 2021. Available from: https://www.ttbbank.com/archive/newsroom/news/pr/view/chemical-fertilizer-market.html. [Accessed: August 11, 2021] (in Thai)

[32] Rattanaprateeptong S. Foreign labor in the Thai agriculture sector. Food and Fertilizer Technology Center Policy Platform. 2020. Available from: https://ap.fftc.org.tw/article/2608. [Accessed: August 11, 2021]

[33] International Organization for Migration. COVID-19 Analytical Snapshot #18: Migrants and Global Food Supply. 2020. Available from: https://tinyurl.com/y7ocan7d. [Accessed: August 11, 2021]

[34] Chalamwong Y, Rattanaprateepthong S. The Impact of Covid-19 Affecting the Management of Migrant Workers in Thailand. Thailand Development Research Institute. Thailand 2020. Available from: https://tdri.or.th/2020/08/covid-19-impact-on-migrant-workers/. [Accessed: August 21, 2021] (in Thai)

[35] Ooi T, Dambul R. Food security challenges during and Post movement restrictions of COVID-19 in Southeast Asia [internet]. Thai Journal of Public Health. 2020;**50**(2):123-131. Available from: https://he02.tci-thaijo.org/index.php/jph/article/view/242553. [Accessed: August 12, 2021]

[36] Chantharat S, Adulthananusak N, Lamsam A, Rattanawararak L, Sangiamnet B, Rittinon C. Thai Agricultural Households in the Covid-19 Crisis. Puey Ungphakorn Institute for Economic Research. Thailand 2020. Available from: https://www.pier.or.th/wp-content/uploads/2020/05/aBRIDGEd_2020_011.pdf. [Accessed: August 13, 2021] (in Thai)

[37] Office of Agricultural Economics. Agricultural Economic Outlook. Bangkok, OAE; 2020. p. 74 p. Available from: https://www.oae.go.th/assets/portals/1/fileups/bappdata/files/Outlook_63_64_Infographic.pdf. (in Thai) [Accessed: August 12, 2021]

[38] NESDB. Gross Domestic Product: Q4/2020. 2021. Available from: https://www.nesdc.go.th/nesdb_en/article_attach/article_file_20210215121719.pdf. [Accessed: August 10, 2021]

[39] Prachachat Business Online. Export "Chicken" to Fight the COVID, Win a Hundred Thousand Tons of Chinese Orders. 2020. Available from: https://www.prachachat.net/economy/news-505923. [Accessed: August 11, 2021] (in Thai)

[40] Ashworth C. Laos 0Temporarily Bans Seafood from Thailand after Covid-19 Outbreak. Thaiger, Thailand. 2020. Available from: https://thethaiger.com/news/national/laos-temporarily-bans-seafood-from-thailand-after-covid-19-outbreak. [Accessed: August 13, 2021]

[41] INN News. Pork-Chicken Shortage of Market after Factory Infected with COVID. 2021. Available from: https://www.innnews.co.th/news/economy/news_158301/. [Accessed: August 12, 2021] (in Thai)

[42] National Health Commission Office. Thailand. Covid-19 Shakes up 'Food Security', Prepares to Develop Proposals for Future Crises. 2020. Available from: https://www.nationalhealth.or.th/en/node/2262. [Accessed: August 13, 2021] (in Thai)

[43] FAO. GIEWS Country Brief: Thailand. Rome: FAO; 2020. Available from: https://reliefweb.int/sites/reliefweb.int/files/resources/GIEWS%20Country%20Brief%20-%20Thailand%2016-December-2020.pdf. [Accessed: August 11, 2021]

[44] National Statistic Office. A Survey of the Impact of the COVID-19 Pandemic Situation on the Economy. 2020. Available from: http://ittdashboard.nso.go.th/img/covid/result_COVID-eco.pdf. [Accessed: August 13, 2021] (in Thai)

[45] Pongutta S, Kantamaturapoj K, Phakdeesettakun K, Phonsuk P. The Social impact of the COVID-19 outbreak on urban slums and the response of civil society organisations: A case study in Bangkok, Thailand. Heliyon. 2021 May 1;7(5):E07161:1-E07161:8. DOI: 10.1016/j.heliyon.2021.e07161

[46] Chanthaphong S, Thasanasoonthornwong W. Workers Returning Home after COVID-19: Turning Point of Thai Agricultural Sector and Accelerating Spreading Prosperity to the Region: Data from Mobile Big Data. Bank of Thailand. Thailand 2021. Available from: https://www.bot.or.th/Thai/ResearchAndPublications/articles/Pages/Article_27Apr2021.aspx. [Accessed: August 12, 2021] (in Thai)

[47] Daily News. People Cry Vegetables, Pork, Eggs Are Scarce - Prices Have Gone up after the Market Is Closed for COVID. 2021. Available from: https://www.dailynews.co.th/news/104739/. [Accessed: August 12, 2021] (in Thai)

[48] Manager Online. Pills Don't Get - No Guidelines - Just Delivery Links. Is This the Standard "Home Isolation" Covid!?. 2021. Available from: https://mgronline.com/live/detail/9640000073168. [Accessed: August 15, 2021] (in Thai)

[49] Tansri K. Labor and Changes in the Thai Agricultural Sector. Bank of

Thailand. Thailand 2014. Available from: https://www.bot.or.th/Thai/MonetaryPolicy/NorthEastern/DocLib_Research/04-Labor%20with%20Agri%20Changing.pdf. [Accessed: August 15, 2021] (in Thai)

[50] Phongprom A. Summary of Land Ownership Situation and Causes of Land Loss among Small Holders in Thailand. Agricultural Land Reform Office. Thailand 2019. Available from: https://www.alro.go.th/tech_trans/ewt_dl_link.php?nid=733. [Accessed: August 16, 2021] (in Thai)

[51] Pongrattananukul S, Sirikanchanarak D. Irrigation System and Thai Agriculture. Bank of Thailand. Thailand 2010. Available from: https://www.bot.or.th/Thai/MonetaryPolicy/Northern/DocLib_Article/ThailandIrrigationAgriSector.pdf. [Accessed: August 17, 2021] (in Thai)

[52] Supawattanakul K, Srisuwan M. Thai Food is in Crisis (2) Seeds are gobbled, Catch the villagers who produce by themselves - the law favors the corporation, Winch to buy to the farm - suggesting that the community must be self-sufficient. Thai Civil Rights and Investigative Journalism. Thailand 2012. Available from: https://www.tcijthai.com/news/2012/29/scoop/654. [Accessed: August 16, 2021] (in Thai)

[53] Boonyanam N. Agricultural policy misspecification in Thailand [internet]. Southeast Asian Journal of Economics. 2016;**4**(1):29-57. Available from: https://www.econ.chula.ac.th/public/publication/journal/2016/Article2_Nararuk.pdf. [Accessed: February 03, 2022]

[54] FAO. National Agro-Economic Zoning for Major Crops in Thailand (NAEZ) (Project TCP/THA/3403). Rome: FAO; 2017. p. 98 p. Available from: https://www.fao.org/3/i7077e/i7077e.pdf. [Accessed: February 03, 2022]

[55] Prachatai. "Food Sovereignty" Politics of Eating. Prachatai, Thailand 2005 . Available from: https://prachatai.com/journal/2005/07/4932. [Accessed: August 16, 2021] (in Thai)

[56] BAAC. BAAC Reveals the Results of Measures to Help Farmers from the Covid-19 Situation. BACC Press Release 29/2020. 2020. BAAC Chatuchak, Bangkok, Thailand

[57] Udomkerdmongkol M, Chalermpao N. Thai Agricultural Sector: From Problems to Solutions. United Nations Thailand. Thailand 2020. Available from: https://thailand.un.org/en/103307-thai-agricultural-sector-problems-solutions. [Accessed: August 11, 2021]

[58] National Food Board. Strategic Framework on Food Management of Thailand. Bangkok: NFB; 2011. 118 p. Available from: http://food.fda.moph.go.th/lgtfdapv/data/Strategy.pdf. [Accessed: August 14, 2021] (in Thai)

[59] Chinvarasopak P. Key Factors Affecting the Success of Organic Agriculture Policy Implementation in Thai Local Communities [Thesis]. National Institute of Development Administration: Bangkok; 2015

[60] Forest Peoples Programme. COVID-19 and Indigenous and Tribal Peoples: The Impacts and Underlying Inequalities. England: Moreton-in-Marsh; 2020. 44 p. Available from: https://www.forestpeoples.org/sites/default/files/documents/JA-450-Covid%20Impacts%20Paper%20ENG%20Single%20page.pdf. [Accessed: August 12, 2021]

[61] The Nation Thailand. Deliver With Safety Campaign' Launched To Boost Global Confidence In Thai Food. Thailand Available from: https://www.nationthailand.com/in-focus/30403815. The Nation Thailand; 2021. [Accessed: August 14, 2021]

[62] National News Bureau of Thailand. Thailand's Industrial Sector Considers "Bubble-and-Seal" System for Factories. 2021. National News Bureau of Thailand Thailand Available from: https://thainews.prd.go.th/en/news/detail/TCATG210824115206493. [Accessed: August 10, 2021]

[63] Sriboonchitta S, Wiboonpoongse A. Overview of Contract Farming in Thailand: Lessons Learned. ADB Institute Discussion Paper No. 112. Tokyo: ADBI; 2008. Available from: http://www.adbi.org/discussion-paper/2008/07/16/2660.contract.farming.thailand/. [Accessed: August 10, 2021]

[64] Suebpongsang P. Contract farming regulations and situations in Thailand. FFTC Agricultural Policy Platform. 2021. Available from: https://ap.fftc.org.tw/article/2842. [Accessed: August 15, 2021]

[65] Chia J. The Real Story about Thai Fruit: Growth of Internet Sales and Pandemic Worries. Thai Enquirer. Thailand 2020. Available from: https://www.thaienquirer.com/14991/the-real-story-about-thai-fruit-growth-of-internet-sales-and-pandemic-worries/. [Accessed: August 15, 2021]

[66] Sereenonchai S, Arunrat N. Understanding Food security behaviors during the COVID-19 Pandemic in Thailand: A review. Agronomy. 2021;**11**:497. DOI: 10.3390/agronomy11030497

[67] Kumse K, Suzuki N, Sato T. Measuring Oligopsony Power in the Thai Jasmine Rice Market; Re-evaluating the Paddy Pledging Program, 2018 Annual Meeting, August 5-7, Washington, D.C. 274198, Agricultural and Applied Economics Association. USA 2018 DOI: 10.22004/ag.econ.274198

[68] NESDB. Poverty and Inequality Report 2019. NESDB: Bangkok; 2020. p. 155 p. Available from: https://www.nesdc.go.th/ewt_dl_link.php?nid=10857. (in Thai) [Accessed: August 06, 2021]

[69] ILO. ILO Brief: COVID-19 Employment and Labor Market Impact in Thailand. ILO Thailand 2020. Available from: https://thailand.un.org/sites/default/files/2020-06/ILO%20COVID19%20impact%20assessment%20Thailand%20report%20-%20UN%20Thailand%20logo.pdf [Accessed: August 22, 2021]

[70] ThaiPublica. Survey the Measures to Cure COVID, Give Away 600 Billion Baht. ThaiPublica. Thailand 2021 . Available from: https://thaipublica.org/2021/02/include-money-giveaway-measures-fight-covid-19/. [Accessed: August 13, 2021] (in Thai)

[71] Ministry of Finance, Royal Thai Government and World Bank. Thailand Flooding 2554 Rapid Assessment for Resilient Recovery and Reconstruction Planning. Bangkok; UNDP; 2012. 288 p. Available from: http://www.undp.org/content/dam/thailand/docs/UNDP_RRR_THFloods.pdf. [Accessed: August 11, 2021]

[72] Treerutkuarkul A. Pandemic Exposes Flaws in Food Supply. Bangkok: Bangkok Post; 2020 . Available from: www.bangkokpost.com/thailand/specialreports/1927564#cxrecs_s. [Accessed: August 05, 2021]

[73] Business B. 'Food Crisis', Fragility in Big Cities in the Situation of 'Covid 19'.

Bangkok: Bangkok Business; 2021. Available from: https://www.bangkokbiznews.com/recommended/detail/2888 (in Thai). [Accessed: August 05, 2021]

[74] Bangkok Business. Rice and Fish: Survival of the Ethnic Groups during 'Covid-190 Crisis. Bangkok: Bangkok Business; 2021. Available from: https://www.bangkokbiznews.com/news/detail/877566 (In Thai). [Accessed: August 14, 2021]

[75] Chatinakrob T. Happiness-Sharing Pantries: An Effective Weapon to Ease Hunger for the Needy during the Pandemic in Thailand. Westminster, Central London Available from: https://blogs.lse.ac.uk/seac/2020/09/16/happiness-sharing-pantries/ LSE; 2020. [Accessed: August 17, 2021]

[76] Wattanasukchai S. 'Pantries of Sharing' mustn't let Dark Side Win. Bangkok Post. Bangkok 2020. Available from: https://www.bangkokpost.com/opinion/opinion/1917012/pantries-of-sharing-mustnt-let-dark-side-win. [Accessed: August 21, 2021]

[77] Porkka M, Kummu M, Siebert S, Varis O. From Food insufficiency towards trade dependency: A historical analysis of global Food availability. PLoS One. 2013;**8**(12):e82714. DOI: 10.1371/journal.pone.0082714

[78] Nyström M, Jouffray JB, Norström AV, Crona B, Jørgensen PS, Carpenter SR, et al. Anatomy and resilience of the global production ecosystem. Nature. 2019;**575**:98-108. Available from: https://www.nature.com/articles/s41586-019-1712-3. [Accessed: August 08, 2021]

[79] Renard D, Tilman D. National food production stabilized by crop diversity. Nature. 2019;**571**:257-260. DOI: 10.1038/s41586-019-1316-y

[80] Egli L, Schröter M, Scherber C, Tscharntke T, Seppelt R. Crop asynchrony stabilizes Food production. Nature. 2020;**588**:E7-E12. DOI: 10.1038/s41586-020-2965-6

[81] Naylor RL, Falcon WP. Food security in an era of economic volatility. Population and Development Review. 2010;**36**(4):693-723. Available from: https://citeseerx.ist.psu.edu/viewdoc/download?doi=10.1.1.472.5979&rep=rep1&type=pdf. [Accessed: September 15, 2021]

[82] Chaiamporn S. Theoretical concepts and personal self-reliance efforts. Journal of Development Administration. 1986. Available from: http://library1.nida.ac.th/nida_jour0/NJv26n4_02.pdf. [Accessed: August 11, 2021]

[83] Von Braun J, Paulino L. Food in sub-Saharan Africa: Trends and policy challenges for the 1990s. Food Policy. 1990;**15**(6):505-517. DOI: 10.1016/0306-9192(90)90041-W

[84] Fonchingong C, Fonjong L. The concept of self-reliance in community disruption initiatives in the Cameroon Grassfileds. Geo Journal. 2002;**57**(1):83-94. DOI: 10.1023/A:1026042718043

[85] Blas J. Food Self-Sufficiency 'is a Nonsense'. Bracken House; London, England: Financial Times; 2009. Available from: https://www.ft.com/content/bad4d152-cd53-11de-8162-00144feabdc0. [Accessed: September 08, 2021]

[86] Chalamwong Y. The impact of the crisis on migration in Thailand. Asian and Pacific Migration Journal. 1998;**7**(2-3):e407. DOI: 10.1177/011719689800700209

[87] Boonyamond S, Punpuing S. The Global Financial Crisis and the Impact of Internal Migration in Thailand. Discussion Paper for UNDP. Thailand: UNDP; 2010

[88] Chareonwongsak K. Pandemic New Normal: Post - Covid Era. NBI Special Session. Bangkok: Senior Executive Program for Nation-Building, National Building Institute; 2020

[89] IPBES. Workshop Report on Biodiversity and Pandemics of the Intergovernmental Platform on Biodiversity and Ecosystem Services. Bonn, Germany: IPBES Secretariat; 2020. DOI: 10.5281/zenodo.4147317

[90] Hoffman J. The Risk of Cyber Attacks on the Food and Agriculture Supply Chain. Minnesota: University of Minnesota; 2021. Available from: https://twin-cities.umn.edu/news-events/risk-cyber-attacks-food-and-agriculture-supply-chain. [Accessed: August 10, 2021]

[91] Chareonwongsak K. Mid-Stream Economic Policy: Direction for the Thai Economy in the Future. Success: Bangkok; 1999. p. 419

[92] Chareonwongsak K. Future Disruption: COVID Revolution Analysis. Success: Bangkok; 2020. p. 320

[93] Chareonwongsak K. Happy Work Happy Life Happy Living. Bangkok: Selom Group Meeting; 2009

[94] RUAF. City Region Food System Toolkit. 2020. Available from: https://ruaf.wbbclient.com/document/city-region-food-system-toolkit/. [Accessed: December 13, 2021]

Chapter 7

Analysis of the Nexus between Coping Strategies and Resilience to Food Insecurity Shocks: The Case of Rural Households in Boricha *Woreda*, Sidama National Regional State, Ethiopia

Adane Atara Debessa, Degefa Tolossa and Berhanu Denu

Abstract

This chapter reports on the coping strategies employed by households in the event of food insecurity shocks and the nexus between the types of coping strategies and resilience to food insecurity in one of the food-stressed woreda from Sidama National Regional State, Ethiopia. The households use various consumption-based coping strategies that run from compromising the quality of food-to-food rationing. Repeatedly occurring food shortage has also forced some households to employ resilience erosive coping mechanisms such as selling reproductive assets. Such coping strategies have an important implication on the household's capacity to cope with the future food insecurity-related shocks, with a statistically significant relationship between the nature of coping strategies utilized in response to previous food insecurity-related shocks and the household's resilience to upcoming shocks. Coordinating crises management based on humanitarian intervention with households' livelihood assets protection and resilience strengthening is the major policy implication of this study.

Keywords: households, coping strategy, resilience

1. Introduction

Food is the most basic need for survival, growth, and good health of human beings. Freedom from hunger is the most fundamental human right that can be attained if an individual is food secure [1]. However, a significant proportion of the world's population still lives under the situation of food insecurity. As it is clear from the FAO et al. [2] report on the state of food and nutrition in the world, even the prospect itself is not sufficiently bright to the extent expected. Five years after the world committed to ending hunger, it has been learned that, the world is still off track to achieve this objective by 2030. Given the current pace, the world is making headway neither towards Sustainable

Development Goal target 2.1, of ensuring access to safe, nutritious and sufficient food for all people all year round, nor towards target 2.2, of ending all forms of malnutrition [2].

Looking at the trends and projections of the state of global food insecurity may help to understand this claim. According to the same report, the number of undernourished people was 690 million in 2019 (60 million more than in 2014), and is expected to exceed 840 million in 2030. When it comes to Africa, the continent's share of undernourishment prevalence for 2019 exceeds one-third of global undernourishment with about 250 million undernourished people. This figure represents about 19% of its overall population and is projected to be about26% in 2030 [2].

Various reports show that Ethiopia hosts a handful proportion of food insecure people. For instance, WFP and CSA [3] report the persistence of poverty and food insecurity despite the country's efforts to counteract the situation. MOFED [4] reported a level of food poverty prevalence of 33.6% in 2014 *versus* 31.8% in 2012/13. However, Ethiopia is moving in a good direction to improve the situation. A joint report of WFP and CSA [5], showed that the country has made tremendous socio-economic progress that resulted in the reduction of the prevalence of hunger and undernourishment to 25.5%. Nevertheless, the country still embraces a noticeable level of food-insecure people.

Response mechanisms to food insecurity shocks varies based on the objectives of the agents responding to it as well as the level at which they are targeted. As active actors/agents/of their own, households employ various coping strategies (response mechanisms) in the event of shocks that challenge their food security. According to Maxwell and Caldwell [6], USAID [7], and Degefa [8], such strategies are not uniform and may also not be equally sustainable, as in some cases they may erode household's capacity to withstand future food insecurity shocks. Although, effects of households' coping mechanisms and resilience to future shocks have been widely discussed, mainly at the conceptual level, empirical statistical evidences on the nexus are quite limited.

For instance, though Carter et al. [9] provide elegant theoretical explanation on the linkage between shock-initiated coping mechanisms and a household's resilience, the unavailability of data on coping strategies constrains them from including this variable in their estimation model. The study of Tran [10] fails to make the distinction between positive and negative coping at the empirical level and focuses only on the immediate positive effects to recover from shocks. However, a particular coping strategy, though resilience erosive, can contribute to smooth current consumption and/or recovery from shocks. Moreover, capturing resilience only through the recovery speed proxy is also too simplistic. Thus, there is an increasing understanding of resilience as an *ex ante* capacity of households to withstand the effect of shocks [11–16]. This way of conceptualizing enables to better capture the essence of resilience as absorptive (buffering), adaptive, as well as transformative capacity in addition to recognizing a futuristic nature. Considering this scenario, this chapter brings forward the linkage between resilience and coping mechanisms, focusing on Boricha woreda as a case study. For that, the following interrelated questions are discussed: (1) how do the study area's households respond to food insecurity shocks? (2) does the resilience level of households vary based on the nature of previously employed coping mechanisms?

2. Linkage between household's resilience to food insecurity and coping mechanisms

Maxwell and Caldwell [6] identify four coping strategies that households employ when they face food shortages or do not have the resources to purchase food. They include taking action on the quality of food to eat, looking for options that help increase food supply, reducing the number of household members that they have to feed through such mechanisms like sending some of them to neighbors' houses, and managing the deficit through mechanisms such as food rationing. Conceptually, these strategies are consumption-based ones having a lesser impact on the households' capacity to cope with future food insecurity shocks.

Carter et al. [9] put the households' actions to cope with shock-induced food security challenges in a certain rational decision-based logical order. As per this source, initially households choose to depend on the markets and other institutions that they have access to. To maintain their consumption standard without further asset depletion, households with financial market access or access to informal finance might borrow against future earnings. Resorting to insurance arrangements, seeking for and receiving disaster aid as well as working for long hours are also coping options that they can exercise before taking action against their productive assets. Households without access to such options may opt to sustain their consumption by drawing down on their assets: the decision which they argue can further increase the sensitivity of assets and weaken the future. Finally, households may cope by reducing consumption. This coping strategy can be the last option for those lacking other assets or options and may also be pursued by households who are reluctant to increase their future vulnerability due to depletion of the stock of assets. However, coping by reducing consumption is regarded unfavorably as it does have multiple costs, i.e., immediate hunger as well as the long-term effect on children's growth and development [17].

To the linkage between coping mechanisms and shocks, it is postulated that adverse events (shocks) may cause a decline in assets and incomes in the short-run and might have negative effects on household livelihoods in the longer-run [10]. However, the extent of the effects, depends on the nature of the shocks, the asset dynamics, as well as on the coping strategies employed. Carter et al. [9] opine that when a given shock happens, it will have both direct and indirect impact on households' resilience to future shocks. Firstly, the shock itself brings direct harm to the quality of households' asset. As households' respond to shocks using their assets and resources, the indirect impact comes via such responses to a particular shock. The whole idea here is that the coping mechanisms used in response to food insecurity-related shocks at a given point can cause a decline in the household's ability to cope with future shocks depending on the strategies employed in between two time periods.

The origin of the concept of resilience is linked to the field of ecology. According to Holling [18], in ecology, the term resilience is used as a measure of systems persistence and capacity to absorb changes and disturbances and still retain the same relationship with state variables. To a household's food security, resilience has been conceptualized as the ability of the household to maintain its food security withstanding shocks and stresses, depending on the options available and its ability to handle risks [11]. Accordingly, resilience is a multifaceted capacity: absorptive, adaptive, and transformative. While explaining the linkage between the nature of coping strategies and resilience, Frankenberger et al. [19] sustain those certain strategies may have negative and permanent consequences to resilience. Positive coping strategies are those based on available skills and resources, to face, manage and recover from shocks and that do not compromise resilience. On the other hand, negative coping strategies, if employed, undermine future options making it more difficult to cope with the next shock or stress [20]. Hence, it can be argued that the resilience status of a household at

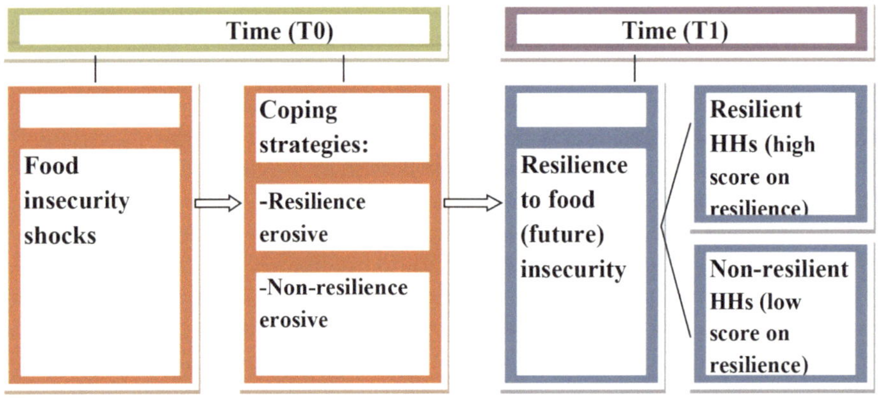

Figure 1.
Conceptual representation of food insecurity shocks-coping strategies-resilience nexus.

a particular time point (resilience to future food insecurity shocks) is partly a reflection of the type of coping strategies previously employed. **Figure 1** represents this conceptualization.

3. Illustrative case

3.1 Description of the study area

The illustrative case is based on the data collected from one of the food-stressed *woredas from* the Sidama National Regional State called Boricha *woreda*. As per the CSA [21] report, Boricha *woreda* has a total population of 250,260 inhabitants, of whom 125,524 are men and 124,736 women. Yirba is the administrative capital. The area has two rain periods a year: the short rainy months (the *belg rain-from March to May*) and the long rainy months (the *kiremnt* rain from June to October). The remaining months constitute the dry season when both humans and animals face water shortages. Besides that, Boricha w*oreda* is known for unreliable rainfall patterns (both in amount and periodicity) for a couple of years and associated food stresses. Mixed subsistence agriculture supports the livelihood of the population. Enset and maize are the two dominant food crops grown at the household level. Khat, coffee, and livestock are also part of the household's economy in the area through their concentration is not uniform across all *kebeles.* Complete dependence on rain-fed farming for subsistence together with rainfall variability exposes people to high risks of harvest loss that easily translates into food insecurity [22]. There are 39 *kebeles (the lowest administrative unit)* in Boricha *woreda*. Of these, three are urban and 36 are rural. According to SNNPR [23] livelihood profile report, these *Kebeles* are classified into three livelihood zones: Sidama Coffee Livelihood, Sidama Maiz Belt Livelihood, and Agro-pastoralist Livelihood.

3.2 Methodological briefing

Based on insights from literature and the resulting framework presented in **Figure 1**, it was assumed that the coping strategies employed by households in response to food insecurity shocks that happened at time (T0), can have an influence on the resilience level at a time (T1) in a way that households with negative coping strategies at T0scoreless on resilience at T1. As the households' coping mechanisms are the response actions to shocks, data can be captured usually *ex post* (or retroactively). Accordingly, the linkage between the level of resilience and household coping mechanisms was examined based on surveys before time T1 in response to various stressors/shocks challenging their food security situation. Conceptually, the study examined the relationship between the nature of coping mechanisms employed at time (T0) and the resilience status of households at the time (T1), the proxy of households' capacity to effectively respond to future food insecurity shocks.

The selection of the illustrative study was based on a cross-sectional survey conducted by using structured questionnaires and key informants' interviews. It involved 420 randomly selected households from three randomly selected *kebeles* (one *kebele* from each livelihood zone). As resilience is a multi-dimensional concept that is not directly observable, it has to be measured through a proxy. To this end, the study adopted the FAO's Resilience Index Measurement Analysis Model (RIMA) originally proposed and used by [11, 12]. The model quantitatively assesses household resilience through latent variable modeling. Accordingly, in the study, resilience was treated as a latent variable to be estimated by using seven indicators (dimensions): agricultural assets, agricultural technology adoption, access to basic services, social capital, social safety nets, adaptive capacity, income and food access. Each of these seven indicators of resilience is a latent variable to be estimated using observable household-level variables. Using the Principal Component Analysis (PCA), the estimation of resilience score (index) was done hierarchically. First, an index for each of the above dimensions of resilience was done separately using observable variables. Then, the resilience score for each household was estimated with PCA based on the indices of those resilience dimensions (indicators) (see **Figure 2**). All the seven indicator variables were strongly loaded on the first component and the component scores were used as resilience index for each household. The following path diagram (**Figure 2**) has been adapted from [12], in order to visually depict this estimation procedure.

At the household level, the resilience index was estimated using the Eq. (1) below, which was further transformed using the weighting mechanisms and applying the Bartlett method of component scoring. The Bartlett method was selected as it generally produces latent variable scores that are unbiased and univocal [24].

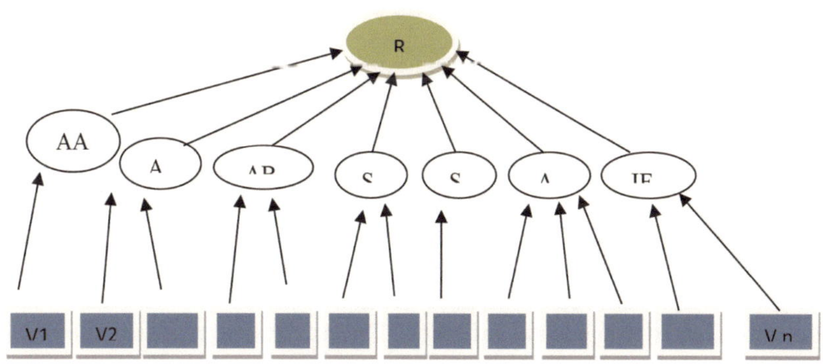

Figure 2.
Household's resilience estimation procedure.

$$R_i = w_{AA}AA_i + w_{ATA}ATA_i + w_{ABS}ABS_i + w_{SC}SC_i + w_{SS}SS_i + w_{AC}AC_i + w_{IFA}IFA_i \quad (1)$$

where:

R_i = resilience of household i, AA_i = agricultural assets, ATA_i = agricultural technology adoption, ABS_i =access to basic services, SC_i = social capital, SS_i = social safety nets, AC_i = adaptive capacity, IFA_i = income and food access, w = Weight for each indicator of resilience.

The surveys to analyze the coping mechanisms measurements included two sets of questions: consumption-based (strategies employed in the last 7 days before the date of the survey) and non-consumption based (strategies used in the last 2 years preceding the survey date). The analysis of data on coping strategies was done descriptively using percentages. The linkage between households' resilience and the previously employed coping mechanisms was examined using contingency table and chi-square tests as well as using the odds ratio. In the analysis, households were categorized into two groups: those who previously employed negative (resilience erosive) coping mechanisms and those who did not employ such coping strategies over the past 2 years. In the current study, such categorization was done based on insights from conceptual literature such as [7, 19]. Hence, based on these conceptual works, coping strategies such as selling of reproductive animals, oxen used for farming, and land, land rental, withdrawal of children from school, borrowing money at the high interest rate, and diversion of loans from MFIs were treated as resilience erosive or negative strategies. Accordingly, households who did use any of these coping strategies over the past 2 years were classified under the negative coping category. Based on Guyu and Muluneh [15] and considering the relative location of the surveyed households on the latent variables (resilience scores,) the study households were categorized into resilient and none- resilient groups.

4. Findings and discussion

4.1 Coping strategies adapted

Literature indicates that the response of households to food insecurity challenges include different coping strategies. These may involve the modification of consumption habits (consumption-based coping strategies) and/or use of the available resources (non-consumption-based strategies). For instance, Christiaensen and Boisvert [25] contend that when they anticipate food shortage people start to consider changing their consumption habits rather than waiting until food is completely exhausted. Though such change in the consumption habits is generally believed to be a short-term adjustments, it could go long as a normal habit even in the situation where non-consumption-based strategies too are activated. This is mainly true in the situation where a given community lives under long standing food stress in terms of availability and/or access. The point here is that though non-consumption-based strategies such as selling key productive assets are used, foods obtained through such actions could still be subject to consumption-based coping such as rationing. This can lead us to safely argue that the two sets of coping strategies, consumption and non-consumption based, should not be seen as completely isolated and mutually exclusive as they appear in the literature. Notwithstanding the complexity here, the analysis of the household's coping strategies was done in light of the general assumption that households are rational decision-makers and thus, the first options are those with the least impact on livelihood or future food security.

Consumption-based coping strategies constitute short-term alteration of consumption patterns. Writers like Watts [26], Corbett [27], and Devereux [28] consider them as easily reversible strategies that do not jeopardize long-term prospects as they mostly do not require a commitment of domestic resources. The households' responses summary (**Table 1**) indicates that 60.2% (253) of the households rely on less preferred foods at least once in a week. 45.5% (191) reported that the consumption of adults was restricted in favor of children. According to one of the elderly key informants "during food shortage, usually mothers take the burden of not having to eat giving priority to children and father". Similarly, a total of 181 (43%) and 141 (33.6%) households limited portion sizes and reduced the number of meals. The proportion of households who reported that they borrowed food or relied on the help from a friend/relative and purchased food on credit was 39.5% (166) and 32.4% (136), respectively. All the remaining coping strategies summarized in **Table 1** were utilized by a small proportion of the households. Only 7.6% (32) of the surveyed households indicated that they relied on wild foods and/or immature crops. Probably, this could be due to the timing of the survey, as it was conducted just after the harvesting period (dry season). Similarly, only a small number of households, 17.9% (75), gave priority to working members at the expense of non-working members, and only 1.7% (7) fastens the entire day. Again, a relatively small proportion of total households, 13.6% (57), consumed seed stocks held for the next season at least once a week. The proportion of households who engaged in the coping behavior of sending family members to eat elsewhere and begging was12.1% (51) and 2.6% (11), respectively. Such findings could be because the experienced level of food inscurity might not be of the extent that forces households to engage in such behaviors or due to the strong local culture that discourages such practices.

Coping strategy	Number/proportion of households employed	
	Count	Percentage (%)
Relied on less preferred foods	253	60.2
Borrowed food or relied on help from a friend/relative	166	39.5
Purchased food on credit	136	32.4
Relied on wild foods, hunt, or immature crops	32	7.6
Consume seed stock held for next season	57	13.6
Household members sent to eat else where	51	12.1
Household members sent to beg	11	2.6
Portion size at mealtimes limited	181	43
Consumption by adults restricted in order for small children	191	45.5
Priority given for working members of household at the expense of non-working members	75	17.9
Meals eaten in a day reduced	141	33.6
Entire days skipped without eating	7	1.7

Table 1.
Consumption based coping strategies.

Complementary and non-consumption-based coping strategies (**Table 2**) included, selling reproductive animals at least once within the last 2 years period (42.6%), and renting (10%) or selling (2.1%) their lands (10%). About 20.7% (87) and 21% (88) of the households had removed their children from school and borrowed

Coping strategies	**Number of households adopted**	
	Count	**Percentage (%)**
Sold reproductive animals	179	42.6
Sold oxen used for farming	98	23.3
Sold land	9	2.1
Rented out land	42	10
Removed children from school	87	20.7
Borrowed money at high interest rate	88	21
Sold small animals	158	37.6
Migrated to nearer areas to wage labor	80	19
Drawing on savings	20	4.8
Selling fire wood	140	33.3
Diverting loans from MFIs to consumption	8	1.9
Appealed for aid	217	51.7

Table 2.
Non-consumption based coping strategies used by households.

Figure 3
Household members taking fire woods collected form forests to market centers.

money at high-interest rates respectively. A total of 37.6% (158) households reported that they coped by selling small animals and about 19% (80) migrated to nearer areas in search of wage labor. Almost none, 1.9% (8), of the households had engaged in the coping behavior of diverting loans from Monetary Financial Institutions (MFIs) to consumption and only 4.8% (20) households had drawn on financial savings to respond to the food insecurity problem. This could be due to a lack of cash savings to draw from and/or limited access to MFIs both of which are common in the rural context. Nearly half, 51.7% (217), reported that they have appealed for food aid to overcome food insecurity within the last 2 years. One-third of the households, 33.3% (140), reported that they used selling firewood as a coping mechanism (see **Figure 3**).

According to the key informants, they collect fire wood from the forest around Bilate River towards the border of Loka Abaya *woreda* and supply to Dila Anole and Balela towns. From our discussions, we further learned that due to persistent food stress, poor people have made collecting and selling fire wood as a regular source of income for food purchase. However, the issue of concern exists. That is, if left unchecked, such a heavily reliance on forests could wipe out the only left over of the ancient forests in the area. Almost all elderly key informants stressed that in the past most of the *woreda* had been covered by dense forests that hosted many wild animals until the downfall of the emperor regime. But, the increasingly growing demand for farm land since then has resulted in the clearance of forests to its demise.

4.2 Relationship between previously employed coping mechanisms and resilience status (level) of the households

As referred above, several authors such as Frankenberger et al. [19], Carter et al. [9], Tran [10], and USAID [7], pinpoint that the types of coping mechanisms employed by households in response to previously happened shocks can affect their resilience to future shocks.

Based on these conceptual backdrops, we have endeavored to understand how the previously used coping strategies of households relate to their resilience status. To this end, households were asked if they experienced one or more shocks challenging their food security situation in the last 2 years preceding the survey and the responses are summarized in **Table 3**. Most of the surveyed households, 79.3% (333), experienced one or more types of shocks that they believe affected their food security situation. Households have also identified a set of coping strategies employed in the past 2 years to cope with food insecurity problems/shocks (**Table 2**).

When it comes to identifying negative coping strategies (erosive resilience), it seems that literatures lack perfect unanimity. With the argument that they undermine future options making it more difficult to cope with next shocks, Pasteur [20]

Variables	Response	Count	Percentage (%)
If shocks affecting ability to feed HHs occurred within the last 2 years	Yes	333	79.3
	No	87	20.7
Number of shocks experienced*	Only one	99	29.7 (23.6% of total)
	More than one	234	70.3 (55.7% of total)

**List of shocks include crop failure, household member death, livestock death, and illness.*

Table 3.
Previously experienced food security situation threatening shocks.

considers strategies such as delaying medical treatment, exploiting natural resources, taking children out of school, eating less, eating less nutritious food, and eroding productive assets as resilience erosive coping strategies. However, some of the strategies considered as negative coping here are consumption-based (temporary adjustments on eating) that are considered by others as easily reversible. Specially, stage 2 and stage 3 coping strategies from the list identified by Watts [26] and Frankenberger [29] are generally treated as erosive coping mechanisms. Based on the literature and on study area's context, selling reproductive animals, oxen, and land, or renting land, taking children from school, borrowing money at high-interest rates, and diversion of loans from MFIs to consumption were considered as negative (resilience erosive) coping in this illustrative case. Accordingly, households were classified into two coping categories (**Table 4**): those who used negative coping in the past 2 years and those who did not. As indicated in the table, 59.5% (250) of the households employed one or more negative (erosive) coping strategies in the last 2 years preceding the date of the survey.

The households' resilience position (status) was determined based on their relative resilience scores and using the criteria of [15]. Based on relative resilience score (index) achieved by households, Guyu and Muluneh [15] classify four resilience categories: Vulnerable (resilience index (RI) < 0.100). Moderately Resilient ($0.100 \leq \text{RI} < 0.250$), Resilient ($0.250 \leq \text{RI} < 0.500$) and Highly Resilient ($\text{RI} \geq 0.500$). Using the resilience scores estimated through the Bartlett method in PCA and applying these cutoff schemes, households are categorized into four categories (**Table 5**). A very significant proportion of the surveyed households (61%) was not resilient (or vulnerable to food insecurity shocks) and only 39% was resilient at different levels. With these pieces of information on the nature of previously employed coping and resilience status, now the discussion turns to examine the relationship between the nature of coping mechanisms and the relative resilience position (status) of the households. Our analysis proceeds with the proposition that the nature of previously used coping strategies can affect the predictive resilience of households (estimated at time T1) in the form that those with prior negative coping strategies scoreless on resilience. Contingency Table and chi-square test statistic, and

		Frequency	Percent	Valid percent	Cumulative percent
Valid	Non resilience erosive (positive) coping	170	40.5%	40.5%	40.5%
	Resilience erosive (negative) coping	250	59.5%	59.5%	100.0
	Total	420	100.0	100.0	

Table 4.
Households by coping type.

Measurement	**Households by resilience category**				**Total**
	Non resilient	**Moderately resilient**	**Resilient**	**Highly resilient**	
Count	256	22	18	124	420
Percent	61%	5.2%	4.3%	29.5%	100

Table 5.
Distribution of household resilience status.

the odds ratio were employed to analyze and test this proposed relationship of the two variables. **Table 6** presents cross-tabulation of previously employed coping types and households' resilience levels. About 59.5% (250) of the households used one or more types of erosive resilience (negative) coping strategies within the last 2 years. From this group, only 19.6% (49) was found to be resilient (scoring relatively high on resilience index) at time T1 (time of the survey). Most households, 80.4% (201), that adapted one or more negative coping strategies were found to be non-resilient. On the other hand, out of the total households who did not previously use negative coping strategies, 67.6% (115) was found to be resilient at time T1 (scoring relatively high on resilience index) against 32.4% (55) scoring relatively low on resilience (non-resilient).

The Chi-Square test was run as a way of checking if the observed frequency (or percentage) differences in the contingency table (**Table 6**) were statistically significant. In statistical terms, it tests the implicit null hypothesis that there is no relationship between types/nature of previously employed coping strategies and the resilience status of the households. That is, it tests the hypothesis that the household's resilience score (status) at time T1 is independent of types of coping methods employed by a household in response to shocks that occurred before time T1. The result of the Chi-Square test (**Table 7**) revealed high significance for $\chi2$ (1) = 98.149, P < 0.001 indicating an association between household's resilience status and types of previously employed coping strategies. Besides the association between these two variables, it does not show the strength of the relationship that has been detected. Therefore, the Phi test for 2 by 2 contingency table, was also performed [30] giving a noticeable level of association between the household's resilience level and types of coping strategies previously employed (**Table 8**). The sign of the relationship is also as expected as the two variables were coded similarly.

			Coping type		Total
			Non-resilience erosive (positive coping)	Resilience erosive (negative coping)	
Resilience level	Resilient	Count	115	49	164
		% within resilience level	70.1%	29.9%	100.0%
		% within coping type	67.6%	19.6%	39.0%
		% of Total	27.4%	11.7%	39.0%
	Non-resilient	Count	55	201	256
		% within resilience level	21.5%	78.5%	100.0%
		% within coping type	32.4%	80.4%	61.0%
		% of Total	13.1%	47.9%	61.0%
Total		Count	170	250	420
		% within resilience level	40.5%	59.5%	100.0%
		% within coping type	100.0%	100.0%	100.0%
		% of Total	40.5%	59.5%	100.0%

Table 6.
Cross-tabulation of households' resilience level and previously used coping strategy.

	Value	Df	Asymp. Sig. (2-sided)	Exact Sig. (2-sided)	Exact Sig. (1-sided)
Pearson Chi-Square	98.149[a]	1	0.000	0.000	0.000
N of valid cases	420				

[a]0 cells (0.0%) have expected count less than 5. The minimum expected count is 66.38.
[b]Computed only for a 2 × 2 table.

Table 7.
Tests of association between resilience status and coping type.

		Value	Approx. sig.	Exact sig.
Nominal by Nominal	Phi	0.483	0.000	0.000
N of valid cases		420		

[a]Not assuming the null hypothesis.
[b]Using the asymptotic standard error assuming the null hypothesis.

Table 8.
Test of the strength of association (resilience level and coping type).

Both association (Chi-Square) and strength of association (Phi test) tests highlighted the existence of meaningful relationships between the two variables under consideration. To further check the strength of association between the two variables the odds ratio was used as a supplement to the Phi test. The odds ratio here refers to the ratio of the odds that a household will be resilient to future shocks with no prior use of negative coping strategies to the odds that a household will be resilient through it previously used some kind of negative coping strategies. Based on frequencies in **Table 6**, the odds ratio was computed as:

$$\begin{aligned}\text{Oddsratio} = {} & \text{Odds of being resilient with no prior use of negative coping} \\ & \div\text{Odds of being resilient with prior use of negative coping}\end{aligned} \tag{2}$$

$$\begin{aligned}&\text{Odds of being resilient with no prior use of negative coping} \\ &\quad = \text{Number of resilient households who didn't use negative coping} \\ &\qquad \div\text{Number of nonresilient households who did not use negative coping} \\ &\quad = 115 \div 55 = 2.0909\end{aligned} \tag{3}$$

This ratio shows that the number of households who are resilient with no prior use of negative coping is as twice as those who are non-resilient though they did not employ negative (erosive) coping before. It is also possible to be resilient or non-resilient to future shocks without prior negative (erosive) coping. However, it is more likely to be resilient than non-resilient given the initial state (previous experience in terms of coping type) is that of no negative (erosive) coping strategy.

$$\begin{aligned}&\text{Odds of being resilient with prior use of negative coping} \\ &\quad = \text{Number of resilient households who did use negative coping} \\ &\qquad \div\text{Number of nonresilient households who did use negative coping} \\ &\quad = 49/201 = 0.24378\end{aligned} \tag{4}$$

The ratio here shows that the number of resilient households experiencing previous negative coping is about four times less than the number of non-resilient households.

Given the two pieces of information (odds ratios presented above) and referring to the first equation, the odds ratio of interest here (the odds that a household will be resilient to future shocks with no prior use of negative coping strategies to the odds that a household will be resilient through it previously used some kind of negative coping strategies) can be computed as follows:

$$Oddsratio = 2.09090 \div 0.24378 = 8.57 \quad (5)$$

The odds ratio indicates that households who did not previously use negative coping strategies were 8.57 times more likely to be resilient to future shocks. So, the clear implication of this finding is that the type of coping mechanisms used in response to given food insecurity-related shocks at a particular point in time can have an impact on households' ability to respond to the upcoming shocks. This finding is in line with the Chi-Square test result above and the extant theoretical literature discussed in the chapter.

5. Conclusion

Depending on the initial state of the households, some of the coping strategies can lead to the poverty trap and erode the ability to cope with similar problems in the future. If left uncontrolled, even the coping mechanisms with no immediate individual impact, like selling firewood, may not be environmentally sustainable. This is especially true in the case of the study area as the source of firewood collection is, mostly, the single leftover of the ancient forest, which is confined to marginal areas around the Billate River. Additionally, the coping mechanisms utilized currently by the households can have important implications on their capacity to cope with future shocks, depending on their resource base. Hence, well-targeted interventions that go beyond saving lives (humanitarian emergency) and focusing on livelihood assets protection and capacity building to future shocks is the recommended policy option.

Author details

Adane Atara Debessa[1*], Degefa Tolossa[2] and Berhanu Denu[3]

1 Addis Ababa University College of Business and Economics, Ethiopia

2 Geography and Development Studies, Addis Ababa University College of Development Studies, Ethiopia

3 Addis Ababa University College of Business and Economics, Ethiopia

*Address all correspondence to: adaneatara@gmail.com

References

[1] Ngongi AM. Food Insecurity and Coping Strategies of Farm Households in Kahama District. Tanzania; 2013. Available from: http://suaire.suanet.ac.tz/bitstream/handle/123456789/581/ANNA%20MARCO%20NGONGI.pdf?sequence=1&isAllowed=y

[2] FAO, IFAD, UNICEF, WFP and WHO. The State of Food Security and Nutrition in the World 2020. Transforming Food Systems for Affordable Healthy Diets. Rome: FAO; 2020. DOI: 10.4060/ca9692en

[3] WFP and CSA. Comprehensive Food Security and Vulnerability Analysis (CFSVA): A Joint Publication between the Ethiopia Central Statistical Agency (CSA) and the World Food Program (WFP). 2014

[4] MOFED. Growth and Transformation Plan Annual Progress Report for F.Y. 2012/13. 2014

[5] WFP and CSA. Comprehensive Food Security and Vulnerability Analysis (CFSVA): A Joint Publication between the Ethiopia Central Statistical Agency (CSA) and the World Food Program (WFP). 2019

[6] Maxwell D, Caldwell R. The Coping Strategies Index: Field Methods Manual. 2nd ed. 2008. Available from: https://www.researchgate.net/publication/259999318

[7] USAID. Livelihood and Food Security Framework. 2011. Available from: marketshareassociates.com/wp ... /LIFT-ES-Framework_8-17-2011.pd

[8] Tolossa D. Causes of Seasonal Food Insecurity in Oromia Zone of the Amhara Region: Farmers' View. Department of Geography, Norwegian University of Science and Technology. Department of Geography, Norwegian University of Science and Technology. 2001. Available from: wmich.edu/~asefa/ ... /Papers/2001%20papers/PaperI19.pdf

[9] Carter MR, Little PD, Mogues T, Negatu W. Shocks, Sensitivity and Resilience: Tracking the Economic Impacts of Environmental Disaster on Assets in Ethiopia and Honduras DSGC Discussion Paper 32. Washington DC: IFPRI; 2006

[10] Tran Q. Household's coping strategies and recoveries from shocks in Vietnam. The Quarterly Review of Economics and Finance. 2015;**2015**:15-29

[11] Alinovi L, D'Errico M, Mane E, Romano D. Livelihoods strategies and household resilience to food insecurity: An empirical analysis to Kenya. In: Conference Organized by the European Report of Development, Dakar, Senegal. 2010. pp. 28-30. Available from: https://europa.eu/capacity4dev/file/13066/download?token=Moifs8j5

[12] Alinovi L, Mane E, Romano D. Towards the measurement of household resilience to food insecurity: Applying a model to Palestinian household data. In: Sibrian R, editor. Deriving Food Security Information from National Household Budget Surveys. 2008. pp. 137-152. Available from: https://europa.eu/capacity4dev/file/13066/download?token=Moifs8j5

[13] Ciani F, Romano D. Testing for Household Resilience to Food Insecurity: Evidence from Nicaragua. 2013. Available from: https://www.siecon.org/sites/siecon.org/files/oldfiles/uploads/2013/09/Ciani-Romano.pdf

[14] FAO. Resilience Index Measurement and Analysis (RIMA-II) Model. 2016. Available from: https://www.fao.org/resilience/resources/resources-detail/en/c/416587/

[15] Daie GF, Woldtsadik M. Household resilience to seasonal food insecurity: Dimensions and magnitudes in the 'green famine' belt of Ethiopia. Applied Science Reports. 2015;**11**(3):125-143

[16] Demeke M, Tefera N. Sustainable Resilience for Food and Nutrition Security: The Case of Farming Rural Households in Ethiopia. 2013. Available from: https://www.researchgate.net/publication/269986227

[17] Hoddinott J. Shocks and their consequences across and within households in rural Zimbabwe. Journal of Development Studies. 2006;**42**(2):301-321

[18] Holling CS. Resilience and stability of ecological systems. Annual Review of Ecology and Systematics. 1973;**4**:1-23

[19] Frankenberger T, Langworthy M, Spangler T, Nelson S. Enhancing Resilience to Food Security Shocks. TANGO International, Inc.; 2012 Available from: https://www.fsnnetwork.org/sites/default/files/revised_resilience_paper_may_28.pdf

[20] Pasteur K. From Vulnerability to Resilience: A Framework for Analysis and Action to Build Community Resilience. Rugby: Practical Action; 2011

[21] CSA. Population and Housing Census of Ethiopia Report for SNNPR. 2007. Available from: http://phe-ethiopia.org/pdf/snnpr.pdf

[22] Atara A, Tolossa D, Denu B. Assessment of food security situation of the rural households: The case of Boricha Woreda of Sidama Zone, Ethiopia. GeoJournal. 2019;**86**(2):711-727

[23] SNNPR. Southern Nation Nationalities, and Peoples Region Livelihood Profiles Report. 2005

[24] DiStefano C, Zhu M, Mîndrilă D. Understanding and using factor scores: Considerations for the applied researcher. Practical Assessment, Research and Evaluation. 2009;**14**:20. Available from: https://scholarworks.umass.edu/pare/vol14/iss1/20

[25] Christiaensen L, Boisvert R. On Measuring Household Food Vulnerability: Case Evidence from Northern Mali. Working Paper. Department of Agricultural, Resource, and Managerial Economics. Ithaca, New York: Cornell University; 2000

[26] Watts M. Silent Violence: Food, Famine and Peasantry in Northern Nigeria. Berkeley: University of California Press; 1983

[27] Corbett J. Famine and household coping strategies. World Development. 1988;**16**(9):1099-1112

[28] Devereux S. Goats before ploughs: Dilemmas of household response sequencing during food shortages. IDS Bulletin. 1993;**24**(2):52-59

[29] Frankenberger T. Household food security: A conceptual review. In: Maxwell S, Frankenberger T, editors. Household Food Security: Concepts, Indicators, Measurements: A Technical Review. New York and Rome: UNICEF and IFAD; 1992

[30] Field A. Discovering Statistics Using SPSS. 2nd ed. SAGE Publications; 2005 Available from: https://www.researchgate.net/publication/247826587

Chapter 8

How to Build Food Safety Resilience in Commercial Restaurants?

Rayane Stephanie Gomes De Freitas and Elke Stedefeldt

Abstract

In this chapter, food safety is portrayed as an intrinsic component of food security and food systems. The objective is to discuss the 'commercial restaurant' system and the 'kitchen worker' subsystem from the perspective of building resilience in food safety. Relationship maps built for the system and subsystem guide the presentation and discussion of structural, organisational, social and symbolic aspects and elements. Resilience investigation is based on the references of the International Risk Governance Centre Resource Guide on Resilience and current and emerging topics related to food safety, such as risk perception of foodborne diseases, cognitive illusions, sociological aspects, social dimension of taste, humanisation and working conditions and precariousness of work in kitchens. In the final section, a list of recommendations for building resilience in commercial restaurants is presented to help researchers, decision-makers and practice agents apply this concept in their fields of expertise.

Keywords: food safety, food systems, restaurants, food handlers, foodborne disease

1. Introduction

There is an urgent need for food safety to be critically rethought in the twenty-first century, considering the breadth of systemic interconnections that predispose food, the environment, animals and humans to known and unknown hazards. These hazards may be present in activities related to food production, processing, distribution, preparation and consumption. One of the barriers to the scientific advancement of food safety is that it is often not treated as an essential and indispensable component of food security in food systems.

However, these three components are inextricably linked. According to the report *The State of Food Security and Nutrition in the World 2021*, food security and nutrition embrace the right of everyone to access quality food based on practices that promote health and are environmentally, culturally, economically and socially sustainable, considering the lenses of food systems as essential to address recent issues [1]. Unsafe food exposes people to several diseases and malnutrition, and there is a greater probability of these conditions worsening among the most vulnerable [2]. Quality food, on the other hand, corresponds to harmless food produced in a way that respects the interaction between man, animal welfare and environmental conservation, provides healthy food choices and encompasses the dimensions of food preference, food preparation, feeding practices, food storage and water access [3, 4]. Food safety should be repositioned, because it is a component that undoubtedly makes up the triad, which includes food security and food systems, guaranteeing the human right to adequate food and health.

The crisis triggered by the COVID-19 pandemic exposed the fragility and unpreparedness of health services and the vulnerability of humans to the deficiencies caused by the current food system in several areas, making the words 'foresight, preparedness, and resilience' the new directive for leaders of global food systems [5]. Therefore, food safety needs to expand its scope of action, i.e. extend beyond the regulations that ensure the prevention of foodborne diseases (FBD) and also cover the long-term threats arising from risks associated with food, which affect the population and ecosystem at a global level [6].

Nowadays, people face an extremely complex paradigm, which will be difficult to understand and solve if it is only comfortably based on digital modelling, artificial intelligence, Big Data, large economic resources and food surpluses [5, 7]. This paradigm is imbricated by social and political aspects, which are erased by the dehumanisation of the people making up the systems due to the use of digital and technological resources in an issue that requires a broad approach on human values [7]. The systems' resilience approach allows for incursion on aspects and elements that permeate multiple domains, such as social, psychological, physical and information [8]. Nonetheless, the structural, organisational, social and symbolic domains that permeate commercial restaurants and kitchen workers, as a system and subsystem respectively, with focus on the issues of humanisation and the precariousness of work in the industry, have been scarcely investigated.

The theoretical references regarding resilience and aspects in relation to social and symbolic dimensions, respectively, which underpin the analyses presented here, are the two volumes of the International Risk Governance Center (IRGC) Resource Guide on Resilience [9, 10] and the social theory of the French philosopher and sociologist Pierre Bourdieu [11, 12]. In light of Pierre Bourdieu's social theory, which describes the constant dialectics between the individual and the social world as modulators of actions, thoughts and judgements [11], the social and symbolic aspects present in the system (i.e. commercial restaurants) and subsystems (i.e. consumers, managers and kitchen workers) are presented and discussed in this chapter.

The National Academy of Sciences defines resilience as 'the ability to prepare and plan for, absorb, recover from, and more successfully adapt to adverse events' [13]. Food safety resilience in commercial restaurants was conceptualised based on this definition and following the proposition by Linkov et al. [8], which states that to operationalise the concept of resilience, it is necessary to describe the resilience of what, for what and for whom. We propose that the concept of 'food safety resilience in commercial restaurants' is the ability of a system to prepare proactively for an adverse event, whether of immediate scope (e.g. FBD, notifications, complaints or fines) or related to globally imminent crises in health and, in its occurrence, have the knowledge, skill and ability to absorb it, recover and adapt to the new state, ensuring the humanisation of individuals at all stages of the process.

Meal expenses outside home favourably influence the economy of a country and represent a significant part of family spending; however, eating out can present risks to the consumers' health [14, 15]. The commercial restaurants of interest in the present discussion comprise establishments outside the institutional scope (e.g. companies, schools and hospitals), focusing on self-service, à la carte, fast food and similar modalities.

We understand the need to view commercial restaurants as a large system to characterise their particularities and interconnections with other systems and subsystems. This broad and detailed knowledge has the potential to provide decision-makers with information capable of minimising the vulnerability of places to external and internal shocks. The reference of resilience fits perfectly into this issue, since it seeks to investigate and manage systemic risks that are not easily detected using traditional risk analysis or that have low probability of occurrence but have serious consequences [16].

The objective of this chapter is to present and discuss the commercial restaurant system and the kitchen worker subsystem (i.e. professionals directly involved in meal production) to provide the means for food safety to be humanised, critically rethought, repositioned in the face of the current interconnected scenario of food systems and resilient in the face of imminent disruptive events.

2. Commercial restaurants as a system

The commercial restaurant system anchors three fundamental subsystems: consumers, managers and employees (i.e. professionals directly and indirectly linked with meal production). The system shown in **Figures 1** and **2** summarises the relations established between the system and subsystems. The construction of this system was based on the current scenario of restaurants in the city of São Paulo, SP, Brazil. São Paulo is recognised as the largest Brazilian metropolis with the largest number of inhabitants in the country, and although it is the economic heart of South America's largest economy, holding the largest stock market and sheltering the headquarters for many companies overall Latin American, it has intense socio-economic and socio-spatial inequalities [17, 18].

In its current conformation, this system is governed by competitiveness, in that each restaurant seeks to maintain its reputation and attract more customers than its competitors. To this end, the order of priorities for commercial restaurants is to guarantee tasty meals, cost-effectiveness in the production of each meal, rapid delivery, quality service, an environment that provides a pleasant experience to the consumer and finally, the safety of the food offered. However, the lack of food safety can ruin the image of a restaurant, causing layoffs, fines, notifications or even the closure.

2.1 Consumer subsystem

The consumer subsystem has an extremely relevant role, as consumers' individual or collective decisions regarding food consumption and production have the potential to impact and even drive new practices towards food systems that provide healthy and sustainable meals [3]. However, consumers often do not recognise their role as protagonists within the system. Their order of priorities for choosing the restaurant is tasty meals, cost-effectiveness, service agility, helpful service, pleasant environment and food safety. Consumers have gaps in the knowledge that they can be sources of external contamination of food in restaurants through practices such as coughing,

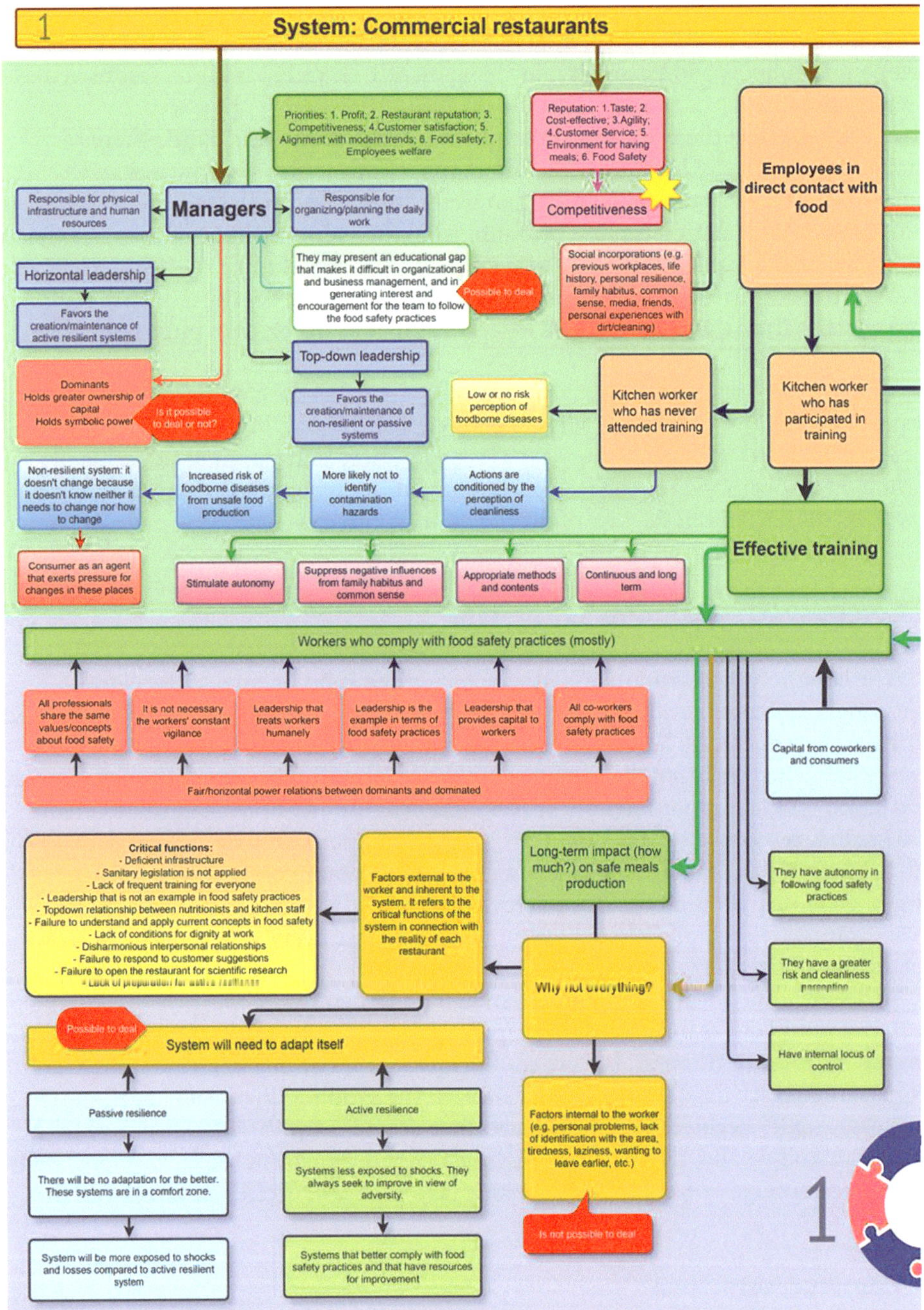

Figure 1.
*Commercial restaurant system map—part 1. For a complete overview, see also part 2 (**Figure 2**).*

sneezing, touching food with dirty hands, among other similar actions, and regarding a broad notion of risky situations and conditions for food contamination presented in sanitary laws. However, in case consumers experience an FBD or witness something that is inconsistent with food safety, they stop going to the place. Although food safety is least prioritised, it is relevant in the determination of the choice of restaurant.

DOI: http://dx.doi.org/10.5772/intechopen.101481

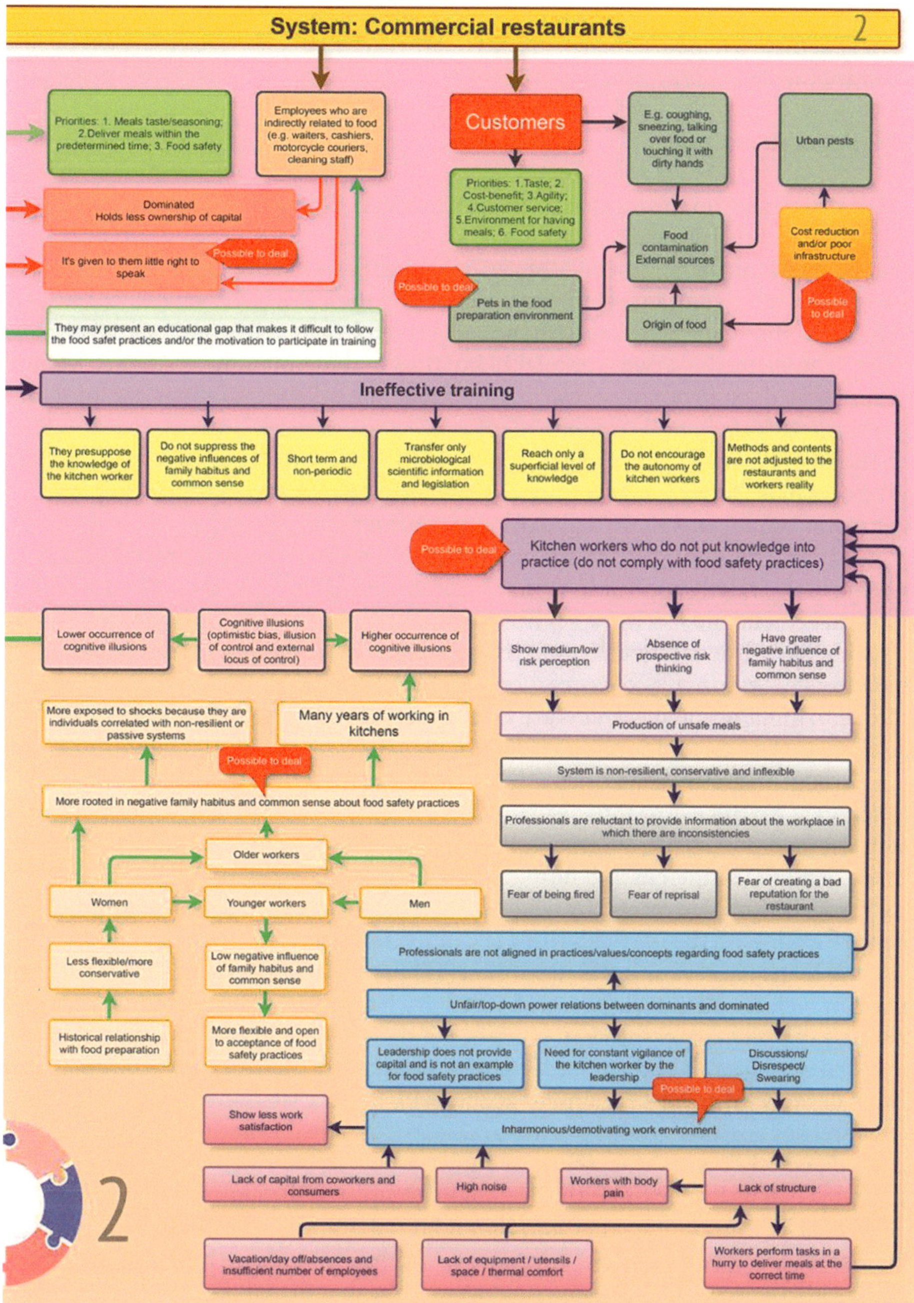

Figure 2.
*Commercial restaurant system map—part 2. For a complete overview, see also part 1 (**Figure 1**).*

We state the need for public policies on food safety to empower consumers as agents of safe practices and advocates for change, through actions that generate knowledge about the impacts of unsafe food on food systems and human health.

Other external sources of contamination, such as the origin of the food, urban pests and the presence of domestic animals in the meal preparation environment, are likely to affect the systems. It is possible to deal with these sources of contamination that threaten food safety, as the infrastructure and economic resources of restaurants are available for such purposes.

2.2 Manager subsystem

Managers make up the most influential subsystem within the system, as they are responsible for organising and planning daily work, physical structure and human resources. For managers, the order of service priorities is established in the following sequence: profit, restaurant reputation, improving their competitiveness, consumer satisfaction, alignment with modern industry trends, food safety and employee welfare. The leadership style is crucial in building and maintaining resilient systems. Horizontal leadership organises the environment in a collaborative manner, provides improvements based on the opinion of all employees, shares food safety values with the whole team and ensures decent working conditions. This leadership model contributes to building resilient systems, as it recognises that food safety requires investing in employee welfare and workplace harmony.

Educational gaps (e.g. difficulties in interpreting texts, concepts and technical language in their daily application) in this subsystem can negatively influence business management and the work environment, decreasing the incentive to follow food safety practices. It is noteworthy that the education of leaders is a step to be promoted constantly in a way that it covers contents beyond food safety. Themes that can be included to build resilient systems are meal production sustainability, water use awareness in the stages of food preparation, management of food quantities to avoid waste through disposal, use of sustainable packaging, reduction of ultra-processed foods in recipes, full use of food, waste management, conscious use of cleaning materials, food purchase from small producers and local traders, combating precariousness of work in kitchens and humanisation of labour relations.

The social world, governed by visible and invisible structures, permeates the sphere of work with the particularities of family, friend and social class experiences and permanence in several areas. Bourdieu [11] proposes that human beings act, think, appreciate and notice the world through a lens called *habitus*, forged through their life experiences and the characteristics of the social class to which they belong. The social world is full of disputes for power positions, which establish the dominant and the dominated agents. Dominant agents with the largest amount of capital, i.e. concrete or abstract assets that are rare, scarce or valuable in their field (work industry), whether economic, social or cultural, govern the rules of the social space analysed [11]. The leadership is the dominant group, and through the recognition of their capital by the dominated group, they hold the symbolic power in restaurants.

However, the symbolic power relegated to dominant agents in this work industry often reverberates in dehumanising practices for the dominated, i.e. kitchen workers. These dehumanising practices, in terms of treatment, social interaction, guarantee of rights, valuation or recognition of work, undermine any possibility of building resilient systems. Resilience requires initiative and proactivity, as they are needed to develop adaptive systems that can respond to unavoidable events [19], and these elements are not likely to be developed in environments that dehumanise work teams. The question 'is it possible to deal or not?' found in the system map (**Figure 1**), was proposed to raise the problem of the secular social paradigm established between managers and employees (dominant and dominated, respectively) on power issues, with the intention of overcoming it and subsequently achieving a desirable level of system resilience.

2.3 Kitchen worker subsystem

This subsystem comprises highly complex relationships and singularities shaped by social, symbolic, educational, generational, cognitive and motivational aspects that are influenced by social incorporations in previous work, the dimensions of the act of cooking and food safety as millennial practices.

For better understanding, this subsystem has been subdivided into employees who have direct contact with food, i.e. who produce the meals, and employees who do not prepare food, but have indirect contact with it, such as cleaning staff, waiters, motorcycle couriers and cashiers. Both groups have common characteristics concerning the high probability of having educational gaps that hinder the monitoring of food safety practices and the motivation to participate in training in the area and having limited right to speak in their workplaces. Emphasis should be given to the fact that food safety can only be implemented in the foreground when all professionals can collaborate with the construction of food safety values and decisions appropriate to their own social contexts, regardless of their professional position at the restaurant [20]. Resilience must be the base of the pillars of a collective construction that does not scold or punish those who speak out and collaborate with their own work and life experiences. It is understood that on a micro scale (i.e. individual), resilience must operate considering human experiences, rights and well-being [21].

The service priorities of the group of employees who produce the meals are arranged in the following order: taste and seasoning of the meals served, agility to deliver the meals within the predetermined time and finally, food safety. In the Brazilian context, it has been noted that knowledge of food safety, having not been stimulated, presented and reiterated throughout the years of basic education, is outdated, creating a gap for its practical application and the recognition of its relevance.

There are two segments within the aforementioned group: kitchen workers who have never participated in food safety training and those who have already participated. Regarding the former, studies show that their level of knowledge about food safety and hygiene and their perception of FBD risk are low [22, 23]. Risk perception refers to the way people understand the likelihood of adverse events [24]. Safe food handling by the workers of this group is mostly supported by their perception of cleanliness of the premises and food instead of the perception of FBD risk. As a result, there is a greater likelihood of not identifying the hazards that cause FBD, whether chemical, physical or biological, and consequently, a greater risk of FBD.

At this point, we would like to conceptualise and characterise a variant of resilience for the commercial restaurant system, the 'non-resilient'. Non-resilient systems are inflexible and disharmonious environments, which undergo major infrastructural, economic, organisational and social impacts in the occurrence of an adverse event, as they lack the technological, human and financial conditions to improve the aspects that make up their systems. They may find themselves in a scenario of food production within the stipulated schedule, but in conditions wherein food safety is at high risk and working conditions can be precarious and dehumanised. The presence of researchers in the area (e.g. Nutrition, Veterinary Medicine, Biomedicine and Food Engineering) is considered a threat to these systems, which do not seek to improve the quality of meals offered to consumers and fear sanitary inspection acts, as they are aware of their non-compliance with food safety practices. Consumers are the main subsystem that can improve these systems through complaints; however, most are not likely to be addressed because of general system disorganisation, lack of resources and lack of food safety education by leaders and employees.

Systems with kitchen workers who never participated in food safety training do not possess the desired characteristics for building and maintaining resilience.

It is essential to note the complex and interconnected web of relationships between elements and aspects belonging to the segments within this subsystem. Kitchen workers who have participated in food safety training tend to present characteristics consistent with the type of training they have received. Effective training seeks, among its specificities, to be continuous, long-term and appropriate in method and content, and it aims to suppress practices that represent an FBD risk arising from family *habitus*, cognitive illusions and common sense regarding food safety, thus stimulating the autonomy of kitchen workers.

Cognitive illusions lead people to have judgements, perceptions or memories that differ from objective reality and occur involuntarily, being difficult to prevent [25]. Optimistic bias is the manifestation of a positive perspective regarding future events, and with it, a person feels protected from negative events or less susceptible to them [26, 27]. The illusion of control causes people to present an illusory perspective of control over situations that is incompatible with reality [28]. Both illusions have been documented in research with food handlers [29, 30]. Internal locus of control reveals whether a person notices that their actions stem from their own behaviours and not from external agents (e.g. luck, chance, fate, powerful people and superior beings) [31]. Research has shown that the internal locus of control is the most appropriate for kitchen workers, as they can take responsibility for the food safety practices adopted in the preparation of meals, which does not occur when they present an external locus of control [22, 32].

Fair and horizontal power relations between the dominant and the dominated created by the stimulus generated in the work team cause a multiplicity of actions and behaviours that positively influence the incorporation of knowledge regarding food safety practices. Harmonious environments that collectively encourage food safety can present resilience in the face of adverse events.

Symbolic gains have an indispensable role in the spheres of individual and collective behaviour. The recognition given by managers, co-workers and consumers, understood here as capitals of this social space, legitimates the value of the work done. Therefore, the amount of capital possessed by each worker determines the positions in which they are distributed, and it may influence the group regarding leadership in food safety and social support. Humanisation permeates symbolic gains, since recognition is inherent to human identity, and its absence can translate into a form of oppression, self-image depreciation and a reductive way of life [33].

Kitchen workers who receive effective food safety training and apply the knowledge in their daily practice tend to have a long-term impact on safe food production, decreasing the risk of FBD. However, some gaps can still occur in the follow-up of safe practices because of both factors internal to the kitchen worker and factors external to them, which are inherent to the systems. Regarding internal factors, we understand that there are action thresholds, such as personal problems, lack of identification with the restaurant sector, tiredness, laziness and desire to leave early. Uncertainty is one of the crucial elements to understand, study and manage risks [34]. Uncertainty associated with the reference of resilience, especially regarding the flexibility of systems, helps understand that it is not possible to have total control of all risks and that adaptations are necessary [8]. Acknowledging the existence of these factors strengthens the means for decision-makers to adjust their actions, practices and training modes to anticipate adverse events that may arise from human limitations relevant to the area.

External factors are correlated to critical functions adjusted to the reality of each place that can result in shocks to commercial restaurant systems. The critical functions identified so far are deficient infrastructure, failure to follow the rules in the sanitary legislations, lack of frequent training for all workers in the system, leadership that is not the example to be followed in food safety practices, top-down relationship of nutritionists with employees, lack of understanding and use of current food safety concepts, lack of conditions conducive to dignity at work, disharmonious interpersonal relationships, lack of response to consumers' suggestions, lack of openness towards scientific research in the place and lack of planning and preparation for resilience.

While recognising the existence of critical functions of structural, organisational, social and symbolic orders, which hinder the construction of resilience, it is also realised that systems need to adapt because of their own characteristics, aiming at better preparation and planning for adverse situations.

Given this fact, two models of action for resilience can be implemented, the passive or the active. Martin [35] conceptualises two types of resilience in view of the referential of safety and risk. Passive resilience is established in the absorption of adverse events, rapid recovery and return to the state of normality or usual functioning, while active resilience, as an improvement, seeks to become stronger with the learning provoked by adversity, generating greater capacity to deal with future disruptive events [35]. Based on this reflection, we developed conceptualisations applied to food safety in commercial restaurants, which are as follows:

Passive resilience: Passive resilience is present in commercial restaurants in which no adaptations to improve the elements and practices are implemented after the adverse event, even though recovery occurs. Meal preparation happens within the stipulated period, but safe practices in food safety are not applied in most of them. A certain accommodation of the individuals of these systems is identified since the meals are delivered without major procedural difficulties, and there is no charge by formal agencies regarding full compliance with safe practices. In these environments, social relations between kitchen workers and managers are often conflicting, and there is no openness to conduct research because of the insecurity generated by the environment. In these restaurants, consumers act as the main agents capable of promoting changes related to food safety.

Active resilience: Commercial restaurants that are active resilient systems have high capacity to recover from and adapt to adverse events. They become consolidated in systems that are more flexible and open to changes that result in food safety and workers' well-being. As a result, there is greater work organisation and higher level of alignment in structural, formative and interactional issues. Active resilience represents the ideal conditions of this type of system. In the occurrence of an adverse event, the restaurants that present this variant recover more quickly, which demonstrates that they have learned and are in better conditions to respond to new adverse events.

In the restaurant context, passive resilience is preferred over non-resilience. However, when active resilience is experienced, restaurants tend to be less vulnerable to internal and external shocks that can disrupt normal functioning generating negative effects on the economy of the place, on workers and on the consumers' health. Hence, it is recommended to manage systems with the construction of active resilience as an objective.

Studying kitchen workers who have participated in ineffective training has shown that it is, among several characteristics, unable to suppress negative influences on food safety arising from family *habitus* and common sense, not periodic and constant, focuses only on passing microbiological scientific information and legislation, reaches a superficial level of knowledge and does not stimulate the autonomy of kitchen workers. They present medium to low-risk perception, absence of prospective risk thinking and greater influence of actions inconsistent with safe practices found in common sense and family *habitus*, such as defrosting at room temperature, reusing leftovers of ready-to-eat food, prolonged exposure of food to room temperature and not disposing of possibly contaminated food.

Moreover, restaurants wherein this scenario is a reality are highly likely to present a 'non-resilient' system, with characteristics of conservatism and inflexibility. These social spaces indirectly cause the suppression of kitchen workers' right to speak about their working conditions and food safety, for fear of losing their job, reprisals or generating a bad reputation for their workplace.

A disharmonic or non-motivating work environment, an aspect that can be changed during the preparation stage for the construction of active resilience, combines inappropriate and unfair conditions between leaders and employees, conflicts, swearing and disrespect among the team and the lack of shared values, practices and concepts in food safety from all those present in the workplace. Disharmonic or non-motivating environments dehumanise workers and cause precarious working conditions since job satisfaction is insufficient, and they have poor infrastructure (i.e. lack of equipment, utensils, space to work, thermal comfort, insufficient number of employees and high noise levels), which can lead to pain and occupational diseases [36, 37]. Furthermore, it is possible to find workers hurrying to meet the schedule for finishing the meals because of the lack of structure, which makes them more susceptible to errors, work accidents and the non-performance of steps essential to food safety.

Throughout the text, and also indicated on the system map (**Figures 1** and **2**), situations in which changes can be made and situations that are difficult to access because of their individual and particular character are highlighted. This holistic and integrated view of elements, factors and aspects enables decision-makers, policy makers and leaders of each system to identify the vulnerabilities present either on a micro (e.g. subsystems) or macro scale (economic sector of out-of-home meals and public health), contributing to food safety and food security in food systems.

3. Social and subjective aspects of the kitchen worker subsystem

Considering its high complexity and multiple singularities, a subsystem map (**Figure 3**) was developed to facilitate the visualisation of the elements pertinent to this subsystem. Only the aspects that have not yet been presented in the system will be depicted.

Meal taste and seasoning have been established as a priority of effort and commitment from the perspective of the kitchen worker. Culinary knowledge comes from the culture of each nation and region passed on from generation to generation and transposed to the *habitus*. The social dimension of taste incorporates the *habitus* with food-related family practices and taste elements characteristic of each social class, reflected in lifestyle and preferences regarding product and food use and consumption [12]. Knowledge exchange between individuals in the restaurants they work or have worked for enables cultural exchange, enriching the result of the meals and the learning of practices that can help or hinder food safety.

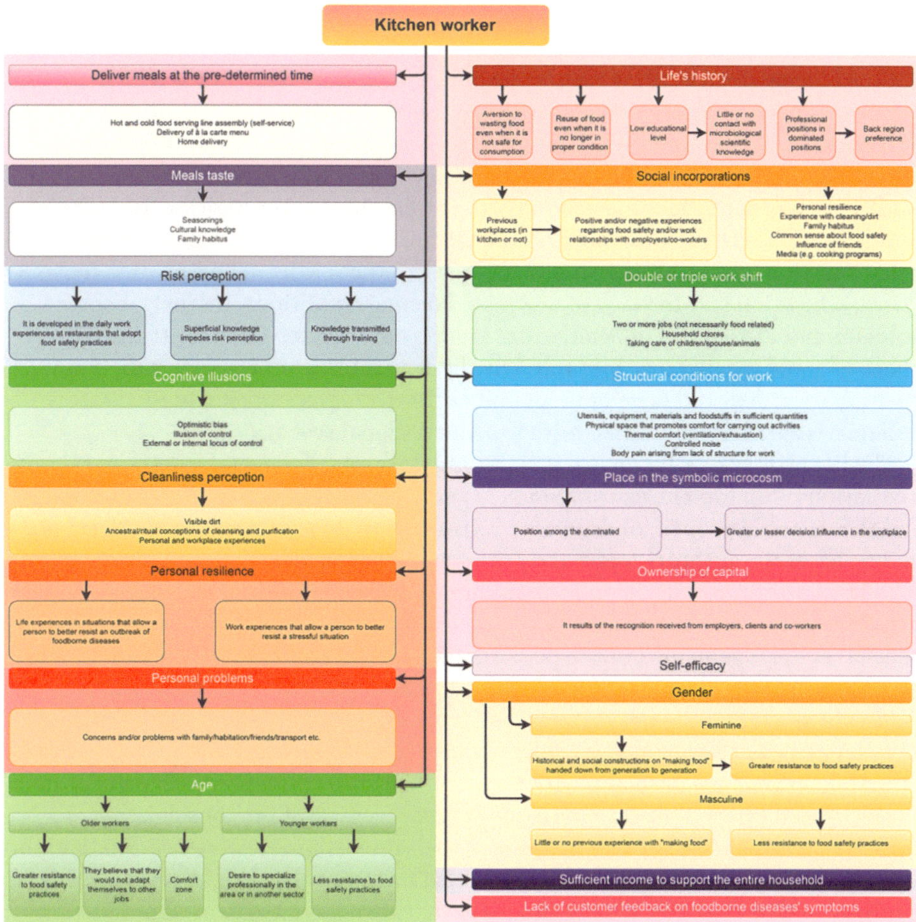

Figure 3.
Kitchen worker subsystem map.

The perception of cleanliness in the work environment and of oneself also acts as a guide for these practices, being shaped in the aforementioned basis and in the referential of dirt and cleanliness (i.e. purification) ancestrally brought by diverse cultures to culminate in what is now understood as hygiene [38, 39].

Self-efficacy, the foundation of human action, refers to how much a person believes in their own ability to control to some extent their functioning and that of the environment, reaching spheres of motivation self-regulation through result expectations [40, 41]. It is believed that self-efficacy can modulate kitchen workers' food safety practices as they envision benefits to consumer health, reducing multiple harms in their workplace and maintaining their jobs. Self-efficacy, when developed favourably, tends to reduce vulnerability to stress and depression and strengthen aspects of resilience in the face of future adversity [41]. In a personal scope, resilience is defined by the Oxford Advanced American Dictionary as 'the ability of people or things to feel better quickly after something unpleasant, such as shock, injury, etc.' [42]. In the context of commercial restaurants, personal resilience is built owing to life and work experiences that enable kitchen workers to better withstand and recover to respond satisfactorily to the occurrence of an FBD, shocks of any order and stressful situations. In a systemic way, micro (individual) and macro (systems) scale resilience are interrelated, and it is not possible to dissociate or compartmentalise them, since one affects the other.

Considering the precariousness present in the meals production sector, it is common to observe kitchen workers having double or triple shifts in order to ensure the livelihood of their families. These shifts can be composed of another work shift, temporary activities related to food production or in another sector and household and family care activities. It is necessary to emphasise that the political and employment scenarios affect the workload and quality of life of these workers. In addition, in the Brazilian context, this group is composed of people from low-income social classes, who often face the lack of adequate housing conditions, urban transport problems and difficulties in health care, among others. Such facts constitute the sphere of concerns that inhabit their daily lives and influence the structure that would be suitable for their full development and performance as workers. In food safety, resilience is also interconnected with broader national scenarios.

The life history of kitchen workers can also influence food safety decisions. Living in situations with food insecurity tends to generate resistance towards discarding food that is not in proper condition for consumption. Making an analysis based on the studies of the anthropologist and sociologist Goffman [43], kitchen workers often dislike interaction with the public, maintain a distance and are shy, which reflects in their preference to work in the back region (i.e. the kitchen) rather than expose themselves to judgements or false performances in the front region (i.e. the dining area with consumers), a fact which is also a product of their social position.

Finally, gender and age issues regarding kitchen workers are relevant in identifying obstacles to food safety practices. Older workers in the sector show an inclination to maintain the *status quo* of their practices, i.e. they are more resistant to changes proposed in view of food safety updates. This tends to occur because of the consolidation of a professional *habitus* throughout the years of their professional experience. Furthermore, because of their social position, they report that they consider themselves incapable of adapting to other jobs, performing functions that are not related to meal production [44]. Male and young workers are usually less resistant to changing their practices, both for being less influenced by the matriarchal reference to meal preparation and for having little or no previous experience with cooking. Knowing these facts enables the designing of strategies aligned to the needs of each profile, aiming to overcome socially constructed barriers and foster new practices for the construction of active resilience.

4. Recommendations for building food safety resilience in commercial restaurants

Table 1 lists recommendations that can improve the development of public policies, legislation and guidelines for the meal production sector to contribute to the construction of active food safety resilience.

The recommendations to build food safety resilience in commercial restaurants are intended to promote the absorption, recovery and adaptation capacity of the systems in the occurrence of adverse events through preparation and planning at multiple levels of dimensions involving people, structure and organisation and by considering the interconnections with sustainability needed in the area. The steps of absorption, recovery and adaptation tend to occur in a more agile and collaborative manner when the people involved in the systems understand the scope of action required to build active resilience and put efforts to achieve it in their daily work practice.

Recommendations for building food safety resilience in commercial restaurants
To provide all workers who make up the system with continuous education that is appropriate to their educational, management and food safety needs
To enable a work environment in which workers can exercise the right to speak without reprimands
To listen to all work team for collective decision-making on food safety organisation, planning and preparation
To share food safety and sustainability values with the entire team, aligning concepts on these topics
To stimulate means to make leaders, in micro or macro scale, a food safety example to be followed to motivate similar behaviour in the team
To provide structural and organisational means to implement food safety practices in the daily working routine
To make efforts to kitchen environments maintain horizontal relations between all positions, based on dialogue and qualitative listening regarding multiple needs and experiences
To combat the precariousness of the meal production sector through decent working conditions
To humanise relations between professionals in all positions based on respect for individuality, appreciation of their work and recognition of the importance of everyone's voice in collective decision-making in food safety
To periodically investigate the system and subsystems for possible vulnerabilities concerning critical functions and new situations that may emerge
To have work plans for resilience preparedness and FBD prevention adapted to the reality of the systems and updated face of relevant changes, without being bound by time frames
To have a vision of the interconnection of systems (field production, food service production, storage, transport, distribution, water resources, environmental preservation, etc.), implementing actions that ensure sustainability at all stages
To become aware that the use of financial resources in measures or infrastructure to ensure food safety is proactive action to prevent financial and other losses to the systems
To develop guidelines and training in food safety that include not only microbiological aspects and sanitary legislation, but also cultural practices and experiences in preparing safe meals in the context of social interaction (i.e. with family, friends, celebrations, common sense, etc.) to contextualise these guidelines
To encourage interdisciplinary research allied to human sciences, which will focus on understanding the factors identified in **Figure 1** as 'is not possible to deal'
To encourage research on resilience in interconnected systems: food purchase, transport, distribution and other systems

Table 1.
Recommendations to build food safety resilience in commercial restaurants.

5. Conclusions

The concepts, elements, factors and knowledge that make up food safety resilience in commercial restaurants point to the fact that its construction needs to be based on a strong foundation to guarantee fair and appropriate conditions for working, learning about food safety and sustainability, humanising interpersonal relationships between professionals and providing an environment that facilitates collective decision-making regarding food safety and its daily application.

As subsystems, consumers, managers and kitchen workers contribute according to their dispositions, capacities and perceptions to mitigate or intensify FBD risks and to create decent working conditions. One of the central characteristics of risk is uncertainty, which permeates the decisions of these three subsystems that can engage in building active resilience through their choices.

When considering resilient food systems that are capable of withstanding adversities, the interconnected systemic vision is the most capable of promoting preparation and planning, as it ensures food safety, food security and sustainability in its broad aspects and particularities.

Acknowledgements

This chapter was funded partly by the Brazilian Funding Agency Coordenação de Aperfeiçoamento de Pessoal de Nível Superior—Brasil (CAPES)—Fund Code 001.

Conflict of interest

The authors declare no conflict of interest.

Thanks

We thank Angelo Bonito for the improvements made in the graphic design of all figures presented in this chapter.

Author details

Rayane Stephanie Gomes De Freitas[1] and Elke Stedefeldt[2*]

1 Postgraduate Program in Nutrition, Universidade Federal de São Paulo, São Paulo, Brazil

2 Department of Preventive Medicine, Universidade Federal de São Paulo, São Paulo, Brazil

*Address all correspondence to: elke.stedefeldt@unifesp.br

References

[1] FAO, IFAD, UNICEF, PMA, OMS. O Estado da Segurança Alimentar e Nutricional no Mundo 2021. Transformando os sistemas alimentares para a segurança alimentar, nutrição melhorada e dietas saudáveis acessíveis para todos. Roma: FAO; 2021. Available from: doi:10.4060/cb4474en [Accessed: 24 January 2021]

[2] WHO—World Health Organization. Food Safety: Fact Sheet No 399 [Internet]. 2015. Available from: https://www.who.int/campaigns/world-health-day/2015/fact-sheet.pdf [Accessed: 08 July 2021]

[3] HLPE. Nutrition and Food Systems. A Report by the High Level Panel of Experts on Food Security and Nutrition of the Committee on World Food Security. Rome: HLPE; 2017. p. 152. Available from: http://www.fao.org/3/i7846e/i7846e.pdf [Accessed: 05 July 2021]

[4] IPC Global Partners. Integrated Food Security Phase Classification Technical Manual Version 3.1. Evidence and Standards for Better Food Security and Nutrition Decisions. Rome: IPC; 2021. Available from: http://www.ipcinfo.org/fileadmin/user_upload/ipcinfo/manual/IPC_Technical_Manual_3_Final.pdf [Accessed: 15 Dez 2021]

[5] Herren HR. Introduction. In: Herren HR, Haerlin B, IASSSTD+10 Advisory Group, editors. Transformation of Our Food Systems: The Making of a Paradigm Shift. Berlin: Zukunftsstiftung Landwirtschaft; 2020. pp. 9-16. Available from: https://www.arc2020.eu/wp-content/uploads/2020/09/FullTextOfTransformationFoodSystems.pdf [Accessed: 05 July 2021]

[6] Swinburn B. The agriculture and health nexus: A decade of paradigm progress but patchy policy actions. In: Herren HR, Haerlin B, IASSSTD+10 Advisory Group, editors. Transformation of Our Food Systems: The Making of a Paradigm Shift. Berlin: Zukunftsstiftung Landwirtschaft; 2020. pp. 130-136. Available from: https://www.arc2020.eu/wp-content/uploads/2020/09/FullTextOfTransformationFoodSystems.pdf [Accessed: 05 July 2021]

[7] Haerlin B. The making of a paradigm shift. In: Herren HR, Haerlin B, IASSSTD+10 Advisory Group, editors. Transformation of Our Food Systems: The Making of a Paradigm Shift. Berlin: Zukunftsstiftung Landwirtschaft; 2020. pp. 17-20. Available from: https://www.arc2020.eu/wp-content/uploads/2020/09/FullTextOfTransformationFoodSystems.pdf [Accessed: 05 July 2021]

[8] Linkov I, Trump BD, Fox-Lent C. Resilience: Approaches to risk analysis and governance. In: Florin M-V, Linkov I, editors. IRGC Resource Guide on Resilience. Lausanne: EPFL International Risk Governance Center (IRGC); 2016. pp. 3-14. DOI:10.5075/epfl-irgc-228206.

[9] Florin M-V, Linkov I, editors. IRGC Resource Guide on Resilience. Lausanne: EPFL International Risk Governance Center (IRGC); 2016. p. 287. DOI:10.5075/epfl-irgc-228206

[10] Trump BD, Florin M-V, Linkov I. IRGC Resource Guide on Resilience, Domains of Resilience for Complex Interconnected Systems. Vol. 2. Lausanne: EPFL International Risk Governance Center (IRGC); 2018. p. 178. DOI: 10.5075/epfl-irgc-262527

[11] Bourdieu P. Coisas Ditas. 1st ed. São Paulo: Brasiliense; 1990. p. 234

[12] Bourdieu P. A distinção: crítica social do julgamento. São Paulo: Edusp; Porto Alegre: Zouk; 2007. p. 560

[13] NAS—National Academy of Sciences. Disaster resilience: A national imperative. In: Committee on Science, Engineering, and Public Policy. Washington: The National Academies Press; 2012. DOI: 10.17226/13457

[14] Santos MV, Proença RPC, Fiates GMR, Calvo MCM. Pay-per-kilo restaurants in the context of healthy eating away from home. Revista de Nutrição. 2011;**24**(4):641-649. DOI: 10.1590/S1415-52732011000400012

[15] IBGE—Instituto Brasileiro de Geografia e Estatística. Pesquisa de orçamentos familiares 2017-2018: primeiros resultados. Coordenação de Trabalho e Rendimento. Rio de Janeiro: IBGE, 2019. p. 69. Available from: https://biblioteca.ibge.gov.br/visualizacao/livros/liv101670.pdf [Accessed: 11 August 2021]

[16] Florin M-V, Trump BD. Resilience in the context of systemic risks: Perspectives from IRGC's guidelines for the governance of systemic risks. In: Trump BD, Florin M-V, Linkov I, editors. IRGC Resource Guide on Resilience, Domains of Resilience for Complex Interconnected Systems. Vol. 2. Lausanne: EPFL International Risk Governance Center (IRGC); 2018. pp. 60-68. DOI: 10.5075/epfl-irgc-262527

[17] Nakano AK. Estimativa da população vulnerável a perdas habitacionais residente na Região Metropolitana de São Paulo. In: Moreira FA, Rolnik R, Santoro PF, editors. Cartografias da produção, transitoriedade e despossessão dos territórios populares [livro eletrônico]. Observatório de remoções. Relatório bianual 2019-2020. São Paulo: Raquel Rolnik; 2020. p. 55-81. Available from: http://www.labcidade.fau.usp.br/wp-content/uploads/2021/01/OR_2020_completo-1-1.pdf [Accessed: 11 August 2021]

[18] Kotkin J, Cox W, Modarres A, Renn AM. Size is not the answer: the changing face of the global city. Research Report. Demographics and Policy. Chapman University and Civil Services College Singapore. 2014. Available from: https://www.chapman.edu/wilkinson/_files/the-changing-face-of-the-global-city.pdf [Accessed: 24 October 2021]

[19] Woods DD. Resilience is a verb. In: Trump BD, Florin M-V, Linkov I, editors. IRGC Resource Guide on Resilience, Domains of Resilience for Complex Interconnected Systems. Vol. 2. Lausanne: EPFL International Risk Governance Center (IRGC); 2018. pp. 167-172. DOI: 10.5075/epfl-irgc-262527

[20] De Freitas RSG, Stedefeldt E. COVID-19 pandemic underlines the need to build resilience in commercial restaurants' food safety. Food Research International. 2020;**136**:109472. DOI: 10.1016/j.foodres.2020.109472

[21] Barrett CB, Upton JB. Resilience as an integrative, measurable concept for humanitarian and development programming. In: Trump BD, Florin M-V, Linkov I, editors. IRGC Resource Guide on Resilience, Domains of Resilience for Complex Interconnected Systems. Vol. 2. Lausanne: EPFL International Risk Governance Center (IRGC); 2018. pp. 39-46. DOI: 10.5075/epfl-irgc-262527

[22] De Freitas RSG, Da Cunha DT, Stedefeldt E. Food safety knowledge as gateway to cognitive illusions of food handlers and the different degrees of risk perception. Food Research International. 2019;**116**:126-134. DOI: 10.1016/j.foodres.2018.12.058

[23] Insfran-Rivarola A, Tlapa D, Limon-Romero J, Baez-Lopez Y, Miranda-Ackerman M, Arredondo-Soto K, et al. A systematic review and meta-analysis of the effects of food safety and hygiene training on food handlers. Food. 2020;**9**(9):1169. DOI: 10.3390/foods9091169

[24] Boholm A. Risk perception and social anthropology: Critique of cultural theory. Ethnos. 1996;**61**(1-2):64-84. DOI: 10.1080/00141844.1996.9981528

[25] Pohl RF. Introduction: cognitive illusions. In: Pohl RF, editor. Cognitive Illusions: A Handbook on Fallacies and Biases in Thinking, Judgment and Memory. Hove and New York: Psychology Press—Taylor and Francis Group; 2004. pp. 1-20

[26] Weinstein ND. Unrealistic optimism about future life events. Journal of Personality and Social Psychology. 1980;**39**(5):806-820. Available from: https://citeseerx.ist.psu.edu/viewdoc/download?doi=10.1.1.535.9244&rep=rep1&type=pdf [Accessed: 12 August 2021]

[27] Weinstein ND. Optimisitc biases about personal risk. Science. 1989;**246**(4935):1232-1233. DOI: 10.1126/science.2686031

[28] Langer EJ. The illusion of control. Journal of Personality and Social Psychology. 1975;**32**(2):311-328. DOI: 10.1037/0022-3514.32.2.311

[29] Da Cunha DT, Braga ARC, Passos EDC, Stedefeldt E, De Rosso VV. The existence of optimistic bias about foodborne disease by food handlers and its association with training participation and food safety performance. Food Research International. 2015;**75**:27-33. DOI: 10.1016/j.foodres.2015.05.035

[30] Rossi MSC, Stedefeldt E, Da Cunha DT, De Rosso VV. Food safety knowledge, optimistic bias and risk perception among food handlers in institutional food services. Food Control. 2017;**73**:681-688. DOI: 10.1016/j.foodcont.2016.09.016

[31] Rotter JB. Generalized expectancies for internal versus external control of reinforcement. Psychological Monographs: General and Applied. 1966;**80**(1):1-28. DOI: 10.1037/h0092976

[32] Stedefeldt E, Zanin LM, Da Cunha DT, De Rosso VV, Capriles, VD, Saccol ALF. The role of training strategies in food safety performance: Knowledge, behavior, and management. In: Ricke SC, Donaldson JR, Phillips CA, editors. Food Safety—Emerging Issues, Technologies and Systems. Elsevier Inc; 2015. pp. 365-394. DOI: 10.1016/B978-0-12-800245-2.00018-6

[33] Taylor C. The politics of recognition. In: Taylor C, Appiah KA, Habermas J, Rockefeller SC, Walzer M, Wolf S, editors. Multiculturalism: Examining the Politics of Recognition. Princeton: Princeton University Press; 1994. pp. 25-73

[34] Boholm Å. The cultural nature of risk: Can there be an anthropology of uncertainty? Ethnos. 2003;**68**(2):159-178. DOI: 10.1080/0014184032000097722

[35] Martin P. The Rules of Security: Staying Safe in a Risky World. United Kingdom: Oxford University Press; 2019. p. 272

[36] Pehkonen I, Takala EP, Ketola R, Viikari-Juntura E, Leino-Arjas P, Hopsu L, et al. Evaluation of a participatory ergonomic intervention process in kitchen work. Applied Ergonomics. 2009;**40**(1):115-123. DOI: 10.1016/j.apergo.2008.01.006

[37] De Freitas RSG, Da Cunha DT, Stedefeldt E. Work conditions, social incorporations, and foodborne diseases risk: Reflections about the (non) compliance of food safety practices. Risk Analysis. 2020;**40**:926-938. DOI: 10.1111/risa.13453

[38] Douglas M. Purity and Danger: An Analysis of Concepts of Pollution and Taboo. New York: Routledge; 1966. p. 193

[39] De Freitas RSG, Stedefeldt E. Hygiene and humanization: Breaking the traditional view of food safety. Food Research International. 2020;**131**:108944. DOI: 10.1016/j.foodres.2019.108944

[40] Bandura A. Self-efficacy: The Exercise of Control. New York: W. H. Freeman and Company; 1997. p. 604

[41] Bandura A. Social cognitive theory: an agentic perspective. Annual Review of Psychology. 2001;**52**:1-26. DOI: 10.1146/annurev.psych.52.1.1

[42] Oxford University Press [Internet]. Oxford: 2021. Available from: https://www.oxfordlearnersdictionaries.com/definition/american_english/resilience [Accessed: 08 July 2021]

[43] Goffman E. A representação do eu na vida cotidiana. 10th ed. Petrópolis: Vozes; 2002. p. 233

[44] De Freitas RSG. Percepção de risco de doenças transmitidas por alimentos: desvelando o habitus do trabalhador de cozinha de restaurantes comerciais [thesis]. Santos: Universidade Federal de São Paulo; 2017

Chapter 9

Legumes Cropping and Nitrogen Fixation under Mediterranean Climate: The Case of Montado/Dehesa System

Fernando Teixeira

Abstract

Climate change contributes to the environmental pressures that the Montado/Dehesa systems are experiencing, leading to an impoverishment of the floristic composition of the understorey. The strongly acidic soils of these systems are associated with nutrient deficiencies, nutritional disorders and the toxicity of metals, especially Mn and Al; these problems are discussed with emphasis on the antagonism between Fe and Mn and the relationship between K concentration and Mg uptake and concentration. The potential for the use of the legume-rhizobia symbiosis to increase biological nitrogen fixation and avenues for research are discussed. The co-colonization of the roots of legumes with arbuscular mycorrhizal (AM) fungi and the effects on P and Mn uptake are discussed. A better understanding of the relationships between soil pH, organic matter content (SOM), microbial community, soil P content and the plant strategies to mobilize it, as well as plant effects on the soil solution concentrations of Mn, is important for the management of these systems. The increase of biological nitrogen fixation in these systems, through the breeding of tolerant cultivars to acidic soils and a stepwise legumes enrichment, alongside soil fertility management, may contribute to increasing biomass production, SOM content and overall ecological plasticity.

Keywords: sustainable agriculture, Montado/Dehesa, legume, biological nitrogen fixation, acid soil, Mediterranean climate

1. Introduction

Plant biomass production is strongly correlated with nitrogen (N) availability which, in most farming systems, is dependent on the use of N-fertilizers. These N-fertilizers are obtained, with few exceptions, from the Haber-Bosch industrial process of atmospheric N_2 fixation which is energy demanding and responsible for 1.44% of the global emissions of carbon dioxide (CO_2) [1]. Contrastingly, most plants of the family Fabaceae (legumes), which comprises 751 genera and 19,500 species [2], can establish symbiotic relationships with rhizobia bacteria capable of fixing atmospheric N_2 into ammonia (NH_3), through the development of root nodules that host the bacteria (bacteroids). This symbiosis has been explored by humankind since the early beginning of agriculture and it still is an essential part of many traditional agriculture farming systems (e.g., see [3]). In the Mediterranean basin and Europe at large, the rise of modern agriculture, which cannot be decoupled from relatively cheap N-fertilizers, has driven the abandonment of legumes in the farming systems. Still, legume usage in the frame of mixed pastures, and forages, did not decline over time as steeply as grain legumes did [4].

The Montado (in Portugal) or Dehesa (in Spain), is an agro-silvopastoral system, typical of the Southwestern part of the Iberian Peninsula, characterized by a savannah-like landscape, where the main tree species are cork and holm oak (*Quercus suber* and *Quercus ilex*, respectively), where it occupies an area of ca. 3.5 Mha [5]. The Montado/Dehesa is the result of the interaction of humans with the land, and it would not exist without it; cork and firewood harvesting, livestock, farming, pastures and cereal crops, among others, are activities that help to maintain the landscape features [5] and contribute to the rich biodiversity [6]. These ecosystems are presently under significant environmental pressures. Projections of the climate change in the Mediterranean basin show that in the decades to come the Iberian Peninsula will experience a reduction in precipitation and higher temperatures throughout the year (e.g., see [7]). Models suggest that these climatic changes will affect the distribution of the cork and holm oak, with an important reduction in the presence of these trees in the regions where they are presently found (e.g., see [8]). Other important environmental pressures on these ecosystems arise from the soil properties, affecting their resilience, namely, the strongly acidic reaction ($pH < 5.5$). In these soils, manganese (Mn) toxicity is often pointed out as the main cause of the low biomass productivity of the pastures (e.g., see [9]). Legumes may help to improve N content and P availability (organic P) through their rich underground biomass and surface plant residues and, thus, increase SOM content and counteract soil acidification. This chapter focuses on the legume-rhizobia symbiosis under rainfed farming in the acidic soils of the Montado/Dehesa systems, conditioned by the Mediterranean climate. The legume-rhizobia and tripartite symbiosis with AM fungi and a set of factors that have been identified as particularly challenging for legumes production are briefly reviewed. Possible avenues of research are identified that may allow, in the future, to enhance biological N-fixation and biomass production in these systems through a stepwise, low-input, legumes enrichment strategy.

2. Root-nodule symbiosis as mitigation of environmental pressures

The biological N-fixation produced by the legume-rhizobia symbiosis may have a profound effect on the Montado/Dehesa ecosystem by increasing the N content of the system and its availability to grasses and other forbs, increasing the overall biomass production and the soil organic matter (SOM) content. The term rhizobia designate diazotrophic bacteria of two different classes of Proteobacteria, encompassing species and strains well beyond those of the genus *Rhizobium*. Rhizobia N_2-fixation only occurs in the frame of the symbiotic relationship with legumes [10]. Legume-rhizobia symbiosis is energy demanding for the plants, and thus, it only happens if there's not enough nitrogen available (nitrate and ammonium) in the soil to meet the plants' needs (e.g., see [11]). The bacteria in the symbiosis receive in exchange photosynthates as a carbon source. The plants control the symbioses, and nodule formation, through regulatory mechanisms, such as the "autoregulation of nodulation" (AON), carbon and nitrogen regulation of nodulation, among others (e.g., [11]). For the symbiosis to occur, both the legume host and the microsymbiont must be compatible [12]. The soil and climate conditions found in the Montado/Dehesa will dictate if legumes sowed, even when inoculated with compatible rhizobia, will produce functional nodules, as the survival and thriving of both symbionts in the following years will only occur if both can cope with those conditions. In the next paragraphs, these environmental pressures are discussed along with the contribution of successful legume-rhizobia symbioses to mitigate them.

2.1 Soil reaction and toxicity of metals

Increasing SOM content may help to counteract soil acidification, to the extent that SOM constitutes an important proton buffer, and SOM depletion and low calcium (Ca^{2+}) saturation of the cation-exchange capacity (CEC) of the soil [13] may constitute one of the main reasons for soil acidification in the Montado/Dehesa system. The high concentration of protons in the soil solution leads to the solubilization of heavy metals that may become toxic to the plants, namely, aluminum (Al^{3+}) and Mn^{2+} (e.g. [14, 15]). The concentration of these toxic elements that plants may endure will vary with species and cultivars but often they have much lower thresholds than their wild counterparts (e.g., [16]). In low pH soils, nodule formation and nodule weight can be reduced by percentages above 90% and 50%, respectively [17]. Rhizobia bacteria can be found in a wide range of proton concentrations, with species (strains) surviving at pH values as low as 4 [18]. Nonetheless, soil acidification might have a profound effect on the survival of the bacterial strains present and thus on the occurrence of matching symbionts [19]. *Bradyrhizobium* spp. are, generally, more pH-resistant (tolerant) than *Rhizobium* spp. [17].

Proton [H^+] concentration in soil solution and the interaction with other elements, namely Al^{3+} and Mn^{2+}, affect plant growth. Aluminum [Al^{3+}] has no known biological function (e.g., [20]) but it can impair plant growth when in relatively high concentrations in the soil solution. The major factor affecting Al^{3+} concentration in soil solution is proton concentration and the presence of other ions that react with the dissolving/precipitating surfaces [15], namely, SOM (e.g., [21]). pH values above 4.5–5.5 are considered as leading to the precipitation of Al^{3+}which in relatively high concentrations affects root elongation and root hair formation likely due to the binding to the pectic matrix of the cell walls, substituting Ca, and hence cell wall thickening and rigidity (e.g., [22, 23]). The aerial part of the plant is also affected by Al^{3+} via induced nutrient deficiencies of magnesium (Mg), Ca and P, phytohormones imbalances and drought stress [22], but transport to the shoots, with some exceptions, is usually limited [24]. Plant Al-tolerance is characterized by the production of root exudates, organic acids and mucilage capable to chelate Al^{3+}, and by a lower CEC of the surface cell walls [22]. Pasture/forage legumes have different tolerance to different Al^{3+} concentrations. For example, the genus *Trifolium* has a higher tolerance than species of the genus *Medicago* (e.g., [25]), and very tolerant species, like *Lupinus luteus* (e.g., [26]), are capable of coping with Al^{3+} concentrations more than 20-fold than the most sensitive legumes. Wood et al. [18], working with *Trifolium repens* (white clover), observed an inhibitory effect of Al^{3+} on root hairs formation and root elongation, at concentrations of 50 μM and at pH 4.3 and 4.7, and no multiplication of *Rhizobium trifolii* and reduced nodulation for Al^{3+} concentrations of 50 μM at pH 5.5. Different rhizobia strains have been shown to grow at much higher Al^{3+} concentrations than the host [27]. Manganese [Mn^{2+}] plays an important role in plant growth, as a cofactor in many processes, from photosynthesis to the control of oxidative stresses (e.g., [28]); plant requirements of Mn are very low and a concentration of 50 μg Mn. g^{-1} shoot DM is considered sufficient for normal plant growth [29]. Mn^{2+} concentration in soil solution is pH related, with concentrations reducing sharply above pH values of ca. 5–5.5 (e.g., [30]), but it is also dependent on the oxidation-reduction conditions of the soil (e.g. [14]), plant characteristics, namely, carboxylate exsudation behavior [30], and the microbiological activity (e.g. [31]). In studies with nutrient solutions, with similar ranges of pH and Mn^{2+} concentrations, it has been reported the inhibitory effect of Mn on the formation of root hairs of important commercial crops, such as soybean (e.g., [32]). Other studies, with similar Mn^{2+} concentrations, did not find any effect of Mn on root hairs formation or root elongation, e.g. in *T. repens* (white clover) [18]. Chen et al. [32] suggest that the soybean responses to Mn toxic concentrations, leading to the inhibition of root elongation, may be due to root cell wall modification and lignification. Many transporters can transport excessive amounts of Mn into the root cells, such as the iron-regulated transporters (IRT1), the "natural resistance-associated macrophage protein" (NRAMP), and many others [28]. The mechanisms of plant Mn-tolerance involve both, the ability to excrete and to store Mn in the cells. Nazeri et al. [33] observed a sharp decrease of Mn concentration in the roots of non-mycorrhizal *Trifolium subterraneum* after the supply of P, consistent with the excretion of Mn as no change in concentration of Mn in the shoots was observed. Although the mechanisms for Mn storage in the shoots are not known for most species, the ability to increase the concentration of carboxylate anions in the cells to chelate Mn is a possible explanation at least for some species [29]. Wood et al. [18] did not detect any effect of Mn at 200 μM on nodule formation in *T. repens*, for a pH range from 4.3 to 5.5. On the other hand, Izaguirre-Mayoral and Sinclair [34] observed that Mn at concentrations of 70 and 90 μM inhibited growth and nodulation of a soybean Mn-sensitive genotype but not on a tolerant genotype. Critical toxicity concentrations for Mn in the above-ground biomass range from 200 to 3500 $\mu g.g^{-1}$ dry weight [35]. Some legume species are exceptionally tolerant to high leaf concentrations of Mn, above 7000 $\mu g.g^{-1}$ dry weight (e.g., *Lupinus albus*) [29]. Keyser et al. [36] found no effect of Mn^{2+} (200 μM solution) in the growth of 23 strains of cowpea rhizobia and 10 *Rhizobium japonicum* (*Bradyrhizobium japonicum*), although a slowed growth was observed when Ca^{2+} concentrations were also low. Wood et al. [18] did not observe any effect of Mn^{2+} (200 μM solution) on the numbers of *R. trifolii*, and no interaction with Ca.

2.2 Soil reaction, nutrient deficiencies and nodulation

Phosphorus [P] is an important element in molecules participating in the intracellular buffering system (the conjugate acid-base pair $H_2PO_4^-$–HPO_4^{2-}), in the energy metabolism of the cells (e.g., ATP, adenosine triphosphate), in the formation of nucleic acids, among others. In acidic soils, low available P in soil solution is mainly due to its retention as adsorbed P on the surface of soil particles of Al- and Fe oxides [37]. Some plant species can exudate to the rhizosphere important amounts of carboxylates that are capable to mobilize Al- and Fe-oxide-sorbed P and also organic P. The organic P is then hydrolyzed by phosphatases, which are exudate to the rhizosphere. The inorganic P uptake by the plant occurs through a high-affinity inorganic

P transporter in the plasma membrane of the root cells, belonging to the PHT1 gene family [38]. This strategy of P-mobilization is accompanied by the mobilization of other nutrients such as Mn [29]. Another strategy most plants follow is the promotion of symbiosis with arbuscular mycorrhizal (AM) fungi capable of scavenging phosphorus (available P) [39]; this strategy will be discussed further ahead. The relative importance of each of these strategies of P uptake, for each plant species/cultivar, and the interactions with the environment, may have an impact on the availability of other nutrients, namely, Mn and their uptake. Plants must possess adequate levels of phosphorus (P) otherwise the N-fixation rate by the microsymbiont will be conditioned by P-availability. For example, the molybdenum-dependent nitrogenase requires for each mol of N_2 reduction, 16 mol of ATP [40]. Nodulating plants allocate a substantial part of the P uptake to the nodules in soils with low available P [41] and P fertilization may have an important effect on biologically-fixated N (e.g. [42]).

Iron [Fe^{2+}] is essential for biological N-fixation, for example, due to its role in the FeMo cofactor of nitrogenase [43] and the prosthetic group of the leghemoglobin. Fe content and availability to plants in acidic soils are usually high, but plant Fe-deficiency can occur in sandy soils with high concentrations of Mn^{2+} in soil solution [44]. Legumes, like all dicots, mobilize Fe through the acidification of the rhizosphere; the mobilized $Fe^{3+}$is then reduced to Fe^{2+} by plasma membrane reductases and the uptake happens through plasma membrane iron-regulated transporters (IRT1), in what is known as the strategy I of iron uptake [45]. Mn and Fe antagonistic relationship has been observed in many studies with legumes and non-legumes (e.g. [46]). Izaguirre-Mayoral and Sinclair [34] observed that: (i) a higher Mn concentration in the leaves of two soybean cultivars when in the presence of low Fe and high Mn concentrations in the culture solution and; (ii) a lower concentration of Fe in the leaves with increasing Mn concentrations in the culture solutions with high Fe concentration. In acidic soils, the Mn-induced accumulation of Fe in the roots may affect nodulation and nitrogenase activity.

Calcium [Ca^{2+}] is an essential nutrient in plant cells, namely, by its structural role in the cell walls and membranes, and the signaling role in the cytosol [47]. Calcium also plays many roles in the nodulation process of legumes, viz., in the root hair deformation and entrapment of rhizobia soon after nod factor release by the rhizobia [48]. The uptake of Ca^{2+} is mediated by plasma membrane transporters, the Ca channels [47]. These Ca channels may be permeable to Mn [28]. Nitrogenase activity can be reduced in acidic soils, particularly, if Ca concentration is low and at the early stages of plant development in common bean (*Phaseolus vulgaris* L. Dobruganca) [49]. Liming, to increase soil pH from 5.2 to 7.3, was shown to increase nodulation, root and shoot weight in 14 lucerne cultivars (*Medicago sativa*) [50]. Muofhe and Dakora [42], working with rooibos (*Aspalathus linearis*), observed a 27.2% increase in biologically-fixed N in response to Ca supply.

Magnesium [Mg^{2+}], besides its role in the chlorophyll molecule, and in a multitude of enzymes, also plays an essential role in ATP; ATP, to become biologically active requires binding with Mg (e.g., [51]). Several studies show a negative effect of K on Mg concentration in the shoot tissues (for reviews see, e.g., [52, 53]. This interaction of K x Mg may be of significance because, in the acidic soils of the Montado/Dehesa, K availability might be high, and low Mg concentration in the plant shoots may have a significant effect on plant growth and nutritional value as feed. The Mg^{2+} transporter(s) responsible for uptake into the root cells is(are) poorly known (e.g., [52]), although there is evidence of Mg^{2+} transport through

Ca-channels [47]. Reduced translocation of Mg from the roots to the shoots, in presence of high K^+ concentration, might be the cause [53]. According to an analysis performed by Rietra et al. [52] on 94 peer-reviewed papers and 117 interactions (synergistic, antagonistic or zero-interactions) on crop yields, no interactions were found between Mg and Mn.

Molybdenum [Mo] is essential for some enzymes found in plants, involved in nitrogen metabolism and phytohormones synthesis [54]. Mo, as seen for Fe, is essential for biological N-fixation due to its role in the FeMo cofactor of nitrogenase [43]. A molybdate transporter type 1 (MTR1), that is a molybdate-specific transporter, has been identified in *Medicago truncatula*, and their expression in the nodules was determined [55]. Mo availability to plants in the soil solution correlates positively with decreasing proton concentration, being highest for soils with pH > 6.6, and with the percentage of soil particles with diameters smaller than 20 μm [56]. Adhikari and Missaoui [50], working with 14 Lucerne cultivars (*M. sativa*), a species particularly sensitive to low pH, observed that plants grown in soils with a pH of 5.2 and Mo supplementation, had a statistically significantly higher number of nodules (53% more nodules) than the control.

2.3 Temperature

In the Montado/Dehesa, biomass accretion happens from fall through winter and spring. The length of the growing period will vary as there is no consistent rainfall pattern from year to year. The daily minimum soil temperatures in the Winter months are often well below 5°C at 2 cm depth (e.g., [57]). In mid-Winter, as the growth rate of legumes increases in responding to favorable temperature and water availability so increases the potential for biological N-fixation. Biomass accretion of the annual species of the understorey ends in late May or early June after soil-available water has been used and the air temperatures are still relatively mild.

The tolerance of rhizobia to low temperatures varies, with different minimum temperatures for growth as low as 5°C, and survival −10°C [58]. Gibson [59] studied the effect of time and temperature in nodule formation of four subterranean clovers (*T. subterraneum*) cultivars and three *R. trifolii* strains, and observed inhibition of nodule formation below root temperature of 7°C, and an increased time to nodule formation as temperatures decreased below 22°C (from 4.1 to 5.7 days at 22°C to 20.2 to 24.2 days at 7°C); the author also observed that for plants with roots at 12°C, time to detect leghaemoglobin in nodules varied between 5 and 8 days (2–4 days for plants with root temperature of 22°C). Peltzer et al. [60], in a study with *Lupinus angustifolius* cv. Yandee, observed that nodule initiation at temperatures between 7 and 12°C failed due to insufficient exudation of flavonoids from the legume to activate nod factors of *Bradyrhizobium*. However, nitrogenase activity in nodules formed at adequate temperatures may occur at a much wider range of temperatures. Dart and Day [61] observed that nitrogenase activity, of nine different species, had a maximum for root temperatures of around 20 to 30°C, and that some species sustained nitrogenase activity for temperatures from 2 to 40°C; these authors also observed that at the temperature range of 2 to 10°C, this activity was only slightly reduced for *Vicia sativa* and *T. subterraneum*. In the winter months, low temperatures and relatively low light exposure of the understorey, as encountered in the Montado/Dehesa, is likely to affect the photosynthetic activity of legumes, and the carbohydrate content in the nodules (e.g., see [11]), affecting plant growth and nitrogenase activity.

2.4 Water stress

Extended periods of low or no precipitation during the growing season are very common in the Montado/Dehesa region and can affect symbiosis. Unsaturated soil conditions, and soil texture (especially in clayey soils), conditioning the diameter and continuity of saturated soil pores, affect rhizobia motility [62]. Thus, in the presence of a low concentration of rhizobia per gram of soil, the initiation of symbiosis may be dependent on transient saturated conditions after rainfall. N-fixation of nodulated legumes may be severely impaired by drought, well before photosynthesis is reduced, and the mechanisms for this response are species-specific and not fully understood; O_2 limitation, C availability and N feedback mechanisms have been proposed as playing an important role in the regulation of nitrogenase activity during drought periods [63]. A better understanding of these mechanisms would allow faster and smarter breeding for drought-tolerant legume species. On the other hand, the Montado/Dehesa systems are located in peneplains, and waterlogging is a common problem in some areas. Waterlogging has a profound effect on aeration and the redox conditions of the soil that can impose high Mn^{2+} availability over time [14]. The nodules, in saturated soils, will be deprived of free O_2, essential for the oxidation of the carbohydrates to produce the energy needed for the nitrogenase activity; also the diffusion of CO_2 and H_2, gases that can inhibit nitrogenase activity, will be hindered [61]. Roberts et al. [64] discuss the model/role of a gas diffusion barrier in the nodules, capable to maintain a microaerobic state, ca. 20 nM O_2, under normal atmospheric conditions, that assure nitrogenase activity at suboptimal rates; changes of the O_2 partial pressure of the atmosphere lead to short term changes of the gas diffusion barrier permeability and the rapid inhibition of the nitrogenase activity (transient and fully recoverable), or long term changes, leading to changes in the cellular and subcellular morphology, including the formation of lenticels and secondary aerenchyma on the surface of the nodules. Depending on the severity of the hypoxic conditions and the exposure time, the adaptation of the legume, regarding the number of nodules and nitrogenase activity, may not be sufficient and, depending on the species/cultivars, the recovery and survival might be compromised. Pampana et al. [65] observed that 5 days of waterlogging during the flowering period were sufficient to reduce the number of pods and seeds of white lupin plants almost three-fold, as well as seed weight and shoot and root dry matter. On the other range of the spectrum, Pugh et al. [66] observed that white clover (*T. repens*) grown under saturated conditions from germination had, after 9 weeks, higher shoot dry matter than normally watered plants; the authors also observed that the plants normally watered had a substantial reduction of the acetylene reduction activity (an indicator of nitrogenase activity) when waterlogged (a reduction to 4%, when compared to previous activity) and that the acetylene reduction activity increased when permanently waterlogged plants were suddenly drained (a 250% increase). Both drought and waterlogging in the Montado/Dehesa are likely to affect the biological N-fixation although the effect of N-fixation on biomass yield requires further experiments allowing the separation of other effects on biomass yield (photosynthetic activity, nutrient uptake and translocation, root anoxia/hypoxia, and so on).

2.5 The importance of tripartite symbiosis

Legumes, besides symbioses with rhizobia bacteria, can establish symbioses with AM fungi in mutualistic relationships where the fungi increase the plant uptake of water and nutrients, in particular phosphorus, and receive photosynthates in exchange [39]. Most plants are co-colonized by multiple AM fungi species and endemic AM fungi, well adapted to the soil conditions, will compete with inoculated AM fungi for mycorrhization of the roots [39]. These symbioses may be important for N-fixation if in the presence of low concentrations of plant-available P. The mycorrhizal component may account for much of the P uptake of legumes and the direct uptake can be residual. Nazeri et al. [33] showed that mycorrhizal plants of *T. subterraneum*, grown under low P-available conditions, had higher P concentration in the roots and shoots, and lower Mn concentrations, when compared with non-inoculated plants, indicating alternative strategies to acquire P. Alho et al. [67], studying the effect of intact extraradical AM propagules, in undisturbed soils, on the infection of *T. subterraneum* by the fungi, observed that plants infected with intact propagules had statistically significant higher P and N concentrations in the shoots (214 to 515% and 203 to 479%, respectively), higher shoots and nodules dry weight (274 to 618% and 398 to 640%, respectively), and much lower concentration of Mn in the roots (34 to 56%) when compared to control (disturbed soil) 42 days after growth started; these authors observed also that the preceding plants, i.e. the plants grown to establish the mycorrhiza, being more or less mycoptrophic, affected the infection of *T. subterraneum*, with non-mycorrhizal species producing statistically significantly lower values for all those variables when compared with plants infected with intact propagules produced by mycotrophic species.

3. Gaps in current research

To increase the soil productivity in the Montado/Dehesa ecosystem, the correction of the soil reaction by liming is expensive but, where economically viable, it is effective, either with calcitic or dolomitic limes (e.g., [13]). However, the economic and social benefits of liming must be balanced with the ecological impact of this practice. From an ecological point of view, liming contributes to the emissions of greenhouse gases (GHG) from mining, transporting and incorporating the lime into the soil. Additionally, liming causes a marked stratification of the soil profile pH and the effects on the forest stand and acidophilic endemic species, in the long term, are unknown. On the other hand, liming potentially yield higher carbon sequestration (SOM), the improvement of several topsoil properties, higher feed production and quality (protein content), just to name a few. Unfortunately, although there are many metric approaches to quantify these variables there is no reliable model to assist in the decision to correct the soil reaction through liming in the Montado/Dehesa.

Alternatively, and although in a wider time frame, the benefits of liming can be achieved through higher SOM content (increasing CEC and the soil buffering capacity) and the management of soil fertility and plant nutritional deficiencies. Endemic legumes species, with cultivars selected for the traits of interest, can increase the N content of the system and N availability to other forbs and grasses, and, along with the correction of plant nutrient deficiencies, enhance biomass production and SOM content. Seeding with no-till systems would allow the preservation of the SOM content, without the exacerbation of microbial activity. It would also allow a sequential introduction of the cultivars of interest, beginning with those species/cultivars that can tolerate the soil conditions and boost soil organic matter (cultivars selected aiming acid soils reclamation and tolerant to the low light conditions of the understorey), creating favorable conditions for the survival of the rhizobia of interest (already present or inoculated) and the preservation of AM fungi, in what can be defined as the first step in a **stepwise legume-enrichment**. These first introduced species/cultivars would be kept through self-seeding by allowing narrow bands to grow to maturity (seed formation) when cutting the pasture for fodder (hay or silage), or by grazing the legume-improved pastures only in the Summer. After achieving a design threshold of SOM content, correlated with higher nutrient availability and soil buffering capacity, pH-sensitive cultivars, capable of higher biomass accretion and adapted for the multi-diverse environments of the Montado/Dehesa, namely, the light/shade exposure, could be sowed. This low-input strategy for legume-rich forage in the Montado/Dehesa would require multidisciplinary research. The next paragraphs will discuss avenues of research readily identifiable: (i) legume species and phenotypic traits; (ii) microsymbionts and symbioses; (iii) soil fertility and nutritional problems.

Legume species and phenotypic traits. In the Montado/Dehesa system, and conditioned by the spatial variability (environmental variability) caused by the forest stand, the best approach to improve biological N-fixation is through the use of mixtures of legumes with different phenotypical traits, capable of occupying these different environments. The plants' genera and species that should be the subject of plant breeding, are not dissimilar from those in the mixtures of the *Sown Biodiverse Permanent Pasture Rich in Legumes* system (see [68]), namely, the genus *Trifolium*, which has many species that are, at least, naturalized in the Iberian Peninsula, and several other endemic genera, including *Ornithopus*, *Lotus* or *Lupinus*; however, breeding for the acidic conditions of the Montado/Dehesa should include traits such as low pH tolerance, Al tolerance, Mn tolerance (the storage capacity or exclusion of Mn), shade tolerance (photosynthetic efficiency), drought tolerance, waterlogging tolerance, high nutrient use efficiency, diseases and pests tolerance, matching rhizobia (the persistence in the soil) and the potential to mycorrhizal symbiosis.

Pastures sowed with mixtures of legumes in the Montado/Dehesa, in soils with pH in water between 4.9 and 5.94, increased the biomass production by more than three-fold, as well as the SOM content, and the protein content of grasses and non-legume forbs [69]. However, the positive effects observed in this study decreased continually from the first year onwards, suggesting the inadequacy of the cultivars sowed. From a stepwise legume-enrichment perspective, lupins may play an important role in the first steps of legume enrichment. The Mediterranean basin is the place of origin of important annual lupin species, with an important genetic pool for plant breeders. For example, in 2009, the number of accessions (landrace and wild types) distributed among different institutions totalled 1804 in Portugal and 5057 in Spain [70]. Lupins are tolerant to acidic soils, with low available P, and can cope with very high concentrations of Mn in the shoot tissues (e.g. [71]). Thus, at least conceptually, well-adapted cultivars of lupins, with good biomass accretion, mixed with other highly tolerant hardy cultivars of other genera could be sowed, increasing SOM and nutrient availability, and establishing/increasing the microsymbionts population, and their ability to survive. In this respect, lupins do not possess very high specificity to their rhizobia microsymbiont, being able to establish symbiosis with several species of *Bradyrhizobium* [72].

Microsymbionts and symbioses. Through screening of acid-tolerant rhizobia strains present in these soils, their matching legume hosts and N-fixation efficiency may lead to the expansion of the area of legume-ameliorated pastures in the Montado/Dehesa systems. In this respect, *Bradyrhizobium* species (and their hosts) may be of particular interest due to their higher tolerance to low pH soils [17]. Concerning AM fungi, when breeding legumes for improved biomass yield, the best cultivars are likely to be deprived of the genetic apparatus that favors symbiosis or alter the regulatory mechanism (the thresholds), increasing the specificity or decreasing susceptibility with the microsymbionts (e.g., [73]). Thus, at least conceptually, breeding new cultivars of legumes from endemic wild types may preserve the ability of these cultivars to establish symbiotic relationships with the different AM fungi present in these soils. In mycorrhizal legumes, the symbiosis may have a profound effect on P and Mn uptake and concentration (e.g. [33, 67]). The work of Alho et al. [67], studying plants and their mycotrophic character, and the highly positive effect of intact mycorrhizal on the infection of *T. subterraneum*, supports the concept of a **stepwise enrichment of legumes in the Montado/Dehesa**, based on the plant species present at the beginning of the process, and by the effect of no-till direct seeding of new cultivars to maximize mycorrhizal symbiosis. For annual legume crops, and especially under the Mediterranean climate and acidic soils of the Montado/Dehesa, the benefits from a tripartite symbiosis may be synergic, with an effect on biomass accretion caused by improved P uptake and N-fixation, much higher than the simple addition of the isolated effect of the microsymbionts, but this is yet to be demonstrated.

Soil fertility and plants' nutritional problems. The management of soil fertility is paramount for increasing the productivity and sustainability of these systems. Where total P is extremely low, P fertilization is needed and may induce higher N-fixation. Nevertheless, as observed by Hernández-Esteban et al. [69], P-fertilization has only a limited effect on pasture productivity, and produced a higher effect when applied to sown legume pastures; the reasons for the low effect of P on natural pastures may have to do with the phenotypical traits of the wild flora which have evolved adaptation mechanisms to thrive in these poor and very dynamic environments. Even in strongly acidic soils, where the P-fertilizers are quickly adsorbed/precipitated in relatively insoluble forms, they will enter the soil's P-pool and will be made available by the plants and microbes in the future. The P-mobilizing strategies of legumes, non-legumes and the microbial community (e.g. [74]), and their effects on Mn availability and uptake of the different groups (legumes, other forbs and grasses), justify a comprehensive study of the relationships between these and other variables. In this respect, the P distribution within the plant (P allocation to the shoots, roots and nodules) can become, as suggested by [37], a tool for the determination of the symbiotic efficiency and/or the adaptation of the legumes (host-bacteria symbiosis) to the environmental conditions. Other plant nutritional disorders that can be detrimental to plant growth and biological N-fixation, such as the Fe and Mn antagonism, or the inhibitory effect of high K^+ uptake on Mg^{2+} uptake and concentration in the shoot tissues, should be further researched, as they can define new approaches to nutrient management, floristic composition of pastures, plant breeding, and others. The complexity of the relationships between different nutrient uptake and the concentrations of these elements in the plant tissues poses many challenges, namely, for screening candidate cultivars. A high-throughput ionomic approach, and the correlations between these elements in the plant tissues, which are highly species- and environmental-specific, can be a very useful tool (e.g. [75]).

4. Concluding remarks

The potential for biological N-fixation with legumes in the Montado/Dehesa systems is lower than in more northern regions in Europe due to the erratic rainfall patterns and the relatively low temperature during part of the growing season, and the poor and strongly acid soils. Increasing the potential N-fixation through liming is expensive and, in these sensitive biodiverse systems, with unknown consequences in the long term.

Legumes bred for tolerance to acid soils and associated metal toxicity, for drought and waterlogging, and for the low light conditions in Winter, could provide biodiversity and the potential to increase N-fixation in the multi-diverse environment, both spatial and temporal, of the Montado/Dehesa. A **stepwise approach**, through the use of no-till direct seeding, starting with the introduction of mixtures of hardy tolerant legume species/cultivars, and adequate soil and plant nutrient management can potentially create the soil conditions necessary for a second phase introduction of more sensitive legumes, but with higher biomass and N-fixation potential. Such a low-input strategy for legume-rich forage has the potential to increase the sustainability and productivity of these systems, by increasing the contents of N, C and organic P.

The avenues of research that are needed may prove beneficial beyond the natural borders of the Montado/Dehesa, by identifying legume cultivars and rhizobia strains tolerant to strongly acidic soil conditions useful in other regions of the world.

Funding

This work is funded by National Funds through FCT - Foundation for Science and Technology under the Project UIDB/05183/2020.

Conflict of interest

The author declares no conflict of interest.

Author details

Fernando Teixeira
MED – Mediterranean Institute for Agriculture, Environment and Development, Institute for Advanced Studies and Research, Universidade de Évora, Polo da Mitra, Évora, Portugal

*Address all correspondence to: fteixeir@uevora.pt

References

[1] Soloveichik G. Electrochemical synthesis of ammonia as a potential alternative to the Haber–Bosch process. Nature Catalysis. 2019;**2**(5):377-380. DOI: 10.1038/s41929-019-0280-0

[2] Christenhusz MJM, Byng JW. The number of known plants species in the world and its annual increase. Phytotaxa. 2016;**261**(3):201. DOI: 10.11646/phytotaxa.261.3.1

[3] Caamal-Maldonado, JA, Jiménez-Osornio, JJ, Torres-Barragán, A, Anaya, AL. The use of allelopathic legume cover and mulch species for weed control in cropping systems. Agronomy Journal. 2001; 93(1), 27-36. DOI: 10.2134/agronj 2001.93127x

[4] Rochon JJ, Doyle CJ, Greef JM, Hopkins A, Molle G, Sitzia M, et al. Grazing legumes in Europe: A review of their status, management, benefits, research needs and future prospects. Grass and Forage Science. 2004;**59**(3): 197-214. DOI: 10.1111/j.1365-2494.2004. 00423.x

[5] Pinto-Correia T, Ribeiro N, Sá-Sousa P. Introducing the Montado, the cork and holm oak agroforestry system of Southern Portugal. Agroforestry Systems. 2011;**82**(2):99-104. DOI: 10.1007/s10457-011-9388-10

[6] Pinto-Correia, T., Guiomar, N., Ferraz-de-Oliveira, M. I. et al. Progress in identifying high nature value Montados: Impacts of grazing on hardwood rangeland biodiversity. Rangeland Ecology & Management, 2018; 71(5), 612-625. doi:10.1016/j. rama.2018.01.004

[7] Giorgi F, Lionello P. Climate change projections for the Mediterranean region. Global and Planetary Change. 2008;**63**(2-3):90-104. DOI: 10.1016/j. gloplacha.2007.09.0

[8] Vessella F, López-Tirado J, Simeone MC, et al. A tree species range in the face of climate change: Cork oak as a study case for the Mediterranean biome. European Journal of Forest Research. 2017;**136**:555-569. DOI: 10.1007/s10342-017-1055-2

[9] Carvalho M, Goss M, Teixeira D. Manganese toxicity in Portuguese Cambisols derived from granitic rocks: Causes, limitations of soil analyses and possible solutions. Revista de Ciências Agrárias. 2015;**38**(4):518-527. DOI: 10.19084/RCA15137

[10] Miller RW, McRae DG, Al-Jobore A, Berndt WB. Respiration supported nitrogenase activity of isolated *Rhizobium meliloti* bacteroids. Journal of Cellular Biochemistry. 1988;**38**(1):35-49. DOI: 10.1002/jcb.240380105

[11] Ferguson BJ, Mens C, Hastwell AH, Zhang M, Su H, Jones CH, et al. Legume nodulation: The host controls the party. Plant, Cell & Environment. 2019;**42**(1):41-51. DOI: 10.1111/ pce.13348

[12] Walker L, Lagunas B, Gifford ML. Determinants of host range specificity in legume-rhizobia symbiosis. Frontiers in Microbiology. 2020;**11**:3028. DOI: 10.3389/fmicb.2020.585749

[13] Ulrich B. Soil acidity and its relations to acid deposition. In: Ulrich B, Pankrath J, editors. Effects of Accumulation of Air Pollutants in Forest Ecosystems. Dordrecht: D. Reidel Publishing Company; 1983. pp. 127-146. DOI: 10.1007/978-94-009-6983-4_10

[14] Patrick WH, Turner FT. Effect of redox potential on manganese transformation in waterlogged soil. Nature. 1968;**220**(5166):476-478. DOI: 10.1038/220476a0

[15] Ritchie GSP. Soluble aluminium in acidic soils: Principles and practicalities. In: Date RA et al., editors. Plant-Soil Interactions at Low pH: Principles and Management. Developments in Plant and Soil Sciences. Dordrecht: Springer; 1995;**64**. https://doi.org/10.1007/978-94-011-0221-6_2

[16] Paschke MW, Valdecantos A, Redente EF. Manganese toxicity thresholds for restoration grass species. Environmental Pollution. 2005; **135**(2):313-322. DOI: 10.1016/j.envpol.2004.08.006

[17] Ferguson B, Lin MH, Gresshoff PM. Regulation of legume nodulation by acidic growth conditions. Plant Signaling & Behavior. 2013;**8**(3):e23426. DOI: 10.4161/psb.23426

[18] Wood M, Cooper JE, Holding AJ. Soil acidity factors and nodulation of *Trifolium repens*. Plant and Soil. 1984;**78**:367-379. DOI: 10.1007/BF02450370

[19] Brockwell J, Pilka A, Holliday RA. Soil pH is a major determinant of the numbers of naturally occurring *Rhizobium meliloti* in non-cultivated soils in Central New South Wales. Australian Journal of Experimental Agriculture. 1991;**31**(2):211. DOI: 10.1071/ea9910211

[20] Exley C, Mold MJ. The binding, transport and fate of aluminium in biological cells. Journal of Trace Elements in Medicine and Biology. 2015;**30**:90-95. DOI: 10.1016/j.jtemb.2014.11.002

[21] Li W, Johnson CE. Relationships among pH, aluminum solubility and aluminum complexation with organic matter in acid forest soils of the Northeastern United States. Geoderma. 2016;**271**:234-242. DOI: 10.1016/j.geoderma.2016.02.03

[22] Horst WJ. The role of the apoplast in aluminium toxicity and resistance of higher plants: A review. Zeitschrift für Pflanzenernährung und Bodenkunde. 1995;**158**(5):419-428. DOI: 10.1002/jpln.19951580503

[23] Sujkowska-Rybkowska M, Borucki W. Pectins esterification in the apoplast of aluminum-treated pea root nodules. Journal of Plant Physiology. 2015;**184**:1-7. DOI: 10.1016/j.jplph.2015.05.011

[24] Ma, JF, Hiradate, S. Form of aluminium for uptake and translocation in buckwheat (*Fagopyrum esculentum* Moench). Planta, 2000, 211(3), 355-360. Available from: http://www.jstor.org/stable/23386009

[25] Andrew, CS, Johnson, AD, Sandland, RL. Effect of aluminium on the growth chemical composition of some tropical and temperate pasture legumes. Australian Journal of Agricultural Research, 1973, 24(3), 325. doi:10.1071/ar9730325

[26] Grauer UE, Horst WJ. Effect of pH and nitrogen source on aluminium tolerance of rye (*Secale cereale* L.) and yellow lupin (*Lupinus luteus* L.). Plant and Soil. 1990;**127**:13-21. DOI: 10.1007/BF00010832

[27] Jaiswal SK, Naamala J, Dakora FD. Nature and mechanisms of aluminium toxicity, tolerance and amelioration in symbiotic legumes and rhizobia. Biology and Fertility of Soils. 2018;**54**:309-318. DOI: 10.1007/s00374-018-1262-0

[28] Socha AL, Guerinot ML. Mn-euvering manganese: The role

of transporter gene family members in manganese uptake and mobilization in plants. Frontiers in Plant Science. 2014;**5**:106. DOI: 10.3389/fpls.2014.00106

[29] Lambers H, Hayes PE, Laliberté E, Oliveira RS, Turner BL. Leaf manganese accumulation and phosphorus-acquisition efficiency. Trends in Plant Science. 2015;**20**(2):83-90. DOI: 10.1016/j.tplants.2014.10.00

[30] Godo GH, Reisenauer HM. Plant effects on soil manganese availability. Soil Science Society of America Journal. 1980;**44**(5):993. DOI: 10.2136/sssaj1980.03615995004

[31] Geszvain, K, Butterfield, C, Davis, RE, Madison, AS, Lee, SW, Parker, DL, Soldatova, A, Spiro, T, Luther, G, Tebo, BM. The molecular biogeochemistry of manganese(II) oxidation. Biochemical Society Transactions, 2012, 40(6), 1244-1248. doi:10.1042/bst20120229

[32] Chen Z, Yan W, Sun L, Tian J, Liao H. Proteomic analysis reveals growth inhibition of soybean roots by manganese toxicity is associated with alteration of cell wall structure and lignification. Journal of Proteomics. 2016;**143**:151-160. DOI: 10.1016/j.jprot.2016.03.037

[33] Nazeri NK, Lambers H, Tibbett M, et al. Do arbuscular mycorrhizas or heterotrophic soil microbes contribute toward plant acquisition of a pulse of mineral phosphate? Plant and Soil. 2013;**373**:699-710. DOI: 10.1007/s11104-013-1838-2

[34] Izaguirre-Mayoral ML, Sinclair TR. Soybean genotypic difference in growth, nutrient accumulation and ultrastructure in response to manganese and iron supply in solution culture. Annals of Botany. 2005;**96**(1):149. DOI: 10.1093/aob/mci160-158

[35] Krämer U. Metal hyperaccumulation in plants. Annual Review of Plant Biology. 2010;**61**(1):517-534. DOI: 10.1146/annurev-arplant-042809-112156

[36] Keyser, HH, Munns, DN. Effects of calcium, manganese, and aluminum on growth of rhizobia in acid media. Soil Science Society of America Journal, 1979, 43(3), 500. doi:10.2136/sssaj1979.03615995004

[37] Mitran T, Meena RS, Lal R, Layek J, Kumar S, Datta R. Role of soil phosphorus on legume production. Legumes for soil health and sustainable management. In: Meena R, Das A, Yadav G, Lal R, editors. Legumes for Soil Health and Sustainable Management. Singapore: Springer; 2018. pp. 487-510. DOI: 10.1007/978-981-13-0253-4_15

[38] Srivastava S, Upadhyay M, Srivastava A, Abdelrahman M, Suprasanna P, Tran L-S. Cellular and subcellular phosphate transport machinery in plants. International Journal of Molecular Sciences. 2018;**19**(7):1914. DOI: 10.3390/ijms19071914

[39] Kobae Y. Dynamic phosphate uptake in arbuscular mycorrhizal roots under field conditions. Frontiers in Environmental Science. 2019;**6**:159. DOI: 10.3389/fenvs.2018.00159

[40] Seefeldt LC, Hoffman BM, Dean DR. Mechanism of Mo-dependent nitrogenase. Annual Review of Biochemistry. 2009;**78**(1):701-722. DOI: 10.1146/annurev.biochem.78.07

[41] Hart AL. Distribution of phosphorus in nodulated white clover plants. Journal of Plant Nutrition. 1989;**12**(2):159-171. DOI: 10.1080/01904168909363943

[42] Muofhe M, Dakora F. Nitrogen nutrition in nodulated field plants of the

shrub tea legume *Aspalathus linearis* assessed using ^{15}N natural abundance. Plant and Soil. 1999;**209**:181. DOI: 10.1023/A:1004514303787

[43] Hallmen PP, Kästner J. N_2 binding to the FeMo-cofactor of nitrogenase. Zeitschrift Für Anorganische Und Allgemeine Chemie. 2015;**641**(1):118-122. DOI: 10.1002/zaac.201400114

[44] Vose PB. Iron nutrition in plants: A world overview. Journal of Plant Nutrition. 1982;**5**(4-7):233-249. DOI: 10.1080/01904168209362954

[45] Rout GR, Sahoo S. Role of iron in plant growth and metabolism. Reviews in Agricultural Science. 2015;**3**(0):1-24. DOI: 10.7831/ras.3.1

[46] Alvarez-Tinaut MC, Leal A, Martínez LR. Iron-manganese interaction and its relation to boron levels in tomato plants. Plant and Soil. 1980;**55**:377-388. DOI: 10.1007/BF02182698

[47] White PJ, Martin RB. Calcium in plants. Annals of Botany. 2003;**92**(4): 487-511. DOI: 10.1093/aob/mcg164

[48] Lei MJ, Wang Q, Li X, Chen A, Luo L, Xie Y, et al. The small GTPase ROP10 of *Medicago truncatula* is required for both tip growth of root hairs and nod factor-induced root hair deformation. The Plant Cell. 2015;**27**(3):806-822. DOI: 10.1105/tpc.114.135210

[49] Vassileva, V, Milanov, G, Ignatov, G, Nikolov, B. Effect of low pH on nitrogen fixation of common bean grown at various calcium and nitrate levels. Journal of Plant Nutrition, 1997, 20(2-3), 279-294. doi:10.1080/01904169709365250

[50] Adhikari L, Missaoui AM. Nodulation response to molybdenum supplementation in alfalfa and its correlation with root and shoot growth in low pH soil. Journal of Plant Nutrition. 2017;**40**(16):2290-2302. DOI: 10.1080/01904167.2016.1264601

[51] Gout E, Rebeille F, Douce R, Bligny R. Interplay of Mg2+, ADP, and ATP in the cytosol and mitochondria: Unravelling the role of Mg2+ in cell respiration. Proceedings of the National Academy of Sciences. 2014;**111**(43): E4560-E4567. DOI: 10.1073/pnas.1406251111

[52] Rietra, RPJJ, Heinen, M, Dimkpa, CO, Bindraban, PS. Effects of nutrient antagonism and synergism on yield and fertilizer use efficiency. Communications in Soil Science and Plant Analysis, 2017, 48(16), 1895-1920. doi:10.1080/00103624.2017.1407429

[53] Fageria VD. Nutrient interactions in crop plants. Journal of Plant Nutrition. 2001;**24**(8):1269-1290. DOI: 10.1081/pln-100106981

[54] Kaiser BN, Gridley KL, Ngaire Brady J, Phillips T, Tyerman SD. The role of molybdenum in agricultural plant production. Annals of Botany. 2005;**96**(5):745-754. DOI: 10.1093/aob/mci226

[55] Tejada-Jiménez M, Gil-Díez P, León-Mediavilla J, Wen J, Mysore KS, Imperial J, et al. *Medicago truncatula* Molybdate Transporter type 1 (MtMOT1.3) is a plasma membrane molybdenum transporter required for nitrogenase activity in root nodules under molybdenum deficiency. New Phytologist. 2017;**216**(4):1223-1235. DOI: 10.1111/nph.14739

[56] Rutkowska B, Szulc W, Spychaj-Fabisiak E, Pior N. Prediction of molybdenum availability to plants in

differentiated soil conditions. Plant, Soil and Environment. 2017;**63**:491-497. DOI: 10.17221/616/2017-PSE

[57] Andrade, J, Alexandre, C, Basch, G. Effects of soil tillage and mulching on thermal performance of a Luvisol topsoil layer. Folia Oecologica, 2010, 37, n°1, 1-7

[58] Bordeleau LM, Prévost D. Nodulation and nitrogen fixation in extreme environments. Plant and Soil. 1994;**161**:115-125. DOI: 10.1007/BF02183092

[59] Gibson A. Physical environment and symbiotic nitrogen fixation. Australian Journal of Biological Sciences. 1963;**20**:1087-1104. DOI: 10.1071/bi9630028

[60] Peltzer, SC, Abbott, LK, Atkins, CA. Effect of low root-zone temperature on nodule initiation in narrow-leafed lupin (*Lupinus angustifolius* L.). Australian Journal of Agricultural Research, 2002, 53(3), 355. DOI: 10.1071/ar01092

[61] Dart PJ, Day JM. Effects of incubation temperature and oxygen tension on nitrogenase activity of legume root nodules. Plant and Soil. 1971;**35**:167-184. DOI: 10.1007/BF02661849

[62] Aroney STN, Poole PS, Sánchez-Cañizares C. Rhizobial chemotaxis and motility systems at work in the soil. Frontiers in Plant Science. 2021;**12**:725338. DOI: 10.3389/fpls.2021.725338

[63] González EM, Larrainzar E, Marino D, Wienkoop S, Gil-Quintana E, Arrese-Igor C. Physiological responses of N_2-fixing legumes to water limitation. In: Sulieman S, Tran L, editors. Legume Nitrogen Fixation in a Changing Environment. Switzerland: Springer International Publishing; 2015. pp. 5-33. DOI: 10.1007/978-3-319-06212-9_2

[64] Roberts DM, Choi WG, Hwang JH. Strategies for adaptation to waterlogging and hypoxia in nitrogen fixing nodules of legumes. In: Mancuso S, Shabala S, editors. Waterlogging Signalling and Tolerance in Plants. Berlin Heidelberg: Springer-Verlag; 2010. pp. 37-59. DOI: 10.1007/978-3-642-10305-6_3

[65] Pampana S, Masoni A, Arduini I. Response of cool-season grain legumes to waterlogging at flowering. Canadian Journal of Plant Science. 2016;**96**:597-603. DOI: 10.1139/cjps-2015-0268

[66] Pugh R, Witty JF, Mytton LR, Minchin FR. The effect of waterlogging on nitrogen fixation and nodule morphology in soil-grown white clover (*Trifolium repens* L.). Journal of Experimental Botany. 1995;**46**(3):285-290. DOI: 10.1093/jxb/46.3.285

[67] Alho L, Carvalho M, Brito I, Goss MJ. The effect of arbuscular mycorrhiza fungal propagules on the growth of subterranean clover (*Trifolium subterraneum* L.) under Mn toxicity in *ex situ* experiments. Soil Use and Management. 2015;**31**(2):337-344. DOI: 10.1111/sum.12183

[68] Teixeira RFM, Domingos T, Costa APS, Oliveira R, Farropas L, Calouro F, et al. Soil organic matter dynamics in Portuguese natural and sown rainfed grasslands. Ecological Modelling. 2011;**222**(4):993-1001. DOI: 10.1016/j.ecolmodel.2010.11.0

[69] Hernández-Esteban A, López-Díaz ML, Cáceres Y, et al. Are sown legume-rich pastures effective allies for the profitability and sustainability of Mediterranean dehesas? Agroforestry Systems. 2019;**93**:2047-2065. DOI: 10.1007/s10457-018-0307-6

[70] Wolko B, Clements JC, Naganowska B, Nelson MN, Yang H.

Lupinus. In: Kole C, editor. Wild Crop Relatives: Genomic and Breeding Resources, Legume Crops and Forages. Berlin Heidelberg: Springer-Verlag; 2011. pp. 153-206. DOI: 10.1007/978-3-642-14387-8_9

[71] Lambers H, Clements JC, Nelson MN. How a phosphorus-acquisition strategy based on carboxylate exudation powers the success and agronomic potential of lupines (*Lupinus*, Fabaceae). American Journal of Botany. 2013;**100**(2):263-288. DOI: 10.3732/ajb.1200474

[72] Jarabo-Lorenzo A, Pérez-Galdona R, Donate-Correa J, Rivas R, Velázquez E, Hernández M, et al. Genetic diversity of bradyrhizobial populations from diverse geographic origins that nodulate *Lupinus* spp. and *Ornithopus* spp. Systematic and Applied Microbiology. 2003;**26**(4):611-623. DOI: 10.1078/072320203770865927

[73] Martín-Robles N, Lehmann A, Seco E, Aroca R, Rillig MC, Milla R. Impacts of domestication on the arbuscular mycorrhizal symbiosis of 27 crop species. New Phytologist. 2018;**218**(1):322-334. DOI: 10.1111/nph.14962

[74] Tian J, Ge F, Zhang D, Deng S, Liu X. Roles of phosphate solubilizing microorganisms from managing soil phosphorus deficiency to mediating biogeochemical P cycle. Biology. 2021;**10**(2):158. DOI: 10.3390/biology10020158

[75] Pii Y, Cesco S, Mimmo T. Shoot ionome to predict the synergism and antagonism between nutrients as affected by substrate and physiological status. Plant Physiology and Biochemistry. 2015;**94**:48-56. DOI: 10.1016/j.plaphy.2015.05.002

Chapter 10

Rust Disease Classification Using Deep Learning Based Algorithm: The Case of Wheat

Shivani Sood, Harjeet Singh and Suruchi Jindal

Abstract

Rusts are plant diseases caused by obligate fungi parasites. They are usually host-specific and cause greater losses of yields in crops, trees, and ornamental plants. Wheat is a staple food crop bearing losses specifically due to three species of rust fungi namely leaf rust (*Puccinia triticina*), stem rust (*Puccinia graminis*), and yellow rust (*Puccinia striiformis*). These diseases are usually inspected manually by a human being but at a large scale, this process is labor-intensive, time-consuming, and prone to human errors. Therefore, there is a need for an effective and efficient system that helps in the identification and classification of these diseases at early stages. In the present study, a deep learning-based CNN (i.e., VGG16) transfer learning model has been utilized for wheat disease classification on the CGIAR image dataset, containing two classes of wheat rust disease (leaf rust and stem rust), and one class of healthy wheat images. The deep learning models produced the best results by tuning the various hyper-parameters such as batch size, number of epochs, and learning rate. The proposed model has reported the best classification accuracy rate of 99.54% on 80 epochs using an initial learning rate from 0.01 and decayed to 0.0001.

Keywords: food security, plant disease detection, wheat rust disease, deep learning, convolutional neural networks

1. Introduction

Rust diseases are the fungal diseases of plants, mainly grasses, caused by fungi. They affect the aerial plant parts especially leaves but can also attack stems and even flowers and fruits. They bear complex life cycles that require two alternative unrelated hosts. Rusts produce spore pustules which vary in color according to the rust species. About 7000 rust species are known to affect a variety of host plants globally. They can cause a wide range of symptoms depending upon the host species like the formation of Galls or swellings on the branches, formation of Canker on the trunks, and formation of Spores on the surface of the leaf. Leaf rust is also known as bown rust due to the brown color of circular urediniospores on the surfaces of the leaf of the crop. Yellow rust or stripe rust is characterized by the yellow color of stripes on the surfaces of the leaf. Stem rust is also brown and characterized by the patches of brown color on the surface of stems. Many approaches are being deployed to combat the problem of these diseases which involves accurate phenotyping which means characterization of the diseases at field level followed by genotyping to find out the genes responsible for its cause. Many germplasm resources are being explored and screened by scientists worldwide to find new sources of resistance. Precision phenotyping is the key requirement to achieve the goals. So far there are manual interventions involved to screen these diseases. But manual scoring of these diseases is a cumbersome job in large pre-breeding and breeding programs. Therefore, there is a strong need for high precision phenomics which involves imaging using high-quality cameras or equipment followed by image analysis using newly developed software and tools. In today's era of artificial intelligence, it is possible to explore high-end phenomics to achieve better yields of important crops like wheat. Many machine learning and deep learning models have been tested and tried to analyze and characterize wheat fungal diseases [1–4]. One of the main reasons for the popularity of these techniques is the use of GPUs (graphics processing units). The classification tools, computer vision, and GPUs are combined in a single framework called deep learning [5]. Deep learning-based models have been used in the various applications of agriculture for end-to-end learning. With the use of GPUs, deep learning can give a better solution to the given problem in a shorter time [6]. The process of building such models is computationally challenging but using GPU power becomes very easy [7, 8]. Fungal diseases have been identified using image processing techniques on different horticulture and agriculture crops. Various feature extraction and classification algorithm have been used to detect the different types of fruits, vegetables, and cereal crops.

Among the various rust diseases, soybean-, coffee-, and wheat-rusts are the most damaging diseases. Therefore, the constant efforts are being done worldwide, to combat this problem. Wheat is one of the staple food crops in addition to rice and maize. The total area under wheat in the world is around 220 million hectares with a production of 772.64 million metric tons (2020–2021). Wheat rusts especially leaf rust, stem rust, and yellow rusts are major fungal diseases that affect the production of the wheat crop throughout the world particularly in South Asian countries [9]. As per the prediction of the Food and Agricultural Organization (FAO) of the United Nations, wheat production might not be fulfilled the requirement in near future due to rapid population growth [10, 11]. In this chapter we discuss the usefulness of deep learning-based algorithms to identify rust using wheat as a case study.

2. Computer vision approaches for plant disease identification

Human perception is based on the interaction between the brain and the eye. On the other hand, computer vision system (CVS) is used to emulate human vision for gathering information without physical interaction [12, 13].

It is also defined as the process of automatic acquisition, and analysis from image data. CVS emulates the dynamic vision system whose operation is very transparent and natural. The data is processed in various stages such as capturing, processing, and analysis of images. **Figure 1** depicts the steps involved during image processing. In the first stage, image acquisition and pre-processing are involved. The images can be acquired using high-resolution cameras and sensors. Further, the images are pre-processed through data cleaning, background removing, adding/removing noise, and also enhancing the quality of images. In the second stage, the images are segmented. The segmentation process involves extracting only important and useful information

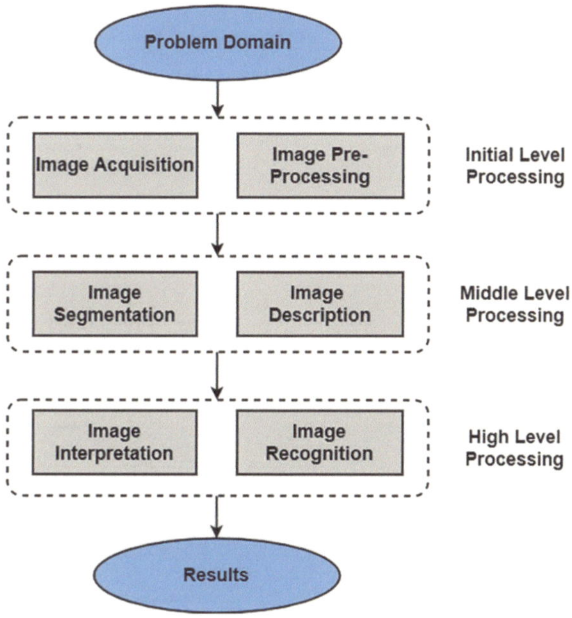

Figure 1.
Steps of image processing techniques.

from the whole image that further helps in the discrimination of classes. In the third stage, the high-level analysis is performed in which direct emphasis is done on the recognition (objects) and interpretation (making results). In a CVS, the following attributes contribute to decision-making: shape, color, texture, and also size. **Figure 2** depicts the utilization of various artificial intelligence algorithms in plant disease detection. These algorithms are further divided into machine learning and deep learning-based classifiers. The description of these algorithms is illustrated in the coming subsections.

2.1 Machine learning based approaches

Classification is the process of dividing the dataset into different categories or groups by adding labels. Nowadays, the machine learning and deep learning approaches are performing well for classifying the algorithm images based on their category. Following are the machine learning algorithms which are used to classify plant disease and are based on supervised learning. Supervised learning is a type of learning where labels (category of images) are given along with input images.

2.1.1 k-Nearest neighbor

It is the machine learning algorithm used for classification and calculated by *k*-neighbors. It is mostly used in image processing, machine learning, and also for statistical estimation. This algorithm worked on the principle of calculating the distance between different data points using Euclidean distance and Manhattan distance [14, 15]. It works with the following steps: (a) getting data, (b) define *k* neighbors, (c) calculate the neighbor distance using Euclidean distance or Manhattan distance and (d) assign new instances to the majority of the neighbors.

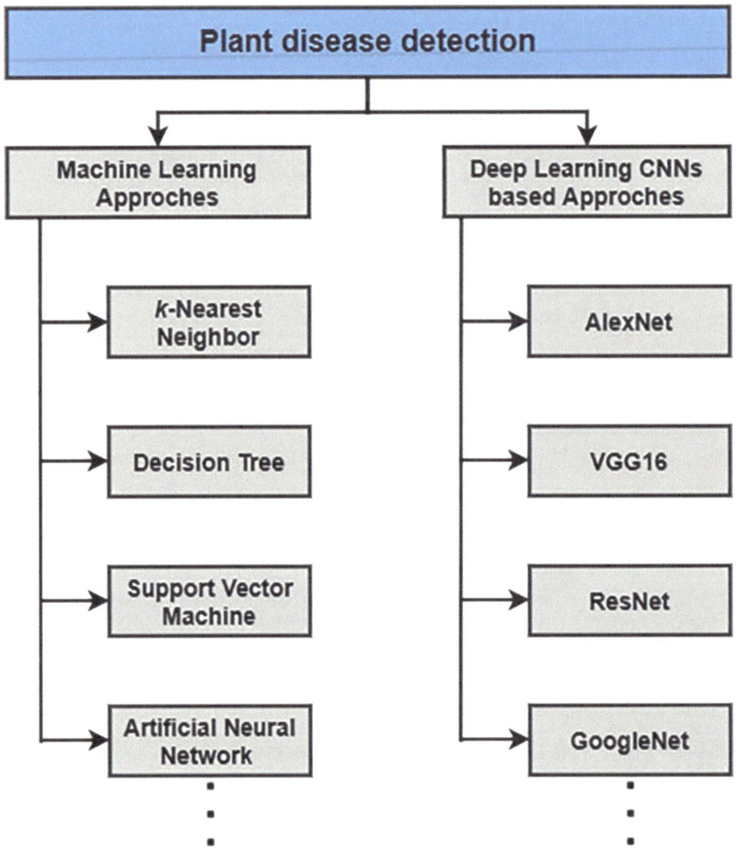

Figure 2.
Description of machine learning and deep learning algorithm used for plant disease detection.

2.1.2 Decision tree

It is the algorithm of machine learning which comes under supervised learning to solve regression and classification-based problems. The decision tree is the graphical representation of pre-defined rules along with the solution. The graph of the decision tree has two types of nodes: one is decision nodes and another is leaf nodes. Additionally, the edges store the information of the answers to the questions, and leaf nodes store the actual output. In Sabrol and Kumar [16], Chopda et al. [17] and Rajesh et al. [18], the authors reported appreciable results in plant disease classification and recognition.

2.1.3 Support vector machine

Support vector machine (SVM) is a very popular classifier used in statistical learning. The classifier aims to discriminate the classes from each other. In SVM, a hyperplane is used to discriminate one class from another. Those points which are close to the hyperplane are referred to as support vectors. The task of the SVM is to classify the different categories based on some features. Additionally, this algorithm performs well in extreme classes. Let us consider, color, texture, shape are some features of a particular plant. If we consider two features such as color and texture to classify diseased and healthy leaves. To classify them, the optimal decision boundary is required. Optimal decision boundaries could result in greater misclassification for the new instance. Therefore, the boundary support vectors are very important than all the training examples. This algorithm works well for linearly separating data points whereas in some cases if the data points are not linearly separable then 2-dimensional (2D) feature spaces are converted into 3-dimensional feature spaces. But the only problem is that it is computationally very expensive. In addition to that, it provides kernel function which can reduce the computational cost to convert 2D feature space to 3-dimensional feature space. Using kernel function the dot product is performed between two vectors. Especially, this is used to transform non-linear to linear transformation space. Various popular kernel functions are polynomial, radial basis, sigmoid kernels used to change 2D data to high dimensional feature space. Choosing the best kernel is a non-trivial task and is a hyper-parameter that can be selected by performing various experiments on the data. The main benefit of using SVM is that it is memory efficient and effective for high-dimensional feature space data.

2.1.4 Artificial neural networks

It is the special type of machine learning algorithm used for classification. The researchers have been working on artificial neural networks (ANNs) since the beginning of the 1980s [19]. ANNs are a special type of classification algorithm and their structure is inspired by the human brain. ANNs takes input from the external world in the form of feature vector or patterns. Each input value is multiplied by their corresponding weights that arc summing with the bias value. Further, the result is mapped to the activation function (binary, sigmoid) and produced the output. Other than these algorithms, there are various algorithms available that reported appreciable results in image recognition such as Random Forest, Naive Bayes, many more. Initially, we started with the study of traditional computer vision approaches used for plant disease detection. Plant disease can be caused by fungi, bacteria, and viruses from which fungi are the common disease organism. It is the type of disease that can be formed by taking energy from plants. The fungal disease has been identified using image processing techniques on different horticulture/agriculture crops [20]. To detect the different types of fruits, vegetable, commercial, and cereal crops that have been utilized using various feature extraction and classification algorithms. They achieved appreciable classification accuracy to identify the disease from horticulture/agriculture crops. Han et al. proposed a novel technique for feature extraction using super-pixel and marker-controlled segmentation methods for the classification of yellow rust and septoria diseases. They have used SVM and ANN for these disease classifications. Their experimentation concludes that SVM classifiers outperformed well than ANN classifiers for the classification of disease [21]. Su et al. experimented with the detection of fungal yellow rust disease on wheat crops. The author collected RGB images with a high-resolution camera and there are a total of three different classes present in region of interest (RoI) as rust, healthy, and background. To monitor the yellow rust, they used the U-Net deep learning architecture and the results were compared with the Random Forest algorithm. They found that U-Net-based segmentation outperformed spectral images. In their work, the average precision of 81.06%, recall of 90.10%, and F1-score of 84.00% have been achieved to segment the disease from spectral images [22]. An application of Fuzzy C-Means clustering has been proposed as the model to identify the wheat leaf disease [23]. In their work, they extracted inter- and intra-class features and further combined them to build a model for identifying the different wheat plant diseases. Although the traditional machine learning-based techniques are performing well for image classification, still there are certain limitations such as it requires manual feature extraction and is only suitable for small datasets, which may lead to the over-fitting problem [23, 24].

2.2 Deep learning-based approaches

Convolutional neural network (CNN) is a popular neural network, designed for solving computer vision problems. The architecture of CNNs is shown in **Figure 3**. The images are represented in the form of pixel values. In the convolution layers, the operation of convolution is performed i.e., the kernel is slide over the input image after choosing the padding and stride values at each layer. Thereafter, the power of non-linearity is to give the non-linear mapping with the input images in such a way that after the non-linear mapping it becomes linearly separable. ReLU activation function is used to change all the negative values to positive values. With this, the pooling layer is used to down sample the different feature maps for getting the most prominent features i.e., the convolution layer performs these triplet operations like convolution followed by ReLU and ReLU followed by pooling one after another. These triplets operations are typically stacked one after another and also based on these triplets, the depth of the neural network has been defined. After these layers, the network is followed by one or more fully connected layers which are responsible for classification.

To build the CNN model, all the above-mentioned parameters play a very important role. To build the custom CNN model, the numbers of convolution layers, max-pool layer, number of filter values, filter size, stride, padding, number of fully connected layers need to be specified. Increasing the number of convolution layers will produce different feature maps and also increasing the fully-connected layers increase the training time of the model. Although, the custom CNN model reported appreciable accuracy. The process of creating a custom CNN model takes more time. Therefore, the concept of transfer learning comes into the picture. Transfer learning is a concept of deep learning where the weights of pre-trained models are reused for a new problem. Every year, there is a competition held on the ImageNet dataset. Many researchers developed new models to classify the different objects of the ImageNet dataset and reported good classification accuracy and reduced error rate. There are variants of transfer learning models such as ResNet, GoogleNet, and EfficientNet varied in terms of the number of layers, filter size, number of filters used, stride, padding, and so on. Some of the few models are elaborated as given below:

AlexNet: AlexNet model is a transfer learning model which is based on CNN's and is proposed by Alex Krizhevsky for classifying the different objects of ImageNet Large Scale Visual Recognition Challenge (ILSVRV). Training can be performed on hundreds of epochs. GPUs are the game-changer in deep learning. Using GPUs, the model

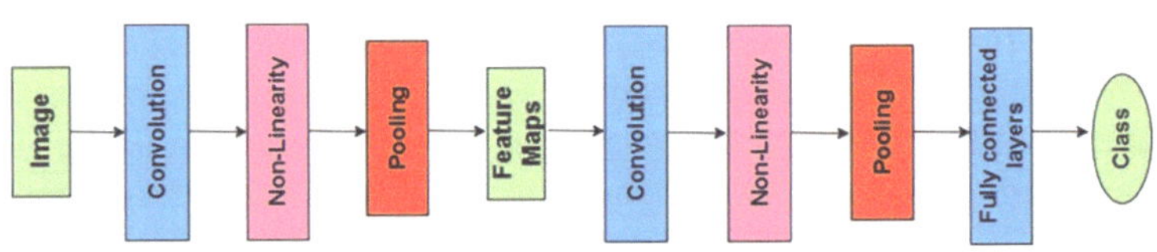

Figure 3.
The basic architecture of CNNs.

will train in very little time and with less effort. AlexNet is the eight-layer network that has a further five convolution layers, and three fully-connected layers including the output layer. It used the ReLU activation function instead of the sigmoid function. In this model, the initial layers used variant sizes of kernels i.e., 11 × 11, 5 × 5, and 3 × 3 to get different features maps as an output. Thereafter, fully-connected layers are used to train the model based on the extracted features.

VGG16: Visual geometry group (VGG) model is the first runner-up of the ImageNet dataset in 2014. It has 13 convolution layers, 5 max-pool layers, and 3 FC layers. The output layer used the softmax activation to classify the 1000 different objects. VGG16 model is different from the AlexNet model in terms of kernel size and the number of layers. VGG16 model used the same kernel size whereas the AlexNet model used the different kernel size. Additionally, the VGG16 model is 16-layered but the AlexNet model is 8-layered architecture. In the present study, the VGG16 model has been utilized to classify the wheat rust diseases and the elaboration is given in Section 3.2.

Modern deep learning architectures are significantly popular to solve agriculture-related problems. Sladojevic et al. developed a CNNs based model for plant disease classification. The model recognized 13 different types of plants. In their work, they used 30,880 images in the training and 2589 images for validation and reported a classification accuracy of 96.30% [25]. Zhang et al. proposed a deep learning model for the detection of rust disease of wheat crop from hyperspectral images. In their work, they automate the process of detecting yellow rust-captured images from unmanned aerial vehicle (UAV). Yellow rust is a fungal disease that can cause 100% loss for the wheat crop. The author used the Inception-ResNet model for feature extraction and reported the highest accuracy of 85.00% when compared with the random forest that was 77.00% [26]. A deep learning model has been built for grading wheat stripe rust disease [27]. In their work, they used different mobile devices to capture images and build their dataset, referred WSRgrading. It contained 5242 wheat leaf images at six different levels. They build and proposed the model by adding an attention layer in the pre-trained DenseNet model and build a new model named as C-DenseNet which has been reported a good classification accuracy of 97.99%. Genaev et al. classify the rust disease from the wheat crop. In their work, they used the CGIAR dataset, containing three classes (healthy wheat, leaf rust, and stem rust). They implemented the DenseNet transfer learning model and reported the F1-score and AUC of 0.90 and 0.98, respectively [28]. Jia et al. in proposed the model for detection and segmentation of fruit features for optimal harvesting of apples using Mask R-CNN. ResNet model was used as the backbone of this network. The model was tested on 120 images and reported precision and recall rates of 97.31% and 95.70%, respectively [29]. The shortage of the wheat disease dataset motivated the researchers to create the dataset which should be publicly available for all [30]. They are motivated to collect more data that will help the research community for conducting the research competitions on wheat diseases classification. Finally, they attempted to prepare their WFD2020 dataset which contains 2414 images. They performed their experiments using the EfficientNet CNN-based model and reported 94.20% classification accuracy.

In the recent decade, deep learning techniques are highly utilized for image processing. Deep learning models are producing appreciable results than machine learning methods [31]. **Figure 4** depicts the utilization of computer vision approaches (i.e., old machine learning methods and modern deep learning approaches) for the wheat crop. These statistics have been built based on work done from the period (2015 to July 2021) for classifying most of the wheat crop diseases. Deep learning approaches include CNN-based architecture such as VGG16, ResNet, Faster R-CNN, and so on. In

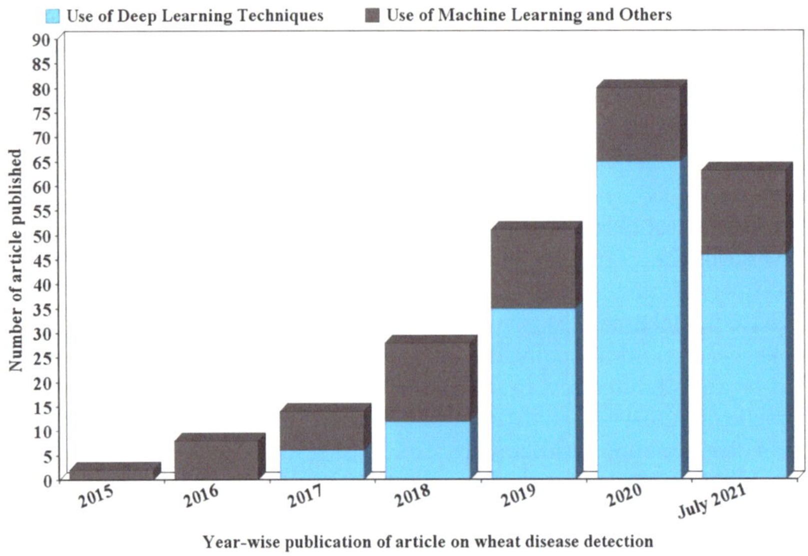

Figure 4.
Year-wise statistics publication of wheat disease detection.

different circumstances, the traditional machine learning approaches include SVM, Random Forest, and so on. The analysis concludes that the modern deep learning architectures have been utilized more for classifying most of the wheat crops diseases as compared to traditional machine learning approaches.

3. Classification of wheat rust disease

3.1 Dataset description

There are standard datasets that are publicly available for research experimentation in the computer vision and image processing domain, such as PASCAL VOC [32], ImageNet [33], IMDB-Wiki [34], CIFAR [35], and PlantVillage [36]. CGIAR dataset is one of the dataset publicly available on https://www.kaggle.com/shadabhussain/cgiar-computer-vision-for-crop-disease [37]. This dataset was further distributed in three different classes of wheat rust i.e., healthy wheat, leaf rust, and stem rust. A sample of each class is shown in **Figure 5**. Most of the images in this dataset were collected by CIMMYT and its partners from Ethiopia and Tanzania. Additionally, a few images were sourced from the Google image database. The images in this dataset have the specific characteristics like (i) all are colored (ii) mixed format, (iii) different orientation, (iv) variable quality, and captured with different resolutions. The datasets are already classified into two categories i.e., 876 images and 610 images for training and testing, respectively. From the training dataset (i.e., 876 images) a total of 863 images have been filtered and considered for training the model. In the present study, the 863 images dataset was further split for training and validation in the ratio of 3:1 (i.e., 75% data in training and 25% into validation). **Table 1** describes the class-wise distribution of this dataset. It is a challenging task to build an efficient model that is capable to classify all three classes of images accurately.

Figure 5.
Sampled images of (a) healthy wheat plant, (b) leaf rust, and (c) stem rust.

Class label	Images	Training set	Validation set
Healthy wheat	142	105	36
Leaf rust	345	258	86
Stem rust	376	283	95
Total images	863	646	217

Table 1.
Class-wise distribution of image dataset.

3.2 Methodologies used for training the model

Deep learning is a popular methodology used for image processing. In deep learning models, features are extracted automatically and little human intervention is required to train the model. Deep learning models are quite efficient to discover the internal structure or patterns of high-dimensional data. However, directly processing the original images leads to inappropriate recognition results, therefore, it is necessary to pre-process the images before feeding them to the model. Pre-processing involves e.g. resizing, enhancing, or removing noise of the input images. It is worth mentioning that CNNs perform better for image recognition and classification. There are various transfer learning models which are based on CNNs like AlexNet, VGG16, GoogleNet, and Inception V3, that are pre-trained on the ImageNet dataset. ImageNet is the standard dataset that contains 1000 different categories of objects. CNN's based transfer learning models reported appreciable results to classify 1000 different objects present in the ImageNet dataset. In the present study, the VGG16 model has been utilized and the architecture is depicted in **Figure 6**. This model is the composition of 16-layers (13 convolution layers, and 3 fully connected layers). In this model, the images are processed in standard size i.e., 224 × 224. The reason for resizing the fixed image size is to extract the uniform or equal feature maps at the end of the convolution process. This model used a fixed size of kernel i.e., 3 × 3. Sometimes, the kernel is referred to as a filter that is responsible for extracting features from the given images. These extracted patterns or features might be horizontal edges, vertical edges, and a combination of both. Initially, a convolution process has been performed to extract the features, and thereafter the classification is done. In the convolution operation, the kernel/filter is sliding over the image starting from the top left to the bottom right corner to extract the features.

The movement of the kernel is either pixel-wise or by skipping some pixels using stride values. If the stride value is 1 then the movement of the kernel is shifted by one pixel after another and if the stride value is 2, then the movement of the kernel

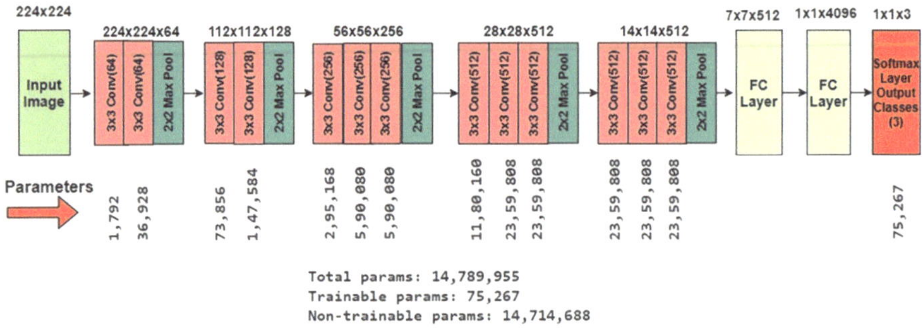

Figure 6.
The architecture of VGG16 for wheat rust disease detection.

is shifted by two-pixel values during the operation of convolution. The convolution layers are used to identify the pattern or features from the images which further help in discriminating the classes. The initial layers extract the general features like edges and the subsequent layers extract the domain-specific features. Each convolution block is followed by the max-pool layer which is used for down-sampling the feature maps. In this process, the dimensionality of the image is reduced by retaining the most prominent feature. At the end of the convolution layers, different feature maps are generated as an output. These feature maps are further flattened and mapped with a fully connected layer in the classification module. Here, the model has a feature vector of size 4096 neurons also referred to as dense layer. This feature vector is further passed to the next dense layer of the same size. Finally, the last layer neurons are fully connected to the output neurons by using the soft-max activation function. However, in the current study, we considered the three classes classification problem. Therefore, the output layer changed to three classes using the soft-max probability function. The actual learning starts from data using forward and backward passes. In the forward pass, input neurons are multiplied with the weight values and also apply the activation function as ReLU. ReLU activation function adds non-linearity to the model i.e., all the negative pixel-values become positive after passing through it. On the other hand, in backward pass back-propagation is used to minimize the loss value. In this process, weights and biases are getting updated from the last to the initial layer by calculating the gradients at each layer using a convolution operator.

To summarize this model, the important and noticeable point is that this model has a total of 14,789,955 parameters but 75,267 are trainable parameters and the rest are non-trainable, the reason is that using transfer learning, the already trained weights have been used during building the model. Therefore, the model is trained in less time with fewer number parameters.

3.3 Hyper-parameter tuning

Hyper-parameter tuning is the backbone of any deep learning model. Finding the best parameters is a very tedious task, it needs many experiments to be performed while building the model. Hyper-parameters include learning rate, batch size, loss function, number of epochs, and optimizer is usually considered for tuning the model. To build the classification model for three classes each hyper-parameter is considered within a specific range. In this way, several experiments have been performed to build an efficient model. After performing some experiments with the variation in the given hyper-parameters, it was concluded that model accuracy is highly dependent on the batch size, learning rate, number of epochs, and size of the dataset. In the present study, the following hyper-parameters has been utilized: *batch size* = *10*, *optimizer* = *Adam*, *loss function* = *categorical cross-entropy*, *initial learning rate* = *0.01*, *decay learning rate* = *0.0001*, *epochs* = *80*. Using these parameters, the model produced good classification accuracy.

4. Experimental results

4.1 Accuracy and loss results

As discussed in Section 3.1 image dataset of wheat disease classification has been utilized to train the model. We used the online google colab platform with GPU support. Among the performed experiments, we discuss the best one, which produces the highest training accuracy. **Table 2** illustrates the training and validation accuracies obtained at different epochs (varied from 10 to 90) along with their loss values. Here, the training accuracy starts with 81.42% on 10 epochs and ends up with 99.54% on 80 epochs. We continued to compute the accuracy for the 90 epochs also but did not get any significant improvement in training accuracy. Although more experiments could be performed by increasing the number of epochs, the accuracy obtained at epoch 80 was quite promising. On the other hand, the validation accuracy fluctuating between 74.76% and 79.05% at different epochs, as shown in **Figure 7**. Similarly, it was observed that the training loss decreases at every increasing step of the epoch (from 10 to 80). Beyond that, the loss has started to increase. In contrast, the validation loss is fluctuating between 0.60 and 0.65 up to 40 epochs. Then, after 70 epochs it starts increasing rapidly (**Figure 8**).

4.2 Model evaluation

To test the performance of the trained model, we performed the test experiments on the validation data (i.e., 25% of the total dataset). In this way, a total of 36 sample images of healthy leaf, 87 sample images of leaf rust, and 94 sample images of stem

Epochs	Training accuracy (in %)	Validation accuracy (in %)	Training loss	Validation loss
10	81.42	74.76	0.50	0.65
20	91.02	79.05	0.33	0.61
30	95.05	77.14	0.22	0.61
40	96.59	78.10	0.18	0.61
50	97.06	76.67	0.15	0.56
60	97.99	78.10	0.12	0.56
70	98.61	74.29	0.09	0.66
80	99.54	77.14	0.07	0.74
90	99.23	74.76	0.08	0.82

Table 2.
Comparison of training accuracy, validation accuracy, and training loss, and validation loss at different epochs.

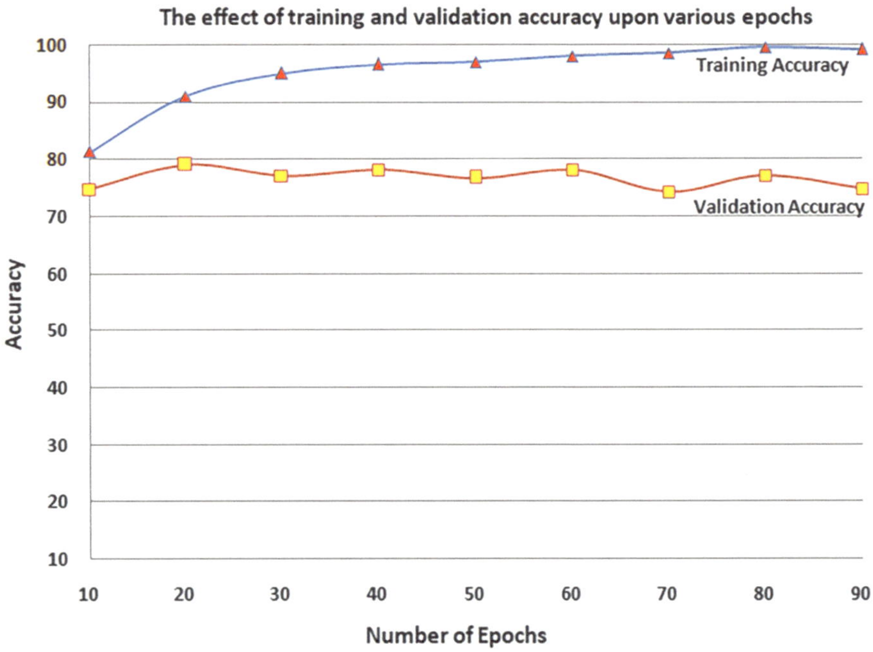

Figure 7.
Representation of the comparison of training and validation accuracy.

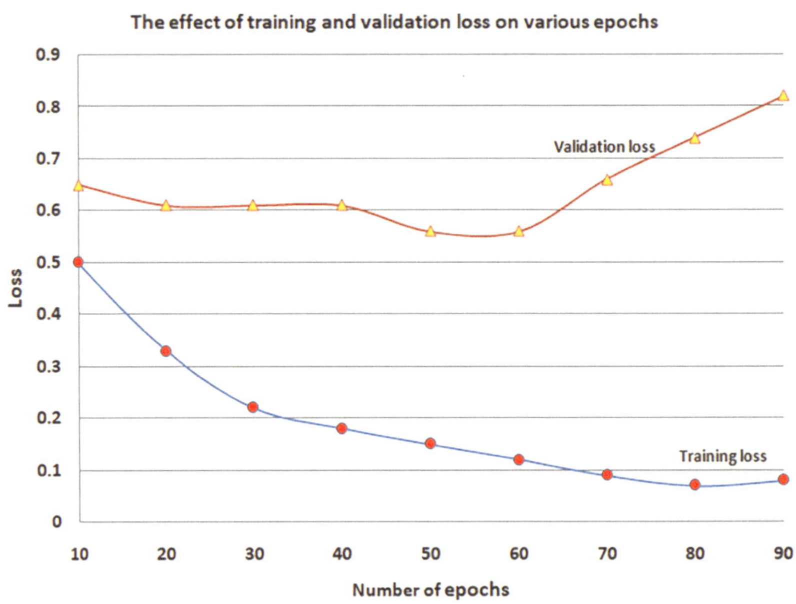

Figure 8.
Representation of the comparison of training and validation loss.

rust have been considered. The evaluation of the testing results was done using a confusion matrix. **Figure 9** illustrates the accuracy and confusion with other intra-classes, wherein, it is shown that leaf rust class samples are confused with stem rust class samples due to less variation between classes.

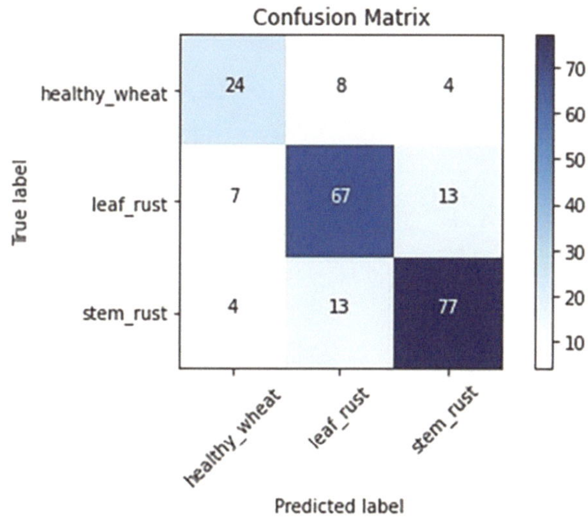

Figure 9.
Confusion matrix at epoch = 80.

5. Conclusions

To summarize this book chapter, different machine learning and deep learning-based models have been discussed to solve plant disease classification and detection problems. Considering a case study of wheat rust diseases, a deep learning-based model is proposed to classify the different wheat rust diseases using a pre-trained VGG16 model. Based on the CGIAR dataset with three classes (stem rust, leaf rust, and healthy wheat), the proposed model has been optimized and produced the classification accuracy of 99.54%, and when evaluated on unseen data it gave a validation accuracy of 77.14%. This model will further help farmers or experts to diagnose disease in the early stages. Although these models give good training accuracy, they were not appropriate to classify stem- and leaf rust when result plot on confusion metrics. This is due to the fact that some images in this dataset contained multiple diseases, meaning that one image contained the features of both leaf- and stem rust. Detection and classification of the wheat rust disease in the early stages lead to high yield at the production level [38]. In the future, we will extend this work by collecting real-time images of wheat rust disease and also incorporating object detection-based algorithms such as Yolov3, Faster R-CNN, and Mask R-CNN [39] to exactly localize the location of the disease in the image.

Author details

Shivani Sood[1], Harjeet Singh[1*] and Suruchi Jindal[2]

1 Chitkara University Institute of Engineering and Technology, Chitkara University, Punjab, India

2 School of Agricultural Biotechnology, Punjab Agricultural University, Ludhiana, Punjab, India

*Address all correspondence to: harjeet.singh@chitkara.edu.in

References

[1] Mahajan S, Das A, Sardana HK. Image acquisition techniques for assessment of legume quality. Trends in Food Science & Technology. 2015;**42**(2):116-133

[2] Sood S, Singh H. Computer vision and machine learning based approaches for food security: A review. Multimedia Tools and Applications. 2021;**80**(18):1-27

[3] Diana Andrushia A, Trephena Patricia A. Artificial bee colony optimization (abc) for grape leaves disease detection. Evolving Systems. 2020;**11**(1):105-117

[4] Kaur S, Pandey S, Goel S. Plants disease identification and classification through leaf images: A survey. Archives of Computational Methods in Engineering. 2019;**26**(2):507-530

[5] Inácio Patrício D, Rieder R. Computer vision and artificial intelligence in precision agriculture for grain crops: A systematic review. Computers and Electronics in Agriculture. 2018;**153**: 69-81

[6] Kirk DB, Wen-Mei WH. Programming Massively Parallel Processors: A Hands-on Approach. Cambridge, United State: Morgan Kaufmann; Nov 24, 2016

[7] LeCun Y, Bengio Y, Hinton G. Deep learning. Nature. 2015;**521**(7553):436-444

[8] Schmidhuber J. Deep learning in neural networks: An overview. Neural Networks. 2015;**61**:85-117

[9] Kumar A, Singh G, Prasad BK, Sharma PK, Kumar R. Genome wide analysis and identification of nramp gene family in wheat (*Triticum aestivum* L.). The Pharma Innovation Journal. 2022;**11**(1):499-504

[10] Charles H, Godfray J, Beddington JR, Crute IR, Haddad L, Lawrence D, et al. Food security: The challenge of feeding 9 billion people. Science. 2010;**327**(5967): 812-818

[11] Chatrath R, Mishra B, Ortiz Ferrara G, Singh SK, Joshi AK. Challenges to wheat production in South Asia. Euphytica. Oct 2007;**157**(3):447-456

[12] Strange RN, Scott PR. Plant disease: A threat to global food security. The Annual Review of Phytopathology. 2005;**43**:83-116

[13] Murillo-Bracamontes EA, Martinez-Rosas ME, Miranda-Velasco MM, Martinez-Reyes HL, Martinez-Sandoval JR, Cervantes-de Avila H. Implementation of Hough transform for fruit image segmentation. Procedia Engineering. 2012;**35**:230-239

[14] Sengür A, Akılotu BN, Tuncer SA, Kadiroğlu Z, YavuzKılıç S, Budak Ü, et al. Optic disc determination in retinal images with deep features. In: 2018 26th Signal Processing and Communications Applications Conference (SIU). Izmir, Turkey: IEEE; May 2-5, 2018. pp. 1-4

[15] Buttrey SE, Karo C. Using k-nearest-neighbor classification in the leaves of a tree. Computational Statistics & Data Analysis. 2002;**40**(1):27-37

[16] Sabrol H, Kumar S. Intensity based feature extraction for tomato plant disease recognition by classification using decision tree. International Journal of Computer Science and Information Security. 2016;**14**(9):622-626

[17] Chopda J, Raveshiya H, Nakum S, Nakrani V. Cotton crop disease detection using decision tree classifier. In: 2018

International Conference on Smart City and Emerging Technology (ICSCET). Mumbai, India: IEEE; Jan 5-5, 2018. pp. 1-5

[18] Rajesh B, Vardhan MVS, Sujihelen L. Leaf disease detection and classification by decision tree. In: 2020 4th International Conference on Trends in Electronics and Informatics (ICOEI) (48184). Tirunelveli, India: IEEE; June 15, 2020. pp. 705-708

[19] Baptista FD, Rodrigues S, Morgado-Dias F. Performance comparison of ANN training algorithms for classification. In: 2013 IEEE 8th International Symposium on Intelligent Signal Processing. Funchal, Portugal: IEEE; Sept 16-18, 2013. pp. 115-120

[20] Pujari JD, Yakkundimath R, Byadgi AS. Identification and classification of fungal disease affected on agriculture/horticulture crops using image processing techniques. In: 2014 IEEE International Conference on Computational Intelligence and Computing Research. Coimbatore, India: IEEE; Dec 18-20 2014. pp. 1-4

[21] Han L, Haleem MS, Taylor M. A novel computer vision-based approach to automatic detection and severity assessment of crop diseases. In: 2015 Science and Information Conference (SAI). IEEE; 2015. pp. 638-644

[22] Su J, Yi D, Su B, Mi Z, Liu C, Hu X, et al. Aerial visual perception in smart farming: Field study of wheat yellow rust monitoring. IEEE Transactions on Industrial Informatics. 2020;**17**(3): 2242-2249

[23] Majumdar D, Ghosh A, Kole DK, Chakraborty A, Majumder DD. Application of fuzzy c-means clustering method to classify wheat leaf images based on the presence of rust disease. In: Proceedings of the 3rd International Conference on Frontiers of Intelligent Computing: Theory and Applications (FICTA) 2014. Bhubaneswar, Odisha, India: Springer; Nov 1-15, 2014. pp. 277-284

[24] Arya S, Singh R. An analysis of deep learning techniques for plant leaf disease detection. International Journal of Computer Science and Information Security (IJCSIS). 2019;**17**(7):73-80

[25] Sladojevic S, Arsenovic M, Anderla A, Culibrk D, Stefanovic D. Deep neural networks-based recognition of plant diseases by leaf image classification. Computational Intelligence and Neuroscience. 2016;**2016**:1-11

[26] Zhang X, Han L, Dong Y, Shi Y, Huang W, Han L, et al. A deep learning-based approach for automated yellow rust disease detection from high-resolution hyperspectral UAV images. Remote Sensing. 2019;**11**(13):1554

[27] Mi Z, Zhang X, Su J, Han D, Su B. Wheat stripe rust grading by deep learning with attention mechanism and images from mobile devices. Frontiers in Plant Science. 2020;**11**:558126. DOI: 10.3389/fpls.2020.558126

[28] Genaev M, Ekaterina S, Afonnikov D. Application of neural networks to image recognition of wheat rust diseases. In: Cognitive Sciences, Genomics and Bioinformatics (CSGB). Novosibirsk, Russia: IEEE; July 6-10, 2020; pp. 40-42

[29] Jia W, Tian Y, Luo R, Zhang Z, Lian J, Zheng Y. Detection and segmentation of overlapped fruits based on optimized mask R-CNN application in apple harvesting robot. Computers and Electronics in Agriculture. 2020;**172**: 105380

[30] Genaev MA, Skolotneva ES, Gultyaeva EI, Orlova EA, Bechtold NP, Afonnikov DA. Image-based wheat fungi diseases identification by deep learning. Plants. 2021;**10**(8):1500

[31] Sujatha R, Chatterjee JM, Jhanjhi NZ, Brohi SN. Performance of deep learning vs machine learning in plant leaf disease detection. Microprocessors and Microsystems. 2021;**80**:103615

[32] Everingham M, Van Gool L, Williams CKI, Winn J, Zisserman A. The pascal visual object classes (voc) challenge. International Journal of Computer Vision. 2010;**88**(2):303-338

[33] Deng J, Dong W, Socher R, Li L-J, Li K, Fei-Fei L. Imagenet: A large-scale hierarchical image database. In: 2009 IEEE Conference on Computer Vision and Pattern Recognition. Miami, FL, USA: IEEE; June 20-25, 2009. pp. 248-255

[34] Mohamed Ali N, Abd El Hamid MM, Youssif A. Sentiment analysis for movies reviews dataset using deep learning models. International Journal of Data Mining & Knowledge Management Process (IJDKP). 2019;**9**(3):19-27

[35] Ngiam J, Chen Z, Koh P, Le Q, Ng A. Tiled convolutional neural networks. Advances in neural information processing systems. 2010;**23**:1-9

[36] Sood S, Singh H, Malarvel M. Image quality enhancement for wheat rust diseased images using histogram equalization technique. In: 2021 5th International Conference on Computing Methodologies and Communication (ICCMC). Erode, India: IEEE; April 8-10, 2021. pp. 1035-1042

[37] https://www.kaggle.com/shadabhussain/cigar-computer-vision-for-crop-disease/. 2019

[38] Sood S, Singh H. An implementation and analysis of deep learning models for the detection of wheat rust disease. In: 2020 3rd International Conference on Intelligent Sustainable Systems (ICISS). Thoothukudi, India: IEEE; Dec 3-5, 2020. pp. 341-347

[39] Sood S, Singh H, Malarvel M, Ahuja R. Significance and limitations of deep neural networks for image classification and object detection. In: 2021 2nd International Conference on Smart Electronics and Communication (ICOSEC). Tamil Nadu, India: IEEE; Oct 07-09, 2021. pp. 1453-1460